THE DEATH OF THINGS

The Death of Things

EPHEMERA AND THE AMERICAN NOVEL

Sarah Wasserman

University of Minnesota Press
Minneapolis
London

The University of Minnesota Press gratefully acknowledges the financial assistance provided for the publication of this book by the Center for Material Culture Studies, the Department of English, and the College of Arts and Sciences at the University of Delaware.

Portions of chapter 3 were originally published as "Ralph Ellison, Chester Himes, and the Persistence of Urban Forms," *PMLA* 135, no. 3 (2020); reprinted by permission of the Modern Language Association of America. Portions of chapter 6 were originally published as "Ephemeral Gods and Billboard Saints: Don DeLillo's *Underworld* and Urban Apparitions," *Journal of American Studies* 18, no. 4 (2014): 1041–67.

Published by the University of Minnesota Press
111 Third Avenue South, Suite 290
Minneapolis, MN 55401-2520
http://www.upress.umn.edu

ISBN 978-1-5179-0977-2 (hc)
ISBN 978-1-5179-0978-9 (pb)

A Cataloging-in-Publication record for this book is available from the Library of Congress.

Printed in the United States of America on acid-free paper

UMP BmB 2020

To my parents—especially my father, Forrest Wasserman.
It's not a donut!

Contents

Introduction

THE DEATH OF THINGS

This is a book about disappearing objects. More precisely, this is a book about books about disappearing objects. While it may seem that fiction has the special ability to preserve lost things, it also has the ability to lose them. After all, American literature is as much about the way the white whale evades capture as it is about the whale. What happens when it's an object's disappearance, its transience, that takes center stage? How does narrative help us reckon with the transient nature of things? And how might that reckoning change our ways of organizing the world, of relating to the objects around us? Why do so many authors tell stories about the death of things?

The Death of Things takes up these questions via a consideration of ephemera and the literature in which these disappearing objects are archived, assembled, and mined for meaning. More narrowly, it examines the transience of things within the context of American postwar fiction, considering how that transience has shaped American cultural production throughout the twentieth century. Although Western aesthetic and intellectual traditions have long featured veneration for ruins, decay, and older forms, both material and literary, postwar American culture has entailed an incessant push toward the new. Consumer habits shaped by a national ideology of progress and innovation have given rise to a frequently binary relationship to objects: either they persist, archived and curated to help stabilize individual and collective memory and identity, or they are disposable, cast out of sight and out of mind. But between these two poles exists a great number of objects that are neither quite lost nor quite present; neither dead nor alive, they are instead *dying*, coming to us in an ongoing state of ceasing to be. It is difficult to make sense of such objects in everyday material relations, but twentieth-century American fiction affords them a privileged place. More specifically, post-1945 American novels trace the long arc of the twentieth century to explain how a consumer culture that once promised plenitude gave way to an endless parade of disappearing objects. These novels are historical in a number of different ways, but they all embed ephemera in the particular settings and moments in which they appear and disappear. The fictions shuttle along scales of different sizes, inviting readers to contemplate the relationship between paper goods and the built environment, between impermanence and infrastructure, and between temporary objects and the social formations they engender. Novelists thinking through transience reveal how things as large as buildings can vanish while minor objects such as pamphlets can have monumental impact. Ephemera thus help reverse and revise Edward Soja's famous diagnosis of the scholarly tendency to treat space as "fixed, dead, undialectical" and time as "richness, life, dialectic."[1] Representations of ephemera in fact remind readers that many objects are living and dying in strange ratios, that things rarely come fully into possession, and just as seldom vanish entirely. This book attends to those representations that allow readers to see how things are not simply either absent or present, but somehow both.

So what, exactly, are ephemera? The word *ephemera* comes from the combination of the Greek *epi,* meaning "on" or "upon," and *hemera,* meaning "day," and the term originally alluded to short-lived flowers and insects like the mayfly, which belongs to the biological order *Ephemeroptera.* In the mid-1700s, the word assumed its contemporary meaning and has been used since to designate written and printed matter not intended for keeping.[2] Air transport labels, bank checks, bingo cards, bookmarks, broadsides, bus tickets, catalogs, envelopes, flyers, lottery tickets, maps, menus, newspapers, pamphlets, paper dolls, postcards, receipts, sheet music, stamps, theater programs, ticket stubs, valentines, and so on: ephemera are as varied as they are ubiquitous. What an initial list like this one makes immediately clear is that, even while so many ephemera wind up in waste baskets and recycling bins, many *do* survive. At Oxford University's Bodleian Library, for instance, patrons can view more than a million printed documents from the eighteenth century to today contained within the John Johnson Collection of Printed Ephemera. Although these materials are carefully preserved and cataloged, the collection's website nonetheless makes the claim that "it offers a fresh view of British history through primary, uninterpreted printed documents, which, produced for short-term use, have survived by chance."[3]

Presumably, this statement describes the way that handbills, greeting cards, or paper fans have made their way into the collection by a chain of unforeseeable events: maybe, for instance, an advertisement saved in a scrapbook is purchased in an estate sale and eventually donated to the library. But such a narrative discloses the fact that it is *care,* as much as chance, that washes a given brochure or board game onto the Bodleian's shores. Mostly, ephemeral objects disappear without a trace, but some of those objects persist, not entirely by accident, but usually because someone somewhere has preserved them. Browsing a collection of ephemera means, ironically, encountering objects that have been rescued from ephemerality. The transient objects that remain with us (whether collected intentionally, folded in with other items, or encountered randomly) work to stabilize history. As John Johnson himself said of ephemera, they "illustrate at one and the same time the historical development of our social life and the development of printing."[4] The fragility of ephemera, however, makes whatever stability and knowledge we gain from them seem shaky, at times just the result of an accident.

Because ephemera vanish in principle and yet so often remain with us, they dramatize the dynamics between the temporary and the permanent, between extinction and longevity, and thus between the valueless and the valuable. This has as much to do with the way that we treat such objects as it does with the material substrate out of which they are made. It makes sense that traditionally ephemera are printed objects, since paper itself is marked by the tension between durability and disappearance. Lisa Gitelman says of paper that its workings "are admittedly complex and even paradoxical. Consider that paper is a figure both for all that is sturdy and stable (as in 'Let's get that on paper!'), and for all that is insubstantial and ephemeral (including the paper tiger and the house of cards)."[5] As convenient for record-taking as it is disposable, paper has long given ephemera their particular status. Mostly, things like paper napkins and gum wrappers disappear without a visible trace, but sometimes, because they have been preserved one way or another, a particular napkin or gum wrapper remains. A fair amount of ink has been spilled about the importance of paper to the study of literature: in *Paper Machine,* Jacques Derrida considers paper as a "body-subject or body-substance," the material that exists in relation to the text, its linguistic code, and the embodied person who writes and reads.[6] Book historians of early modern and Renaissance texts, such as Margreta de Grazia and Peter Stallybrass, have made it clear that the material embodiment of a text is crucial to the way that it makes meaning.[7] And Jonathan Senchyne's research on the history of the book and print culture in early and nineteenth-century America proposes a new literary periodization based on materiality and paper production.[8]

Given conventional ephemera's printed nature, paper occupies a privileged place in this study. However, I am less interested in the materiality of paper—its weight, grade, or opacity—and more concerned with the figurative relationship between paper ephemera and the novels in which they are represented. The many paper objects such as stamps and signs described in novels raise questions about the paper books in which they appear. They are literary proxies, asking to be read and staging the vexed drama of the novel's own (im)permanence. The question of whether or not the novel today is disappearing or simply shifting shape as it migrates into digital forms is one that is raised later in this book; for now, I want to stress that the novel serves as a storage medium for ephemera, even as novels themselves come to seem increasingly ephemeral. And the novel stores ephemera in more ways than one. When writers represent ephemera in their fiction, they create a record of stamps, world's-fair souvenirs, or magazines that will disappear or have already vanished. In focusing on these objects, they enact the kind of care that ephemera require to survive the ravages of time. In this peculiar way, a novelist's attention to vanishing objects can be said to *create* ephemera. Even as a writer "stores" a newspaper or train ticket in a narrative, they invest those fictional objects with the dynamics of ephemera, the push and pull of disappearance and permanence. The novels in this study draw readers' attention to the vexed status of ephemera as things that usually vanish and endure only with care, attention, or representation. These novels do not simply include descriptions of ephemera; they ephemeralize their objects.

Though this book centers on postwar novels, I want to start with an iconic American novel from the turn of the twentieth century to show how the phenomenon of ephemerality has always shaped postindustrial America and its appearance on the page. Theodore Dreiser's *Sister Carrie* (1900) casts into vivid relief the effects of industrialization and its attendant object relations. It initiates readers in the challenges of a transient object world, challenges that accelerate and intensify as the twentieth century marches onward. Dreiser's novel about Carrie Meeber, the country girl who makes her way to the city of Chicago, catalogs the fashion and finery of downtown department stores, but it also attends to a class of objects that have little to do with accumulation and display. Alongside the "slippers and stockings, the delicately frilled skirts and petticoats, the laces, ribbons, hair-combs, and purses" that Carrie hopes will transform her into a "fine and fortunate lady," Dreiser tells of the ephemera that also shape his characters' urban existence.[9] The tickets, playbills, newspapers, and letters that accompany Carrie on her journey register the uncertainty and transience that are hallmarks of the sprawling, expanding city. Such an object appears in the novel's very first sentence: "When Caroline Meeber boarded the afternoon train for Chicago, her total outfit consisted of a small trunk, a cheap imitation alligator-skin satchel, a small lunch in a paper box, and a yellow leather snap purse, containing her ticket, a scrap of paper with her sister's address in Van Buren Street, and four dollars of money" (2). That scrap of paper, a seemingly insignificant detail, grows in importance while Carrie "looked at the little slip bearing her sister's address and wondered," as if the slip itself contains all the mystery and danger of the approaching city (2). Unlike the commodities that affirm the American myth of the self-made man, the novel's paper ephemera capture something of Dreiser's view of fate, the mercurial forces that cannot be bent by an individual's efforts or desires. Residing in the simple scrap of paper are ephemera's complex dynamics, those restless renewals that sweep Dreiser's characters along on the currents of their uncertain destinies.

When social hierarchies are upended, domestic order undone, and class and morality untethered from one another, the whole of Carrie's existence, along with that of the city, endures in a constant state of vanishing. The sweep of Dreiser's novel shows how "ephemera" names a dynamic as much as it names a kind of object. This is the dynamic that informs the artifacts in Don DeLillo's novels, the houses in Marilynne Robinson's, and the streetscapes in Chester Himes's. These novels necessitate expanding the definition of the term "ephemera" so it includes the variety of objects that appear in postwar fiction to help readers confront the way that things often refuse the categories we assign matter. In *The Death of Things*, ephemera include letters, billboards, world's-fair buildings, temporary memorials, and even city blocks. As

Caitlin DeSilvey points out in her work on the conservation of cultural heritage, it can be difficult to "tell stories about the unraveling of bigger things," as we are conditioned to see our buildings and environments as immutable.[10] Novels often remind us that even these objects are subject to disappearance: transience happens at many scales.

If even buildings vanish, how can ephemera be delimited at all? Neighboring terms assist in this task: "trash," for instance, is an object of another kind, one that must be displaced or destroyed.[11] "Obsolescence" leaves behind a remainder that is outmoded. Raymond Malewitz has written about what he calls the "literature of misuse": fictional portraits of the creative reuse of objects classified as obsolete or as waste, forms of artistic recycling that harken back to Claude Lévi-Strauss's celebrated *bricoleur.*[12] Ephemeral objects, on the other hand, are often keyed to specific occasions that they outlast. Unlike the stubborn fact of the obsolete object, ephemera are a fleeting currency. Unless cared for or accidentally preserved, they vanish into an unknown or unseen horizon. Defined by their imminent disappearance or destruction, ephemera call into question our most basic assumptions about matter. Their transience confounds our notion of objects as static and stable.

But who really thinks of matter as static and stable anymore? These days, objects are anything but inert. Objects, in fact, are out and *things* are in. Martin Heidegger distinguished between *objects,* as artifacts defined by their sensible properties, and *things,* matter that has entered into a relational dynamic, and thus exceeds its own physical characteristics.[13] In his latest book, *Other Things,* Bill Brown traces how "thingness and objecthood have been distinguished resolutely" by Heidegger's efforts to understand being as it takes shape with and through *das Ding.*[14] To put the distinction more plainly, the book you are holding right now is an object insofar as it is a series of ink-printed, bound pages made of paper. It is a thing if it becomes something more, like when it causes you to frown or, more optimistically, when it beckons to you from its place on the shelf asking to be finished. Lately it seems that Heideggerian *things* are everywhere. Just take a scene from DeLillo's novel *Zero K* (2016), in which the narrator examines an art installation that consists of one large rock positioned in the center of a gallery. While his teenage companion wonders whether "rocks are" or whether "they exist," the narrator notes, "what I did not tell him was that these ideas belong to Martin Heidegger."[15]

DeLillo's reference here is just one sign that Heidegger's ideas have had a renaissance of late, especially in the recent philosophical trends that attempt to shift away from epistemology toward ontology, where things have being of their own. "Object-Oriented Ontology," "Actor-Network Theory," and "Speculative Realism," despite their differences, have all challenged the centrality of the subject within the humanities, often drawing upon Heidegger's theories of the thing to do so.[16] Posthumanist work frequently treats the human as object or assemblage; the environmental humanities remind us that our planet is an object in need of care; the new materialisms identify the force of agentic objects, hyperobjects, and networks of matter. One reason these theories have been gathering force is that, ironically, things appear to be on their way out. Though work in media studies and on the history of the book continues to illuminate our material relations to printed matter and technological forms, our attention drifts to the app, the tweet, or the cloud.[17] We know that our digital devices are made of glass, copper wiring, and silicon chips, but apps nonetheless seem immaterial and Instagrams weightless.[18] Digital Humanities and forays into "big data" translate words, books, even paintings into intangible code and archival work is increasingly likely to require a VPN (virtual private network) rather than a pair of white gloves. As our surroundings appear ever more immaterial, we look to better understand materiality. The ongoing scholarly attraction to things at the moment of their supposed disappearance is certainly an advance recognition that the persistence of the material will come to have serious consequences for the planet and the humans who inhabit it.

Given the overwhelming sense that we must reckon with things because they seem to be simultaneously assuming agency of their own (from the ATM to the drone) *and* dematerializing (from the disappearance of video-rental stores to melting ice caps), it may feel odd to turn back to fiction written decades ago. But the novelists who catalog the rapidly vanishing object world of postwar America give us crucial insight into the path that has led to the present. Their portraits of fluctuating material relations offer a prehistory to our digital moment, a history that remains resonant today. Ephemera are important precursors to digital bits and online bots with lessons to share about the tension inherent in things that seem simultaneously excessive and elusive. Internet users who post photos or share messages can have the strange sense that their content is never really theirs to possess, nor theirs to erase. Even the most strenuous efforts at deleting a profile or account seem to leave some indelible trace. The methods of media archaeology can show how new media often revive and recirculate older materials and technologies; following this line of thought, we can see how the twenty-first-century avalanche of immaterial data that must be algorithmically sorted finds its antecedent in the twentieth-century surfeit of stuff, most of which appears to vanish but revisits us in this or that object preserved in an album or a museum, or in the cases that interest me most, a novel.[19]

In *The Tears of Things: Melancholy and Physical Objects,* Peter Schwenger demonstrates literature's capacity to represent the peculiar sense that even resolutely material objects are always receding from our grasp. His reading of modernist and postmodern texts suggests that objects are never quite what we want them to be, never wholly ours, and thus "fundamentally distant from us."[20] For Schwenger, writers depict "the undertone of melancholy" that persists in all things, a melancholy he says is "felt by the subject and is ultimately *for* the subject."[21] However, the portraits of ephemera offered by the writers in this study (Michael Chabon, Don DeLillo, E. L. Doctorow, Philip K. Dick, Ralph Ellison, Chester Himes, Thomas Pynchon, Marilynne Robinson, and Philip Roth) insist that melancholy is only half the story. Their novels attest to the way that ephemera can be exuberant and transience transformative: these novels show that loss, like possession, is often only partial.

Reading for ephemera entails an approach to material culture that can address *both* the material and immaterial dimensions of the novels' object world. The scholarly treatment of things—from the material culture methods developed within museum and conservation studies to the most recent variants of object-oriented ontology—focuses on the presence, animacy, and agency of objects. So far, it has left us little room to attend to the death of things. To remedy this, I bring insights borrowed from psychoanalysis to bear on material culture studies in order to make sense of the ongoing losses that shape postwar American fiction. Fiction has always stored and cataloged the objects that populate our world, but it also depicts the decay and disappearance of objects, leaving us a literary history of ephemera that has gone largely unchronicled. As Anne Cheng argues in *Ornamentalism,* attention to objects often dismissed as insignificant, superfluous, and trivial can in fact "alter how we think about the indispensability and expendability that inform labor and life, people and things."[22] My readings show how ephemera can inspire generative responses to the disappearance of things: readers encounter new uses of urban space, new forms of visibility for marginalized groups, and new conceptions of the marginal itself. In my account, post-1945 U.S. fiction responds to the vanishing object world in ways that are both melancholic and transformative. It explores how attachments to disappearing objects reveal new conceptions of time and social affiliation. And it asks us to consider how we might hold onto the world and one another differently if we recognize the ways in which we cannot always hold onto objects.

The Death of Things also makes visible the many ways in which the vanishing object is constitutive of the enduring subject, not incidental to it. In this way, my project sits uneasily amidst the majority of object-based studies, which have become enamored with the object's potential to usher in a liberating and ethical post-humanism. A little-known essay by Freud that I will turn to later in this Introduction has become a key text for me because of the way it gives us a language for describing the way that neither subjects nor objects can be known wholly to themselves or to others. There is no shimmering object to liberate the human from struggle and no authoritative subject who persists unperturbed by the material world. Object-oriented ontology, thing theory, and other discourses seeking to decenter the human in favor of the material world stress notions of relationality but often overlook the distinct and differential character of the entities in given relations. Representations of ephemera help us see these shades and grades more clearly. Some of the most resonant interactions in postwar literature are those between a compromised subject and a fading, fleeting object. The turn to things as they appear in the works of American writers from Ralph Ellison to Philip Roth helps us make sense of who we are when we cannot legitimately claim to constitute ourselves independently of chaotic and unequal regimes of production, consumption, and disposal.

READING FOR DISAPPEARANCE: THE RISE OF MATERIAL CULTURE STUDIES

Because ephemera point to a future in which they no longer exist, they evoke the strange sense that they are artifacts of a projected past. This peculiar *durée* requires a method for approaching dying things that can account for temporal disjunction. What are the reading practices that allow us to think not just about material but about its dematerialization, about the way that some objects signal their dissolution and point toward a time in which they will no longer exist?[23] Although the methods of material culture studies offer many leads, the field's longstanding focus on production has been one obstacle to understanding the fleeting character of ephemera. Anthropologists and archaeologists have been studying material culture since at least the 1870s, but it was taken up in literary and cultural studies only toward the end of the twentieth century. The key theories developed in the 1970s demonstrated that objects are more than mere props in the drama of human development; they are in fact the physical determinants of imaginative and cultural life. Drawing heavily upon Marx's ideas of the commodity, scholars like Jean Baudrillard and Pierre Bourdieu examined the ways in which production under capital involves a projection of the human into the made world.[24] This intense focus on production meant that eyes were turned toward objects' birth and proliferation, leaving little room to consider their decay and death.

During the 1980s and 1990s, however, the attention paid to things shifted as many scholars relinquished a version of Marxist ontology that insisted on the subject's constitution through production. Instead, in part through the influence of the Birmingham School of Cultural Studies, consumption became the new center of attention, the key process by which subjects entered into meaningful relations with objects and with one another. Purchase, barter, exchange, and use stole the spotlight from production as scholars grew more interested in the social functions of objects.[25] In his introduction to the seminal volume, *The Social Life of Things: Commodities in Cultural Perspective* (1986), Arjun Appadurai insists that "commodities . . . can be usefully regarded as having life histories."[26] He adds that the commodity phase of an object's "life history" does not exhaust its biography. But despite his recommendation that scholars assess the commodity's "total trajectory from production, through exchange/distribution, to consumption," Appadurai has very little to say on what we might call an object's final chapter.[27] Confined largely by the parameters of sociality, or the way an object mediates relations between humans, anthropologists and social historians like Appadurai conceive of objects first and foremost on the basis of their presence, as matter that reifies labor, is assigned value, and changes hands in complex webs of exchange. In the late 1990s, consumer historians turned their attention to one category of object that seems to speak to the "total trajectory" of objects as they fall out of the commodity phase.[28] Work on unusable goods and trash began to consider the commodity's afterlife, though not the moment or process of its death.

Alongside efforts to narrate the social histories of things, work in museum and conservation studies began to formalize ways of approaching objects outside of what might be called their "natural" social context. What is a student of material culture to do when faced with an unknown artifact that does not disclose its function or significance, be it a canister of Civil War–era gunpowder or an eight-track tape? In his 1982 essay "Mind in Matter: An Introduction to Material Culture Theory and Method," Jules David Prown laid out a method for examining and extracting cultural evidence from "mute" objects.[29] This approach, now known as the "Prown method" entails three steps—description, deduction, and speculation—that are intended to help an observer move from observation of an object's physical properties to an analysis of its function in a particular cultural context. The Prown method and other strategies have emerged from the hands-on efforts of curators and conservators to acknowledge the dense network of meanings that can inhere in an artifact. But they take the desire to conserve, to collect, and to contextualize an object as a given. As a result, these methods can do little to help explain the strong, sometimes unexplained, and often queer attachments that we form to the things around us. In a volume edited by Prown, Jennifer Roberts's discussion of a lava lamp generatively pushes the Prown method past its limits. In Roberts's reading, the lava lamp illuminates the dialectic relationship between mainstream and counterculture in the 1960s. But the essay hinges on the lamp's entrancing glow and psychedelic flows that kindle a desire on the part of the researcher to uncover this dialectic.[30]

That things should be objects of study precisely because they are objects of desire is a claim explored by Susan Stewart already in 1984 in her influential book *On Longing: Narratives of the Miniature, the Gigantic, the Souvenir, the Collection*.[31] Stewart's book made it clear that subjects come to know themselves through a number of different material relations and practices, many of which cannot be neatly aligned with Marxist theories of value, and hence Stewart's use of psychoanalytic and semiotic criticism. *On Longing* also makes a compelling case for literature as a space in which some of these enigmatic relations are best described. One of the book's most significant and lasting interventions is that it not only explains how certain objects can give meaning or shape to a subject; it also shows how the narration of these objects can give form or shape to literary expression. This is an argument echoed by Diana Fuss in *The Sense of an Interior,* where she notes that "the everyday friction between people and things reminds writers both of the literary potential of objects and the material limits of subjects."[32]

There is, of course, a long tradition of scholarship about objects in literature: books that track mountains in German romantic texts, the rose or the hillside in pastoral poetry, a French cookie or a lighthouse in texts of high modernism, or the car or the road in midcentury American novels. But the turn that interests me and that I see largely inaugurated by Stewart's *On Longing* entails less a following of literary details and more a reckoning with the thorny work objects can perform in fiction. After all, doesn't holding a stone in your hand differ from reading about holding it? What is to be gained, then, from investigating the objects in a novel as more than mere scene setting or realist description? Can representations of things help us understand our relations to them? And can things give rise or meaning to particular literary forms? Such questions have long animated Brown's work. In *The Material Unconscious* (1996) and *A Sense of Things: The Object Matter of American Literature* (2003), Brown explores how changes in the material culture of late-nineteenth- and early-twentieth-century America found their way into the literary imagination and how literature itself became a vehicle for giving meaning to the object world.[33] Brown's work helped illustrate how *reading* things in and out of literature, reading their histories, their biographies, and their affective and aesthetic dimensions, could be a fruitful endeavor. Subsequent books such as Elaine Freedgood's *The Ideas in Things* (2006), John Plotz's *Portable Property: Victorian Culture on the Move* (2008), Mary Jacobus's *Romantic Things* (2012), and Matthew Mullins's *Postmodernism in Pieces* (2016) draw on Brown's insights and expand on them within different literary fields.[34]

While it should be clear by now that *The Death of Things* is inspired and informed by the work done by literary critics who have extended the reach of material culture studies, it also diverges from the field's conventions in significant ways. Ephemera, I argue throughout this book, don't just call for a new mode of reading things. They also return us to the subjects who interact with them, who watch them vanish, and who encounter them in fiction. This is ground that has been cleared by thing theory but has been largely overwritten by subsequent work on objects and their animacy, agency, and life. The new materialisms, such as work by Jane Bennett, Diane Coole and Samantha Frost, and Bruce Braun and Sarah Whatmore, are interested in the force or vitalism of materiality, its potential to act independently of humans.[35] Bennett, for example, writes of "thing power" as "the agentic capacity of a matter that is alive and whose ontology needs to be taken into account."[36] Taking this ontology into account is a central goal of object-oriented ontology (OOO), which maintains that objects exist independently of human perception and are not exhausted by their relations with either humans or other objects. Graham Harman, Levi Bryant, Timothy Morton, and Ian Bogost are among the scholars whose work has explored the "private lives" of nonhuman and nonliving entities, attempting to elucidate how objects might experience their existence in a way that lies outside a human definition of consciousness.[37] While this work has given us provocative new ways to evaluate the importance of objects, especially in relation to geography, bioethics, environmental science, and politics, it prizes liveliness over death or disappearance and elides the inevitably important role that humans play vis-à-vis objects in each of these realms.

I have alluded to my sense that the new materialisms represent an overcorrection against universalizing discourses of the subject, against the idea that humans are the only beings worthy of attention, and against the sense that objects are utterly inert. It is time, I think, to correct this overcorrection, to practice a mode of reading that recognizes the importance of objects without elevating them to the role of subjects and, thereby, replicating the very discourses that object-oriented thinking is meant to repudiate. Maurizia Boscagli makes a similar plea when she writes that "we cannot stop at the ecstatic response: the chief affects of new materialisms cannot be just fascination in front of the vibrancy and the marvel of a materiality that works by itself, because we declare that its mobility always produces something new."[38] Attention to ephemera and the literary works that preserve them is a useful antidote to this kind of ecstasy. Many of the best-known American novelists of the twentieth century use ephemera to think about the past that always inheres in what appears new and about the future that may be far from vibrant. Instead of positing objects as the aim and end of inquiry, these writers depict objects as nodes in densely webbed networks of historical, political, and environmental forces.

The novels examined here tell readers about the death of things; they can tell critics about the death of thing theory. Or, more accurately, they tell us that both things and theories are meaningful not only when they persist but also when they dissipate. As the lessons of thing theory and other forms of object-based study migrate into environmental, digital, and posthumanist paradigms, they might cease to exist in a familiar form but do not necessarily lose force. Attunement to ephemera pushes existing paradigms of object study in new directions because they vanish and are, therefore, in some key sense, *not there.* Even though the ephemera we encounter in an archive or a novel have been preserved through curation or representation, they retain their message of disappearance, reminding us of their intended absence. Even at its most abstract, material culture studies turns around a definite, "real" object. And "real" objects, whether trash or treasure, consumable or collectible, retain their solidity and there-ness even when scholars show them to be socially constructed, historically contingent, or dynamic in their use and meaning. Whether these objects of study exist in an archive, in an art gallery, or on the terrain of everyday life, it is taken for granted that they do, indeed, exist. This is why work in material culture studies, even in its more literary branches, frequently assumes a role that feels anthropological or curatorial. Materiality can serve as the generative source of innovative work, but it can also set a limit, particularly if our object of study is imagined or evoked—the "material" inventory of novels.

As they move between presence and absence, ephemera push against these limits. Taking things seriously means attending to their form and their unique physical properties. In the case of ephemera, it is transience as much as any material quality that makes these objects unlike others and challenges familiar temporal frameworks. Here for now, announcing their disappearance and then narrativized in novels, ephemera make visible time's competing vectors. The perplexing tangle of past and future is a hallmark of the twentieth-century production regimes that began to mass-produce ephemera. Diagnosing this change, Walter Benjamin argued that the modern dynamic of commodity circulation produced a unique experience of time. The core insight of his *Arcades Project* that the "confrontation of the most recent past with the present is something historically new" has informed work across literary and media studies.[39] But Benjamin's approach does not directly address the distinct way that transience works on and through the human psyche. Ephemera often feel like animate objects because they have "lifespans" that remind us of our own mortality. This is especially surprising given the way we turn to objects as ballasts against our impermanence. The ephemeral object's disappearance rebuffs this attempt, chiding us for imagining we could slough off our human values including our transience. So while current work in thing theory and object-oriented ontology tends to focus on the agency of objects and how that agency can reorganize or dissolve the concept of the human subject, this book investigates why an object might be treasured for its passing or pastness. The ephemera that survive ironically cue us to the disappearance of so many other objects. It is intuitive to think that an object that vanishes might be seen as rare or precious; but what if it's the vanishing itself that's precious? In this case, literature, as opposed to a museum exhibit or history book, can mimetically reproduce a loss, even a whole art of losing.

READING FOR DISAPPEARANCE, PART TWO: ON FREUD, ON TRANSIENCE

The novels I consider do not animate objects in order to describe a world of posthuman agency. Rather they chronicle ephemera as a way to contemplate the confusing, often compromised agency of humans at particular moments in history. Authors as different as Chester Himes and Philip K. Dick, I argue, are concerned with collapsing boundaries between subject and object only insofar as that collapse changes the conditions of subjectivity. I therefore spend little time tracking (or policing) the distinction between subject and object and more time uncovering how particular kinds of objects might inspire or demand a different type of subject. Thing theory and object-oriented ontology do not neglect the subject: scholarship in the field often intends to spur humans into ethical or environmentally-conscious behavior. Such scholarship nonetheless promotes things in an apparently new way that decenters and at times eclipses the human. But psychoanalysis has long blurred the distinction between subject and object, offering a useful vocabulary for exploring their entanglement. Because it is seen as a problematic, pseudo-science of the subject, psychoanalysis is rarely brought to bear on material culture studies.

Although Brown's reading of Lacan in *Other Things* demonstrates one way that thing theory might be reoriented around psychoanalytic principles, psyche and stuff remain largely separate scholarly terrain. In the present book, I do not perform psychoanalytic readings that track drives, anxieties, or symptoms; instead, I use insights about attachment, loss, and grief to recast current vocabularies and approaches for apprehending matter. A short, largely overlooked essay by Freud exemplifies how psychoanalytic thought, when seen through the prism of material culture studies, illuminates the significance of ephemera to the subject and its material formation.

In the same year that Freud published "Thoughts for the Times on War and Death" (1915), he also penned an enigmatic, shorter essay that has received comparatively little attention. In the autumn of 1915, Freud was asked to contribute to a special publication, *Das Land Goethes,* which was intended to raise money for German libraries (Figure 1). Conceived in part as wartime propaganda, the volume was dedicated to Goethe, and it was supposed to demonstrate the civility of German character that was vilified by its enemies at the time. The contributors to the volume made for impressive company: Albert Einstein, the writers Gerhardt Hauptmann, Arthur Schnitzler, and Jakob Wasserman, the composers Max Reger and Richard Strauss, and more than a hundred other writers, artists, scientists, and politicians. It was planned as a lavish production, with expensive reproductions of artworks, manuscripts, and autographs, all bound together in yellow silk.

Freud's contribution is very short compared to his major works, just over a thousand words that would fill two pages. The essay, "On Transience," is both like and unlike most of his writing. Though his theme, the origin of mourning, is psychoanalytic, the essay is lyrical, meditative, and elegiac. The original German title of the essay is simply the word *Vergänglichkeit,* with no article or preposition. James Strachey's addition of the "on" in the English title signals immediately that this is a writerly piece: a meditation or reflection rather than an exhaustive clinical text.[40] In the text, Freud describes a walk through the countryside with two companions that prompts him to ruminate on the "transience of all things." The two companions are generally agreed to be Lou Andreas-Salomé and Rainer Marie Rilke, both of whom Freud met in Munich during the Fourth International Psychoanalytical Congress of 1913.[41] Freud tells us in the essay that, while the three friends admire the beauty of their surroundings, the "young but

Das
Land Goethes
1914–1916
Ein vaterländisches Gedenkbuch
Herausgegeben vom Berliner
Goethebund

Der Reinertrag ist für die Errichtung von
Volksbüchereien in Ostpreußen bestimmt

1 9 1 6
Deutsche Verlags-Anstalt
Stuttgart/Berlin

FIGURE 1. Title page of an original edition of *Das Land Goethes* 1914–1916*: Ein vaterländisches Gedenkbuch.* Published in 1916 by Deutsche Verlangsanstalt.

already famous poet" grows melancholy. He realizes that all the things he sees are transient, fated to extinction. For him, beauty is eclipsed by its negation and therefore has no value or meaning.

Freud is sympathetic to the poet's view but cannot accept his conclusion. For Freud, an object's transience does not detract from its beauty. He claims instead that "the value of all this beauty and perfection is determined *only by its significance for our own emotional lives*" and therefore "has no need to survive" (emphasis mine). For Freud, transience gives things value because it reinforces the subject's significance. The fading blossom, the vanishing leaves—each object grants its beholder pastoral pleasures. As Freud puts it: "Transience value is scarcity value in time. Limitation in the possibility of an enjoyment raises the value of the enjoyment." The poet's inability to enjoy the objects he sees, therefore, appears pathological to Freud, who concludes that it shows an unreasonable fear of mourning. All of this makes "On

Transience" an interesting enough document to prompt a rethinking of "Mourning and Melancholia," but before we get there, I want to say something about the specific objects in the essay.

Freud gives us a wide range of objects: under the broad headings of "nature and art," we read of landscapes, flowers, pictures, statues, poems, and philosophy. The human form is also named; all are said by Freud to vanish at different speeds, some during the course of our own lives, others in a different time. A whole range of scales appears intrinsic to transience; ephemera may be discrete objects or whole environments. There is no specificity. Freud never mentions a particular statue or picture, nor are we told the location of this countryside or given a sense of how it might look. The essay does not acknowledge the qualities that give an object its beauty or makes its disappearance so painful. Instead, Freud sets the human observers apart from a tableau of transient objects, attempting to shore up a subject who may lift his head optimistically and await restoration. Thus, we might say that, in this essay, Freud *subjectivizes* objects, imbuing them with importance pegged entirely to human subjects. In many psychoanalytic texts, objects are treated in this way, with things maybe vibrant and nearly agentic; just think of the famous sardine can that does not "see" Lacan in "The Line and the Light" or of the curiously shaped table with carvings of crocodiles that come to life in Freud's essay "The Uncanny."[42] But these things, even when vividly drawn, matter only because they are props in the psychic drama that psychoanalysis wants to capture. In short, there's no need for Freud to be specific about the objects at hand because his real interest is in subjects. This would be straightforward enough if it were not also true that psychoanalysis also treats subjects as objects.

The various uses of the term "object" (*das Objekt*) in psychoanalytic literature stem from the Freudian notion of the instinct. In his essays on the theory of sexuality from 1905, Freud explains: "I shall now introduce two technical terms. Let us call the person from whom sexual attraction proceeds the *sexual object* and the act towards which the instinct tends the sexual aim" (emphasis mine).[43] Tracking the term from this instance forward, Jean Laplanche and Jean-Bertrand Pontalis conclude: "[The] object is understood as a sense comparable to the one it has in the literary or archaic, 'the object of my passion, of my hatred, etc.' It does not imply, as it does ordinarily, the idea of a 'thing,' of an inanimate and manipulable object as opposed to an animate being or person."[44] Of course, it is not only that the love object, the target of an object-choice, may be an animate being or person. We also know that the ego can split and treat itself as an object, as in melancholia, when "one part of the ego sets itself over and against the other, judges it critically, and as it were, *takes it as its object*."[45] And in the most basic sense, the analysand is herself the *object* of analysis. To be the subject of one of Freud's case studies is to be subjected to his method, not so much an agent as an object of the doctor's inquiry.

If the psychoanalytic move of turning subjects into grammatical objects is a familiar one, less clear is the exact role of material objects. I claimed earlier that, in "On Transience," the object matters only insofar as it illuminates the processes at work in the melancholy poet's mind. But wouldn't the essay feel different if the poet's sadness was prompted by an urban landscape instead of a pastoral one? Or a painting of that landscape? Or something entirely different: a library, a coat, a gold coin? To return briefly to the carved table of "The Uncanny," if we swap the crocodiles for chickens or the table for a tapestry, surely Freud's story would have a different effect. While plenty of ink has been spilled about Freud's mystic writing pad, many of the objects animating his other writings have received little attention. "A Note Upon the Mystic Writing Pad" ties together the transience of writing on cellophane and the deeper inscription of text on the wax pad underneath, but the object there is a metaphor for human memory, one of Freud's usual subjects. In "On Transience," though, even as he discusses human desire and grief, Freud is thinking about things themselves.

The poet refuses to take pleasure in the beauty of the "smiling countryside" that he knows will not survive. If the poet is indeed Rilke, we know that by 1913 he had already developed the *Dinggedicht*, or "thing poem," his own attempt to present objects with factual precision. In poems like "Blue Hydrangea," "The Carousel," and most famously, "The Panther," Rilke describes surfaces and minute details to try to convey the essential nature of things. "The 'thingness' of these poems," explains Erich Heller, "reflects not the harmony in which an inner self lives with its 'objects'; it reflects a troubled inner self immersing itself in 'the things.'"[46] On the one hand, these poems seem to show Rilke's willingness to find pleasure in things; on the other, the detached expression of the *Dinggedicht* suggests a dispassionate observer who refuses to feel for the beauty around him. This refusal, Freud says in the context of their countryside walk, is a preemptive strike against mourning. But the refusal leaves the poet melancholic, already bereft of the objects he is loath to mourn and trapped in an impoverished world of his own making. The objects here are not lost: the countryside is *right there* as the poet looks on. So we cannot speak of "libido attached to a lost object and drawn into the ego," as Freud does in "Mourning and Melancholia."[47] "On Transience" does not describe a reaction to loss, a retrospective process; instead it tells of a prospective one.

The poet's "aching despondency" aligns with the usual understanding of melancholia in that both arise when the subject refuses to mourn. But, in "On Transience," it is a refusal to mourn in the future. It is also a refusal made although the imagined loss may never happen fully or absolutely; it is always only *happening,* but articulated as if it has already taken place. This is where I think the significance of the countryside *as an object* begins to emerge. After diagnosing the poet's fear of mourning, Freud reflects:

> My conversation with the poet took place in the summer before the war. A year later the war broke out and robbed the world of its beauties. It destroyed not only the beauty of the countrysides through which it passed and the works of art which it met with on its path but it also shattered our pride in the achievements of our civilization, or admiration for many philosophers and artists and our hopes of a final triumph over the differences between nations and races. It tarnished the lofty impartiality of our science, it revealed our instincts in all their nakedness and let loose the evil spirits within us which we thought had been tamed forever by centuries of continuous education by the noblest minds. It made our country small again and made the rest of the world far remote. It robbed us of very much that we had loved, and showed us how ephemeral were many things that we regarded as changeless.[48]

By describing the many losses left in the wake of the First World War, Freud enacts the very mourning that his companions hope to avoid. "Look," he tells his readers, "I am not afraid to mourn!" He compiles this extensive list in an effort to demonstrate that love and attachment are meaningful even, or especially, if we know that the objects of those attachments are temporary.

But Freud's performance of mourning strains at the essay's conclusion. After this list of losses, Freud writes: "We cannot be surprised that our libido, thus bereft of so many of its objects, has clung with all the greater intensity to what is left to us, that our love of our country, our affection for those nearest us and our pride in what is common to us have suddenly grown stronger." Even if we put aside the overtones of nationalism and the belief in shared sentiment that look so misplaced in light of the Second World War and Freud's ultimate flight from his native Austria to England, we are still left to wonder whether the end of this essay really does demonstrate "healthy" mourning. It reads instead like Freud's own refusal even to acknowledge what has been lost; his hasty mourning requires a focus not on what is transient but on what endures. The last two sentences of the text present yet another contradiction: "When once the mourning is over, it will be found that our high opinion of the riches of civilization has lost nothing from our discovery of their fragility. We shall build up again all that war has destroyed, and perhaps on firmer ground and more lastingly than before." Freud himself demonstrates how difficult it is not to think in absolute terms about presence and absence, the past and the future, the object that is lost and the object preserved. His struggle here illuminates the challenge any writer faces in narrating a history of losing instead of loss.

The poet looks at the countryside and sees what he will lose; Freud looks at the countryside and sees what will be rebuilt. So, on the one hand, Freud's vision of rebuilding (*Alles wieder aufbauern*) comes only after "healthy" mourning has been completed. On the other hand, doesn't this fantasy of rebuilding compromise the very acceptance of transience that Freud advocates? This fantasy is, after all, one of preservation wherein all that has been lost is replaced on firmer ground. The difference between the melancholic poet who denies the beauty in the world because he cannot bear to witness its destruction and the doctor who endures this destruction by imagining the eventual resurrection of beauty starts to dissolve. This collapse reveals the central challenges to thinking about transience: how specific must we be about objects that vanish and the ones we hope will take their place? How can we hold on to the knowledge there are many objects we cannot hold on to, even if they do not vanish entirely?

Though he must imagine a countryside for Rilke, Freud's own mourning focuses instead on "the riches of civilization" that can be rebuilt.[49] He occludes this difference so as to posit himself a symmetric foil to Rilke.[50] In “On Transience,” it would initially seem that loss is loss is loss. The object matters less than the subject’s response to it, whether prospective or retrospective. But what I hope my attention to the contortions of Freud’s text has shown is that the apparent insignificance of objects’ particularity is in fact an admission of their importance. Freud cannot fully pin down the objects that prompt mourning, and so he seems to write over them multiple times, creating images that feel overdetermined in their ambiguity. In “On Transience,” the objects cannot be entirely assimilated into a subject-centered narrative; here their ontic energy thwarts the psychoanalytic tendency toward mastery. The crucial lesson of this essay is that neither subjects nor objects emerge unscathed, known wholly to themselves or to others: no shimmering object to liberate the human from his struggles, no authoritative subject who can persist unperturbed by the material world.

If object-oriented ontology, thing theory, and other discourses seeking to decenter the human in favor of the material world have overlooked this point, then representations of ephemera help us see it more clearly. Freud’s essay cues us to read for the imbrication of subject and object, for the messy entanglements between persons and things.[51] This type of reading takes seriously the fact that loss is not only retrospective. It is counterintuitive to think in the future tense of an item as lost; can I really mourn the absence of something still here? But there are many reasons to contemplate future losses: historical conditions (fear of imminent war), design principles (planned obsolescence), and individual experience or temperament (anxiety about personal illness or tragedy), to name just a few. Despite the narrative of the United States as an optimistic and forward-looking nation, the sense of impending disasters military, climatological, political, and so on has made the future a source of anxiety and given rise to what Paul Saint-Amour calls “a pre-traumatic stress syndrome.”[52] Even now, many of us probably have more in common with Freud’s version of Rilke than we care to admit.

AMERICAN EPHEMERA, AMERICAN NOVELS

The insights drawn here from Freud illuminate how the postwar novel serves as techne and tutelage for readers thinking about their relationships to the object world. We tend to expect that fiction depicting the disappearance of beloved objects or the transience of the material world will be nostalgic or elegiac. And it is true that, because ephemera announce their own decay, disappearance, or destruction, they frequently function as apt ciphers for expressing melancholic feelings. But ephemera are not only flickering illusions hovering on the horizon of loss. They are just as likely to be excessive, obtrusive, and enduring in the memories and practices they engender, and in the fiction that depicts them. The literary treatment of ephemera captures these different sentiments and explores how the different affects associated with transience constitute the subject. The novels I consider investigate what it means to be human when being human entails confronting a perpetually shifting material world. When we turn our attention from the life of things to the way things die, we see that perpetual—but never absolute—loss is fundamental to the experience of many American novels.

The American literary fascination with ephemera is in part a response to what has always been understood as a constitutive feature of the national landscape and character. It was the radical mutability of the United States, especially its cities, that defined the country for many thinkers. In 1904, when Henry James returned to the United States after living abroad for more than twenty years, he marveled at New York's "restless renewals," which seemed to him a caustic element of the city's destructive essence.[53] Le Corbusier, on the other hand, celebrated Manhattan as "a provisional city," marveling at how the new world seemed to require a whole lot of newness.[54] As Michel de Certeau put it, "[America's] present invents itself, from hour to hour, in the act of throwing away its previous accomplishments."[55] Such remarks already illustrate the range of responses that creative destruction writ large can inspire. The tendency to view impermanence and disposability as part of an American ethos might be said to have begun already with Alexis de Tocqueville, who cataloged what he saw as Americans' dismissive attitudes toward history and tradition in *Democracy in America*: "Among democratic nations new families are constantly springing up, others are constantly falling away, and all that remain change their condition; the woof of time is every instant broken and the track of generations effaced. Those who went before are soon forgotten; of those who will come after, no one has any idea."[56] This "falling away" is usually associated with a kind of national historical amnesia; it might also help to explain the nation's enduring love affair with transience.

The stories of industrialization, urbanization, and mass consumption that are crucial to the post-1945 novels that interest me thus begin much earlier. Douglas Mao, in *Solid Objects,* examines the ambivalence modernists had about new production techniques; Schwenger discusses the self-conscious forms of expression used by modernists to reflect on the object of their art; Brown writes of modernism as an aesthetic strategy that aims to liberate objects from the confines of modernity. Where mid- and late-nineteenth-century writers like Dreiser focused on the potential to "build a self" with the help of consumer goods and new technologies, American modernists reflected the increasingly porous relationship between reality and fiction that came to characterize life in twentieth-century America.[57] Turning briefly to F. Scott Fitzgerald's canonical work of American modernism, we can see that Carrie Meeber's "innate taste for imitation" culminates in the form of Jay Gatsby, who has transformed himself into a glittering playboy reigning over an estate as synthetic as the identity he has created for himself.[58] Gatsby is a provisional king in an empire of images, and Fitzgerald's novel does for those images what Dreiser's did for factories and department stores. In constructing the perfect image for himself, the one that he believes will help him win Daisy's love, Gatsby has discovered the power of "enchanted objects."[59] He surrounds himself with things that lend him (and the novel) glamour meant to incite desire. Lavish clothing, cars, and mansions are not ephemeral in the conventional sense of the word, but in *The Great Gatsby,* they are hollow objects, fragile ornaments that lend the novel not only its glitz but also its melancholy.

The "enchanted objects" in *The Great Gatsby* inspire a grief that thrums underneath the novel's high notes. It may revel in the excesses of the jazz age, but the novel reminds readers at every turn that, in this era of decadence, objects have usurped people as the means of communication, of emotional and sexual exchange. While Fitzgerald depicts the city as a geometric grid of streets where subway trains rumble beneath hotels, movie theaters, and throbbing dance halls, the real emblem of twentieth-century urban life watches over the commuters who make their way between Manhattan and the wealthy enclaves of Long Island. From a fading billboard of a long-forgotten oculist, the gigantic eyes of Dr. T. J. Eckleberg preside over "the valley of ashes," the "gray land and the spasms of bleak dust which drift endlessly over it" (23). Like Freud, Fitzgerald is attuned to the disjunction between material and psychic registers: the way that humans can experience expansion and excess as a process of loss. The eyes, "dimmed a little by many paintless days," expose the empty promise of images; they also lay bare the wasteland that springs up as a direct consequence of twentieth-century urban development. The billboard speaks to the concerns with accumulation that intensified during the second half of the twentieth century, with the sense that lingering objects might threaten us with their staying power, while also asking readers to reflect on what has been lost in the push toward "progress."

Fitzgerald's novel also gives us an image that evokes the strange temporality of ephemera. Like Eckleberg's eyes bearing down on the present with their patina of the past, the famous green light that beckons from the end of Daisy's pier shines on a goal that recedes as Gatsby approaches it. In the famous lines that close *The Great Gatsby,* which hardly need to be quoted, Nick says that, though "Gatsby believed in the green light, the orgiastic future that year by year recedes before us," he fails to see "that it was already behind him, somewhere back in that vast obscurity beyond the city, where the dark fields of the republic rolled on under the night" (189). The green light is an illusory promise of the future, one that Fitzgerald tells us is built on the wreckage of the past. The green light captures the way that vanishing objects can convey an impression of folded, knotted, looping time. Fitzgerald's novel thus concludes in the same vexed position as Freud's essay, with a subject who sees the desired object eluding his grasp as it moves endlessly into an unreachable future. The green light is an ephemeral object moving through the relays of newly kinked time.

Freud and Rilke, Dreiser and Fitzgerald: these earlier thinkers in Europe and in America were responding to what we could call the first phase of consumer culture, the development and expansion of museum culture, department stores, and mail order catalogs. Whether we call these writers late-Victorian, *fin de siècle,* or modernist thinkers, they all chronicle a culture on the cusp of dramatic material change. This is also Benjamin's terrain; his studies of Parisian arcades and world's fairs lead him to articulate a mode of reading objects for their anachronistic powers. In the form of the "wish image" (*Wunschbild*), Benjamin locates objects that could express collective fantasies by reaching back into the past. In *The Arcades Project,* Benjamin suggests that the wish image "is that wherein what has been comes together in a flash with the now to form a constellation."[60] Examples of these images could be found in the shop windows of the arcades, in the pavilions of world's fairs, and even in metro stations, displayed as part of an enchanted scene.[61] Their "exhibition value" (*Ausstellungswert*), as he called it, was not divorced from the economic principles of production and exchange. But exhibition value speaks to the special visibility of certain objects, and to the value that can be exposed only through perception. Thus, where Freud understands transience as "scarcity value in time" and attempts to understand its impact on the individual human psyche, Benjamin sees transience as a fundamental property of modernity, one that can lead to a collective encounter with the past. Though Benjamin is a theorist of loss and losing, he imagines a nonmelancholic relation to objects that recede forever beyond our grasp but never disappear altogether. Benjamin's treatment of modernity's objects and the way they can store the past regardless of their transitory nature anticipates the work that ephemera do in more recent texts. His insights, like Fitzgerald's and Freud's, illuminate the cultural forces shaping object relations, forces that later writers see accelerated and intensified in postwar America.

In *The System of Objects,* Baudrillard taxonomizes and investigates the "ever-accelerating procession of generations of products, appliances, and gadgets" that twentieth-century capitalism brought to the consumer's door.[62] His claim that "production speeds up the lifespan" of objects is a fundamentally Marxist one. It echoes the famous passage of the Communist Manifesto in which Marx and Engels proclaim that "the bourgeoisie cannot exist without constantly revolutionizing the instruments of production, and thereby the relations of production, and with them the whole relations of society."[63] This ceaseless production generates a seemingly endless march of new objects and new desires to own them. By the time Baudrillard was writing in the 1960s, the incessant turnover described by Marx and Engles was a marketing strategy, a conscious motivation in the manufacture of goods. In Baudrillard's account, "production has now emerged as an all-surpassing agency with the power not merely of life but also of death over objects."[64] By the postwar era, planned obsolescence and ever-shorter cycles of fashion enforced the maxim that "the object cannot be allowed to escape from ephemerality."[65] The history of postwar America is undeniably a history of more things that die more often. This story has been wonderfully told by several historians: Lizabeth Cohen narrates the inextricable link between mass production after World War II and the conception of U.S. citizenship in *A Consumer's Republic;* in *Waste and Want,* Susan Strasser details the boom in disposable goods in the United States that not even the Depression could dent; Ellen Ruppell Shell chronicles the expanding surfeit of cheap goods and the related activity of "bargain hunting" that took off in the second half of the twentieth century in her book *Cheap.*[66]

The short lives of consumer goods, the mutability of cityscapes and skylines, and even the temporary structures of film and television sets converged to make ephemerality a dominant paradigm of the late-twentieth-century object world. It's not difficult to see how this fed into the postmodern sensibility of fragmentation and inauthenticity, of temporary images and objects swirling together in dizzying eddies. Regardless of their differences, the many definitions of postmodernism tend to agree that American consumer culture—its pervasiveness, its excesses, its seeming ability to commoditize everything—contributed to the literary style that emerged after World War II. According to Fredric Jameson, the flood of goods onto the market under late capitalism and the liquid fungibility of the market itself made all things appear interchangeable.[67] Though commodities appear displaced by the market, which becomes a substitute for itself, still structures of labor, distribution, and exchange are responsible for what Jameson calls postmodernism's "crisis in historicity." Another way to gloss this crisis (in reverse) is to say that, once objects become predominantly disposable and transient, so too is history. We find this kind of correlation in Jameson's thought in passages like this one: "The post-modern must be characterized as a situation in which the survival, the residue, the holdover, the archaic, has finally been swept away without a trace. In the post-modern, then, the past itself has disappeared."[68]

The Death of Things is both literal (it's about ephemera) and literary (it turns to the fiction in which they are represented), and so I argue that postwar U.S. novels frequently question the persistence of the past *through* representations of the residues and traces Jameson is so quick to efface. Literary portraits of ephemera include the details of their disappearance, but they also preserve the objects and their disappearance in narrative form. If literature shows that commodities still have particular features and particular histories, if all that is solid leaves its mark even as it melts into air, then it makes sense that the individual subject never fully disappears, as Jameson claims, but rather emerges altered as she wanders through the terrain of the late twentieth century.

Novels that critics call postmodern are not all or only ironic, devoid of history and sentiment, pressing objects into empty simulacra and humans into empty shells. As I will argue throughout this book, these novels frequently, and with earnestness and urgency, tackle the role of the subject against a landscape littered with the detritus of American material culture.

But no books, including this one, escape the market logics that they might seek to diagnose or critique. The question of which books circulate in which markets is one that has received significant attention of late, as scholars including Jim English, Mark McGurl, Laura McGrath, and Dan Sinykin track the tangled web of publishers, prizes, book clubs, school curricula, online reviews, and algorithms that work together to deliver certain books into certain readers hands.[69] Kinohi Nishikawa's *Street Players* maps the circuits that black pulp fiction traveled during the twentieth century, showing how porous the boundary between ephemera and literature truly is and how profoundly magazines, pulp paperbacks, and hardcover literature are all subject to the period's material conditions.[70] Given that books are subject to capitalism's rhythms of production and disposal, it is logical that the stories within them consider the effects of such ubiquitous and accelerated object relations. Under these conditions, ephemera survive usually as the result of a rescue mission; when they appear in novels, they often testify to the ravages of capitalism and its consequences. Boscagli aptly describes the stakes of such narratives in her discussion of "stuff": "[Stuff is] made up of objects that have been brought through the mill, have interacted with the world and its subjects, and have a story to tell. This story, which all matter, as it were, knows is its destiny in modernity, is both that of the dynamism that infuses all relations of modern subjects with every kind of materiality, and that of the dehiscence of this complex, hybrid materiality into the valueless."[71] The novels I consider record both parts of this story through their attention to ephemera, both the dynamism and the dehiscence, and most importantly, how subjects operate when they are pulled between these poles.

But why focus on the *novel* as the form that addresses the ephemeral with such acuity? Poetry has long stored and cataloged the objects that populate our world; Achilles's shield and Keats's well-wrought urn might even be said to concretize the Western canon.[72] William Butler Yeats even wrote a poem called "Ephemera" in 1884. In it, Yeats narrates a conversation between lovers in the moment of their waning love. They stand hand in hand beside a lake, and the autumnal scenery seems to register the melancholy of their loss. The poem ends with a claim that human existence itself is defined by its transience: "Before us lies eternity; our souls / Are love, and a continual farewell."[73] Despite its title, Yeats's poem is interested in the leaves only insofar as they effectively metaphorize love and its declension. Novels, on the other hand, especially the postwar texts that I consider, are filled with details that never rise to the figurative grandeur of Achilles's shield or the urn, but this does not make them meaningless. In his expansive study of eighteenth-century English fiction, J. Paul Hunter argues that the novel subsumes and contains many forms of popular thought and everyday materials that surround it. He calls this "the novel's imperialism": "Its ability to take over features from other species and assimilate them into a new form is well known, but we have to be clearer about what those features are and where they come from."[74] The postwar novels that interest me store the ephemera that flooded American homes and markets during the second half of the twentieth century and also draw on the dynamics of ephemera that writers saw inflecting the world around them. In depicting transience, these novels also address the possibility of their own vanishing.

Postmodern literature in particular, with its emphasis on dizzying networks, emerging communication technologies, and the proliferation of both objects and images, seems to hail the death of print culture. Scholars eager to proclaim the end of postmodernism seem reactive to the way that its literature stages print, and literature itself, as a transient object. Perhaps this is why recent critics have been so eager to proclaim the end of postmodernism: it is the rare literary scholar who can comfortably admit that the novel is dying. But writing *The Death of Things* has shown me that to live in the time of the novel's *dying* is not to live in the time of its death. The alarm bell about the death of books has been sounding for some time: as Kathleen Fitzpatrick notes, "questions of the book's ostensible decline have hounded it for decades, if not centuries."[75] The printed novel may not be as alive as we would hope, but it continues to make meaning as it changes shape and perpetually dies. Jessica Pressman has tracked the move from the book to "bookishness," a term she uses to "describe an aesthetic practice and cultural phenomenon that figures the book as an artifact rather than just as a medium for information transmission."[76] Even so, it is likely that most of our books in printed format, if not all, will come to seem like ephemera before too long. Novels self-reflexively comment on this material transience through representations of ephemera, speaking as if they are native informants from a land of printed objects.

In part, postwar U.S. novelists write of ephemera such as playbills and newspapers, and even makeshift memorials because such objects simply made up the object world around them. A realistic description and a finely grained scene setting might well include the transient or disposable items that were characteristic of the times. In his 1993 essay "E Unibus Pluram," David Foster Wallace remarks that "one of the most recognizable things about this century's postmodern fiction was the movement's strategic deployment of pop-cultural references—brand names, celebrities, television programs—in even its loftiest high-art projects."[77] But, beyond a drive toward the mimetic, writers grant central roles to ephemera in their novels in order to contend with their disappearance. Such objects have beguiled writers like Thomas Pynchon and Michael Chabon, elegists of the waning promises of American modernity. These elegies don't simply express the "traditional lament for the ephemeral object" in which the passing of beauty inspires lingering woe.[78] I have already argued that novels can serve as a particular kind of archive for ephemera *and* for their disappearance; they represent this duality that shows readers the generative capacities of loss.

The postwar novels that I discuss frequently construct portraits of the compromised and therefore timely subjects who must navigate the world into which they are written. The novel, a form committed to novelty but thought to have a monumental or memorializing function, catalogs vanishing objects but also instructs readers on the necessity of letting things go. Letting go of objects in these novels means letting go of fantasies: of permanence, of national coherence, of a universal subject, of a particular future.[79] Unlike an artifact in a museum display or a keepsake in a personal collection, an object in literature can be *there and not there.*[80] Novels about ephemera know this and they help readers see the many ways in which the vanishing object is most meaningful in its vanishing, not in its death but in its dying. In his discussion of the changing form of the book, Andrew Piper writes that "thinking historically rests on the contradictory notion of something being both simultaneously present and absent, on grasping and letting go."[81] Fiction that reckons with ephemera facilitates this historical operation, presenting readers with paradoxical objects that they cannot hold onto, even while insisting that those objects never completely disappear.

THE STRUCTURE OF THIS BOOK

Given the curious, anachronistic vectors of time that ephemera themselves express, this book does not unfold in a neat chronological order. I examine pivotal developments in twentieth-century American history through the postwar novels that depict them. Although I have organized this book chronologically according to these historical developments, the fiction about them is not similarly ordered across time. A novel written in 2000 about an event in 1939, for instance, precedes the discussion of a novel written in 1962 about the late 1950s. Historical time chafes against literary time, a meaningful irritation, given the temporal contortions of transience itself. Each chapter explores the fictional life and death of objects, and each situates fictional ephemeral objects in historical context with archival research before exploring the broader dynamics of ephemera in novels. This is a delicate dance: moving between historical objects and fictive ones, between historical events and novels that question the status of history. *The Death of Things* uncovers the trenchant historical importance of ephemera while also insisting that American writers in the second half of the twentieth century turn to ephemera to revise history and to reorient readers toward an unfamiliar past that fades, recedes, and challenges the conventional sense of what endures and why.

The first chapter, "Yesterday's Tomorrowland: E. L. Doctorow, Michael Chabon, and the 1939 World's Fair," examines world's-fair novels to explore the duplicity of their future visions. Although a number of scholars have studied the nationalist and imperialist dimensions of world's fairs, none have considered how the ephemerality of the fairs and their objects complicate their implied political allegories. The 1939 New York World's Fair, erected on what F. Scott Fitzgerald called "the valley of ashes," staged monuments to a better future that paradoxically highlighted their own transience. Returning obsessively to this site of loss, E. L. Doctorow's *World's Fair* (1985) and Michael Chabon's *The Amazing Adventures of Kavalier and Clay* (2000) reveal the fair's promises for a better future to be fantasies, their objects already dissolving into debris. Because world's fairs display objects while also functioning as temporary objects themselves, they illustrate the powerful appeal of the ephemeral: its capacity to inspire grief but also to organize material and sensory experiences toward the future.

Chapter 2, "Counterhistory, Counterfact, Counterobject: Philip K. Dick, Philip Roth, and the Second World War," takes up the troubled time immediately following the 1939 world's fair in order to examine the link between national ideals and transient materials. I move from celebratory world's fairs to a period of explicit menace, exploring the role of ephemera in literary responses to World War II. In counterfactual historical novels that imagine alternative outcomes to World War II, including Dick's *The Man in the High Castle* (1962) and Roth's *The Plot Against America* (2004), ephemera become charged with the nostalgic task of preserving and reanimating a lost past. But by placing prewar Americana such as advertisements and postage stamps at the heart of their novels, Dick and Roth suggest that the past supposedly lost to us may not be the past we imagine. Using "real" artifacts in their counterfactual worlds, the novels confound the distinction between authentic and fake objects and between historical fact and fiction.

The third chapter, "Zoned Out: Chester Himes, Ralph Ellison, and Urban Infrastructure," considers narratives that engage transient objects in order to depict anxieties about the racial life of neighborhoods in 1950s and 1960s New York. Ellison and Himes responded to the challenge of representing both permanence and loss in a changing Harlem. Reading Himes's *Harlem Cycle* (1957–69) alongside Ellison's *Invisible Man* (1952) by the light of ephemera illuminates relays between the two authors that have been largely overlooked. Objects like signs, newspapers, and blueprints serve as proxies for the built environment, allowing readers to more readily grasp Harlem's transience. Himes, long-positioned as a genre writer and only recently emerging as an important figure of study, has much more in common with the canonical giant Ellison than has previously been noted. Ellison and Himes both confronted the paradox of gentrification, depicting Harlem in the mid-twentieth century as a black space undergoing a perpetual and unfinished process of gentrification. A reading of the ephemera within their novels also sheds light on what I call the "infrastructural racism" that underlies the physical changes wrought by gentrification, seeking a language to name spatial and racial relations that are, in fact, never fully transformed.

Chapter 4, "Time, Stamped: Thomas Pynchon's Media Systems," analyzes the waste and ephemera that circulate in Pynchon's early novels *V.* (1963) and *The Crying of Lot 49* (1966). I argue for the centrality of material ephemera to postmodern literary form: the aesthetic project of the novel is shaped by the transience of its objects. Like the stamps collected by the narrator in *The Plot Against America,* the stamps that compose the novel's titular object, Lot 49, point to an alternate world that may or may not be real. But Pynchon's stamps are just one set of objects amidst many that vanish or mislead in the same fashion as his novels' language and plots. Pynchon's fiction, I argue, does not just use stuff to indict consumer excess or the American infatuation with "empty" cultural performances. Rather, Pynchon's dying objects insist upon a human sense of ethical responsibility, despite our almost universal understanding of his work as a ludic and postmodern treatment of the disappearing human subject. This chapter suggests that the time is right for a new reading of Pynchon, one that has not been properly knowable until now, when the novelty of his investment in the dazzlement of accumulation has itself begun to fade.

Turning from Oedipa's errant quest to make sense of transient objects, in the fifth chapter, "The Disorder of Things: Marilynne Robinson's Transient Women," I examine *Housekeeping* (1980), in which women themselves seem to become transient. The novel is a paradigmatic American narrative of self-fashioning that established Robinson as one of the most successful writers of late-twentieth-century domestic fiction. I consider recent feminist and queer theories of feeling and objecthood alongside the Freudian double logic of transience. Taken together, these theories give shape to Robinson's distinctive prose style, which finds a newly gendered and nonurban language that manages not just to describe the transience of things, but to enact it. *Housekeeping* neither hallows nor disparages small-town life in rural 1950s America. The novel's copious ephemera of dress patterns, women's magazines, pressed flowers, and newspaper clippings challenge the domestic order that women are expected to maintain. Robinson's portraits of transient objects make visible a longer lineage of women's writing on ephemera and point to the vexed status that the writing of women has long had *as* ephemeral.

In the last portion of the book, I move from literary texts that reflect on dying objects in a late industrial age to texts that speak to our increasingly digital, "immaterial" culture. My sixth chapter, "Ephemeral Gods, Billboard Saints: Don DeLillo's Apparitions," studies the phenomenon of religious apparitions in city spaces. I ask what kind of communities form around instances in which faith becomes material. Reading the apparition with which Don DeLillo concludes *Underworld* (1997) alongside a "real-life" image of the Virgin Mary that appeared in April 2005 in Chicago on the wall of a highway underpass, the chapter follows the experiences and consequences that such visions effect. The emergent objects engender material practices that work, at least temporarily, against the destructive and dehumanizing forces of modernization. The apparitions reveal the malleable nature of urban structures taken to be permanent, thereby dismantling the difference between waste and relic, loss and restoration. And, in a coda, I consider the digital afterlives of stuff, asking what impact the technology that extends objects' lives has on our interpretive practices and our desires. Can preserving ephemera in digital archives long past their "natural lives" strip them of a unique power they otherwise possess? One effect of considering the digital through the lens of the ephemeral is disciplinary: media studies, I suggest, has much to learn from literary studies. The current tends to flow in the other direction these days, but the novels on transience that I consider productively blur the line between the two disciplines.

OBJECT POSITIONS

The central lesson of ephemera when they appear in novels, the lesson of not imagining that we possess things fully or can preserve them indefinitely, has become more timely than ever. The dangerous nostalgia of right-wing and white-supremacist politics in the United States relies on a melancholic relationship that some Americans have to their disappearing objects. As Rebecca Solnit points out, "More Americans work in museums than work in coal, but coalminers are treated as sacred beings owed huge subsidies and the sacrifice of the climate."[82] The inability to accept the dying away of certain objects, lifeways, and national ideals is undeniably related to the country's racial divisions: residual and sentimental attachments to a largely fictional former America reflect the fear that increasing equality for some means less prosperity for others. As a result, a strange shift is taking place in the discourse of marginalization. Instead of marginalized groups demanding equal rights, we see a bitter, multifront battle unfolding over who in fact is marginalized. Not so long ago, those at the center fought ferociously to hold the line and force back those at the margins. But now an additional conflict rages about who occupies the margins and whose grievances "count." The goal of the conflict remains reaching the center: the space of visibility, rights, and reparations. As the concept of the margins becomes a battleground in an ongoing so-called culture war, it is important to ask whether marginal *objects* can really teach us anything useful about marginalized *subjects*.[83]

Literary portraits of ephemera frequently revolve around issues of marginalization for several reasons: because infrastructural changes to urban space disproportionately affect minorities; because the material archive of "historiographic metafiction" often attempts to renarrate history from the perspective of those who have been silenced; because loss and grief are woven into American nationality as embodied traces of slavery, immigration, uplift, and assimilation, even when, and perhaps especially when, those narratives are subtextual or buried in artifacts; because, in other words, American nationality is founded on ideals whose betrayals have been repeatedly covered over.[84] In the novels that interest me, the attempt to uncover those betrayals reveals surprising intersections and constellations. For example, the literary catalog of transience in this book makes visible a link between African American and Jewish American texts. Black and Jewish citizens have been subject to very different forms of discrimination and marginalization, but fiction's running concern with ephemera reverberates across those differences. The disappearance of objects ironically becomes a connective tissue between cultures and communities stretched across distance in space and time in the decades that spanned the aftermath of the Holocaust and the advent of the Civil Rights Movement.

Minor objects also challenge our understanding of "major" works. In novels that strive toward the monumental and lean into the grand narratives of history, such objects can have unexpectedly disruptive energy. Since the canon itself might be said to be the corpus of works that escapes transience, reading for ephemera can highlight impulses in these works that pass under the radar. So, while I devote most of my attention to canonical novels, most of them by men, I understand reading for disappearance to be, at heart, a feminist undertaking. This is not only because many of our best theorists of the relations between subjects and objects are feminist thinkers, but because ephemera point to entangled, embodied ways of being. Transient things, properly understood in the amber of great fiction, remind us to look askance at heroic and punctual—often masculinist—narratives of origins and ends. In this way, their appearance in fiction that might otherwise seem to neglect issues of gender brings to the narrative foreground certain forms of temporary community and fleeting resistance that have long been the province of women.

Attention to ephemera also affords an opportunity to interrogate the whiteness of the material turn. Revisiting canonical fiction reveals that it is often in the detail, the discard, and the disappearing object that a novel's concerns with ethnicity, class, and minority status reside. While scholars in performance studies, including Sandy Alexandre, Robin Bernstein, and Tavia Nyong'o have written about race and material culture studies as they intersect in archives, in museums, and on the stage, less of this kind of work has been done within twentieth-century and contemporary literary studies.[85] In an essay from 2015, Uri McMillan examines "the failure to interrogate critical race studies in much of new materialist thought and the resultant and ongoing violence of such an occlusion particularly when theorizing blackness has long required considering existential questions of life and death, the limits of humanity, and a stultifying thingness."[86] As I consider the objects in postwar American novels and what they have to tell us about subjects embedded in particular historical moments, I have tried to acknowledge the harm in that history and the way that even the most vibrant objects can tell stories of cruel dehumanization. Reading for the vulnerability of things is one way to comment on the injuries of history in relation to social difference more generally, on the uneven distribution of vulnerability that has been the hallmark of capitalism in twentieth-century America. Glossing Jameson's famous statement that "history is what hurts," Alexander Galloway elaborates:

> History hurts because history is full of the violence of capitalism, or what Jameson described as 'the scars and marks of social fragmentation and monadization, and of the gradual separation of the public from the private' and 'the atomization of all hitherto existing forms of community or collective life.' History hurts because of unemployment, proletarianization, and 'pauperism.' History hurts whenever material necessity wins out over social collectivity.[87]

In the following chapters, I expose the "violence of capitalism" that inheres in ephemera; I also attend to the forms of social collectivity that writers imagine might grow out of and around those objects, in the places where transient objects and marginal subjects come together.

That social collectivity is possible because of the transience of ephemera, not in spite of it. Their temporary, often fragile nature points to the necessity of human care. The novels in which they appear so often lament the way that humans have been poor stewards of the objects around them or have been overattentive to things at the expense of other humans. In what follows, I try to resist the siren song of the artifact, the dead and knowable object that offers a sense of stability, as well as that of the agentic object, wholly alive and singing of vibrant networks in which we could shift the tiresome burden of care onto rocks or robots. The postwar fiction in this study denies these two poles and instead asks readers to linger on the world-embedded and thing-entangled humans who must give care and who need to receive it.

Letting go of things and doing away with fantasies of durability means rejecting damaging nostalgia and accepting constant change; it also means recognizing that even temporary formations can carry within them the possibility of real action. I believe ephemera encourage a nondominative orientation to the object world, one in direct opposition to Freud's assertion of superiority when he suggests that a fleeting object enhances the subject's pleasure in it. What postwar fiction shows instead is that encounters with fleeting objects allow us to recognize that all objects and subjects are, in crucial ways, and for all time, transient. Without care, and a good measure of chance, neither survive. In that spirit, I can say that putting these ideas into print is simply the only way to let them go.

1

Yesterday's Tomorrowland

E. L. DOCTOROW, MICHAEL CHABON, AND THE 1939 WORLD'S FAIR

THE THING ABOUT FAIRS

In July of 1896, the Viennese weekly paper *Die Zeit* published a brief review of a grand trade show that had opened in Berlin a few weeks earlier (Figure 2). The article's author wrote that the trade show could be understood only in the broader context of the fin-de-siècle expositions that had been taking place throughout Europe. He argued that these expositions were "momentary centers of world civilization which assembled the products of the entire world in a confined space as if in a single picture."[1] The exhibition gave its author, a young sociologist named Georg Simmel, a site to consider the effects of commodification that would come to inform his later work.[2] Simmel diagnosed the fairs "intended for temporary use only" as essential features of modernity: sites that revealed urban space and visualized consumer culture as condition and consequence of late-nineteenth-century globalizing processes. In his studies of late-nineteenth-century world's fairs, Walter Benjamin reflects on how the many artifacts on display illuminated both the present and the past more brightly. For Benjamin, the world's fair, a "monument on another planet" where "the world from old fairytale . . . had come to life," seemed uniquely poised to educate visitors about the material conditions of the dynamic modernity in which they lived.[3]

The rise of the world's fair in the nineteenth century is an infrastructural tale surpassed in scale and drama, perhaps, only by the story of the fair's demise. Once spectacles that riveted the world's attention, from the Great Exhibition of 1851 that gave London the Crystal Palace to the Exposition Universelle of 1889 that motivated the construction of the Eiffel Tower, world's fairs had an enormous influence on architectural, technological, and cultural developments. But they have by

FIGURE 2. Poster for the Industrial Exhibition in Berlin, Germany, 1896. Designed by Ludwig Sütterlin.

now nearly vanished altogether. While trade shows continue to promote awareness and sales of various goods (everything from flowers to guns), Disney-style theme parks repeat some of the fairs' entertainment strategies, and the Olympic Games fulfill their recurrent, nationalistic pattern, none of these contemporary exhibitions have the kind of widespread impact of early fairs. It is difficult to grasp the scale of that impact, but one statistic here is illustrative. The Chicago Columbian Exposition of 1893, which ran for a wildly successful six months, welcomed over twenty-seven million distinct visitors, which was equivalent to about half the U.S. population at the time.[4] The last world's fair to be held in the United States was the 1984 Louisiana Exposition, which was so poorly attended that it earned the dubious distinction of being the only world's fair in history to declare bankruptcy *during* its run.[5] But no matter how passé these fairs are now, they continue to capture the American imagination, making their way into novels, films, and scholarly texts.

In the field of material culture studies, world's fairs occupy a prominent place. Seminal work by Tony Bennett, Timothy Mitchell, and Robert Rydell argues that world's fairs did important cultural and political work, consolidating national narratives and imperialist ideas through their innumerable displays. Derek Gregory and John Pickles have also written about the important work that fairs did in constructing the world as exhibition, a visual field that was "from the beginning spatialized, globalized, and gridded."[6] These scholars' Foucauldian approach helped illuminate the power dynamics of mass entertainment and the role that fairs played in shaping urban culture. Fairs came into focus as an object of study around the same time that other scholars such as Arjun Appadurai and Daniel Miller were developing more general theories about objects. These new theories argued that objects were the physical determinants of human life, objects with social dynamics and life histories of their own. World's fairs, stocked with all kinds of objects, from the mundane to the marvelous, and reasonably well-documented in archives, make tempting fare for anyone looking to understand the constitutive role that objects have had on modernity and its subjects.

For all the work that has been done on the fairs and their many objects, there is little consensus as to whether the exhibitions have a homeopathic relationship to modernity or an allopathic one. Did fairs help visitors acclimate to the shocks of an accelerating world or give them a temporary illusion of control over changing conditions of production and consumption? Bill Brown has argued that world's fairs at the end of the nineteenth century offered visitors "object lessons." He returns to Simmel's better-known work on the metropolis, writing that the fairs were meant to "treat the hyperesthesia that Simmel understood as the pathological condition of modernity."[7] Neither Brown nor most other scholars of the fairs, however, mention one significant condition of that modernity: it was excessive and taxing to the senses, but it also bred practices, structures, and goods that became increasingly ephemeral under industrial capitalism. And this fact is central to the logic of world's fairs. An ephemeral world required ephemeral world's fairs: temporary landscapes that did not eradicate the unconscious sense of accelerated accumulation for modern subjects, but instead staged that feeling as uncanny amusement. Although they provided seductive glimpses of an imaginary world that seemed close at hand, it was clear from the outset that the fairs' grand structures and endless displays would be dismantled. The expositions were always, as Burton Benedict describes, "rituals of abundance ending in property destruction."[8] In this respect, the very transience of the fairs reflected the nature of the commodities they showcased, especially their temporary novelty and the rapidity of their worldwide circulation.

But this fact and the important affective work transience performs have been largely overlooked, precisely because scholars most often examine the "object lessons" that fairs offered visitors. Focus on the fairs' pedagogic dimensions and what Appadurai would call the "life histories" of the fairs' commodities has obscured the final chapter in those histories, the dying things housed in temples of modern production that inevitably became mausoleums of modernity. The fairs' transience is no trivial fact: it lent these expositions their near-mythic status and appeal, but it also prompted at the time of the fairs, and in retrospect, grief for the utopian visions that would inevitably be dismantled and demolished. Turning from Freud's countryside to the fairgrounds, the present chapter examines what we might paradoxically call a monumental instance of ephemera. I focus on the 1939 New York World's Fair because it is the focus of postwar American novels that attempt to make sense of the fair's legacy, or rather of the legacy it failed to leave. E. L. Doctorow's 1989 novel *World's Fair* and Michael Chabon's 2000 *The Amazing Adventures of Kavalier and Clay* address the 1939 fair's transience from a distinctly Jewish American perspective. In this chapter, I set forth three interrelated claims about the way that these novels depict the fair. First, I argue that their emphasis on transience captures a dimension of the fair that historians and archivists often miss but that was central to the fair-going experience and is central to the artistic aims of these fictions. Second, I read the novels' attention to ephemera as a form of critique, one that disputes the fair's evident nationalism and often blaring narratives of progress. These critiques are historically situated, given shape by the novels' Jewish protagonists who experience the fair's American fantasies at a certain remove, an angle of skepticism reinforced by their growing awareness of the war abroad. My third aim is to consider how these novels help explain why world's fairs still captivate us although they have become a thing of the past. The novels archive the fair and its objects so that we can understand the collectively imagined future on display, and so we can feel the impact of that future, not only on those who encountered it in 1939 but also on readers in the present who wonder how the twentieth century has shaped the twenty-first. The vanishing materials of historical futures still have much they can tell us today. Can Doctorow's and Chabon's novels on transience prime us to better understand them?

World's fairs appear in a number of novels, frequently as a kind of dramatic set piece or backdrop in historical fiction and nonfiction alike. The 1893 Columbian Exposition, for instance, is the setting for Sesh Heri's 2005 science fiction novel *Wonder of the Worlds,* in which Nikola Tesla, Mark Twain, and Harry Houdini pursue Martian agents who have stolen a powerful crystal from Tesla at the fair. Erik Larson's 2003 best-seller *The Devil in the White City* interweaves the "true" story of the fair's architect Daniel Burnham with the lurid tale of Dr. H. H. Holmes, a pharmacist and serial killer who lured his victims to their deaths in an elaborately constructed murder chamber he called the "World's Fair Hotel." The Columbian Exposition is also the setting of the first chapter in Thomas Pynchon's byzantine 2006 novel *Against the Day.* The 1939 fair is the subject of James Mauro's 2010 narrative-nonfiction *Twilight at the World of Tomorrow.* In a chapter of his 1988 novel *Prisoner's Dilemma,* Richard Powers flashes back to 1939, narrating the twelve-hundred-acre fairgrounds from the point of view of Bud Middleton, the gawking son of the world's fair's model American family. The graphic novel *Whatever Happened to the World of Tomorrow?* by Brien Fies also prominently describes a father taking his wonder-struck son to the fair. Perhaps the most critically acclaimed text about world's fairs is another graphic novel, Chris Ware's meticulously drawn book from 2000, *Jimmy Corrigan, or the Greatest Kid on Earth.* Ware, like Doctorow and Chabon, foregrounds the Chicago World's Fair's ephemeral character. The novel turns around the trope of abandonment: fathers abandon their sons, the fair abandons its laborers, and the dream of the White City abandons all those who dare to believe it can endure. What this brief overview of "fair fiction" suggests is that, even as they draw upon their utopian promises, writers find world's fairs apt settings for sinister happenings and potent ciphers for melancholic reflection.

Fiction is therefore an especially poignant medium for representing world's fairs; the novel's capacity to hold notions of both the monumental and the miniature—the grand arc of history with the minor details of a particular scene—makes it suited to the multiple scales of the fairs' drama. Chabon's and Doctorow's novels navigate these scales and take up the question of transience with particular urgency. In addition to offering new readings of their novels, this chapter illustrates why postwar fiction gives us important insight into world's fairs, even if it has been largely overlooked by material culture scholars. Most studies of fairs focus on plans, buildings, displays, advertisements, and the data of finances and attendance: the materiality that can be reconstructed through archival and historical research.[9] But like the pedagogical focus, this mode of study occludes the transience that was central to the fairs and to fairgoers' experiences of them. Fiction, which represents objects but never gives readers the objects themselves, is therefore uniquely suited to this topic. The novels I turn to here depict the fair in incredible detail, but they also emphasize the transience of the fair and its many objects. Doctorow and Chabon thus allow readers to see the future on display at the fair as one that was mourned at the very moment it emerged. The vexed temporality of the ephemeral object informs the narrative time of these novels and troubles familiar generic and periodizing categories. Doctorow, who lived through the fair, writes from an autobiographical perspective, while Chabon casts a retrospective look as a member of a different generational cohort.

Contemporary digital practices have also had an impact on the afterlife of the world's fair and its many objects. As scholars of material culture respond to digitization and a range of web-based innovations, the central dynamics of ephemera shift and take on new urgency. What happens when we preserve ephemeral objects long past their natural lives? To arrive at one answer to this question, we can consider the fairs as a technology for managing the present, as the kind of management Simmel described. We can see, in fact, that the fair was a technology for managing the *transience* of the present, its accelerating collapse into futurity. Understanding that the 1939 fair never presented visitors with a tidy vision of the future, but rather gave them something more fraught, more uncanny, will prepare us to explore the novel as a technology that still helps us manage our own sense that modernity's infrastructures require constant revisiting and renovation.

EPHEMERAL WORLDS

Almost every world's fair has prompted debates among its creators and architects about what should become of the magnificent structures and displays once the exposition ended. One of the Chicago Columbian Exposition's architects, Charles McKim, for instance, wrote to a friend in 1893 that he and the chief architect, Burnham, agreed that the fair "should be swept away in the same magical manner in which it appeared." He added that "the most glorious way would be to blow up the buildings with dynamite, or to destroy them with fire. This would be the easiest and grandest spectacle except for the danger of flying embers in the event of a change of wind from the lake."[10] It is unlikely that McKim or Burnham actually believed that the fairgrounds should be dynamited or set aflame, but this talk of conflagration speaks to the despair that many felt in watching the dream staged by the fair come to an end. A writer for *Cosmopolitan* said of the exposition's White City: "Better to have it vanish suddenly, in a blaze of glory, than fall into gradual disrepair and dilapidation."[11] Promoters certainly seized on the fair's ephemeral character in order to urge visitors to come and partake in the "limited time only" phenomenon before it magically vanished. But the imminent disappearance of the fair's grand structures, such as the eighty-meter iron wonder that was George Ferris's rotating wheel and the massive Beaux Arts buildings of the White City that were, in Burnham's words, designed to be "as pliable, temporary, and unified as sand castles," also highlights the discrepancies between the fair's promises and the legacy it actually left behind.[12] The vision of an aesthetically pleasing nation marching triumphantly into the future neglected the racism, poverty, and brutal labor conditions that defined reality for so many Americans at the end of nineteenth century. Indeed, Ida B. Wells came to Chicago in 1893 to protest the exclusion of African Americans from exhibits, insisting that "the exhibit of the progress made by a race in 25 years of freedom as against 250 years of slavery, would have been the greatest tribute to the greatness and progressiveness of American institutions which could have been shown to the world."[13] The text she wrote and published with Frederick Douglass on the topic attests to the entrenched racism of the exposition's organizers and the audience they catered to. Racialized bodies could be displayed as exotic spectacles, but any testament to the achievements of formerly enslaved people was unwelcome.

The fairgrounds' beauty also did little to help the thousands of workers who joined the swelling army of the unemployed after the exposition's formal closure, or the homeless people who took up residence among the abandoned palaces of the fair. In his 1900 novel *The Web of Life,* Robert Herrick described the cold face of the fair's broken promises:

> The poor had come lean and hungry out of the terrible winter that followed the World's Fair. In that beautiful enterprise the prodigal city had put forth her utmost strength and, having shown the world the supreme flower of her energy, had collapsed. . . . The city's huge garment was too large for it; miles of empty stores, hotels, flat-buildings, showed its shrunken state. Tens of thousands of human beings, lured to the festive city by abnormal raises, had been left stranded, without food or a right to shelter in its tenant-less buildings.[14]

The despair that writers like Herrick noted after the end of the 1893 Chicago Exposition is a sentiment that one encounters repeatedly in the context of fairs' closures, regardless of the historical moment in which they transpired. In 1939, the "beautiful enterprise" of the New York World's Fair seemed in dissolution even before its gates were closed in 1940.

During the four years it took to develop the New York World's Fair, its planners settled on the thematic slogan "Building the World of Tomorrow," and they worked to create this world on the site of a former garbage dump in Queens, the grim location described by F. Scott Fitzgerald in *The Great Gatsby* as a "valley of ashes."[15] While prior fairs held in the United States were designed to awe visitors with the plenitude of the present and cast a backward glance at the years of "progress" defining the nation's history, the architects of the "world of tomorrow" hoped to dispense with the past altogether in favor of a broadly appealing model of an American future shaped by technological innovation and commerce. Spreading outward from the iconic futuristic theme buildings, the conic Trylon and the globe-shaped Perisphere (Figure 3), a profusion of exhibits offered previews of how the fair's engineers and its corporate sponsors imagined the coming decades in twentieth-century America. The architects, including Norman Bel Geddes and Raymond Loewy,

FIGURE 3. Fountains with Trylon and Perisphere in background at the 1939 New York World's Fair. Photograph by Samuel H. Gottscho.

used the "streamform" style throughout: structures were smoothed down into seamless and aerodynamic shapes resembling airplanes, and inside the streamform structures, landscapes lifted from science fiction came to life. The America on display featured rocket-ports, radio-controlled superhighways, electrified farms and even talking, cigarette-smoking robots (Figures 4 and 5).

As if to confirm the World of Tomorrow's relation to science fiction, H. G. Wells weighed in on the fair in a special March issue of *The*

New York Times. He offered a set of strange instructions for potential fairgoers:

> . . . the visitor who wants to get the most out of this World's Fair will do best *not to regard it as a show of things* but as a collection of hints and let his imagination off the leash of discretion a bit. Then he may really get a glimpse of the realities of tomorrow that lurk in this jungle of exhibits. It will cease to look like a collection of things for sale and reveal its real meaning as a gathering of live objects, each of which is going to do something to him, possibly quite startling, before he is much older.[16]

FIGURE 4. Detail from the General Motors Futurama exhibit at the 1939 New York World's Fair. Photograph by Richard Garrison.

FIGURE 5. "The Middleton Family at the New York World's Fair," Westinghouse advertisement from *Life Magazine,* March 31, 1939. Original print advertisement.

Wells's advice is both enthusiastic and menacing. Lurking in a jungle of exhibits, the fair's objects come alive, transformed into energetic creatures preparing to act upon the men, women, and children who have come to gaze upon them. By calling the fair a gathering of live objects, Wells ironically allows us to think about what may in fact be their most startling behavior: that the objects themselves will not have the chance to grow older, that they will perish before their promises are fulfilled. But this is not to say that these fleeting objects do not "do something" to the fair's visitor; it is rather to insist that what Wells calls their "real meaning" is constituted as much by their projected absence as by their sensational presence. Wells's curious account thus clarifies the distinct nature of world's fairs: unlike the department store and the trade show, their goods are not explicitly for sale; unlike theme parks and museums that house entertainment and cultural artifacts in permanent spaces, fairs teach visitors how to be consumers of the future more than students of the past. Most significantly, as Wells observes, the fairs' objects point toward a near future in which they will exist even as the fair ceases to.

Wells's text also raises a methodological question that is central to this book: how we can read a world's fair, or any collection of objects, not only for its excess but also for its disappearance? Archives give us extensive visual and narrative records of the buildings and exhibits of the "world of tomorrow," and newspaper articles, guidebooks, and advertisements testify to the importance of the fair's transience, drawing on the logic of "a limited time only" to encourage attendance (Figure 6). But it remains difficult to access that which cannot be archived in the conventional sense: the meaning made by the fair's transient nature. Fiction in this case forms a different kind of archive, a non-indexical repository of the fair's ephemera. Novels can preserve an image and experience of the fair's objects while also cataloging their destruction and absence. Fiction expresses something like the fair's unconscious—the forced encounter with transience that contrasts with the stabilized futurity sold at the gates. Doctorow's *World's Fair* and Chabon's *Kavalier and Clay* reveal the fair's promises for a better future as carefully orchestrated fantasies, their objects fading too soon into ruin and dissolving into debris.

DOCTOROW'S COMPLICATED TOYS

The plot of Doctorow's *World's Fair* is fairly simple. The first-person narrator, a child sharing the author's first name, Edgar, who lives with his parents and brother (who also share the names of Doctorow's real family), looks back on his Depression-era childhood in the Bronx. The book opens in the early 1930s during the Depression and ends at the 1939–40 fair in Flushing Meadows. Edgar recollects his boyhood, offering up vivid details: a visit to the kosher butcher, the decline of

FIGURE 6. "It's the Greatest Fair of All Time: Don't miss it!" Pennsylvania Railroad advertisement from *The Saturday Evening Post,* 1939. Original print advertisement.

Edgar's Yiddish-speaking grandmother into senility, and the disappointment of an austere Hanukkah. Critics usually describe Doctorow as a postmodern author, "a leftist political writer concerned with the shadowy border between history and myth as well as a writer who engages in postmodern experiments."[17] Despite this consensus view of Doctorow the experimental ironizer, most critics also tend to see *World's Fair* as an outlier. For instance, Michael Robertson writes that, although Doctorow "achieved fame for his imaginative playfulness with history in his 1975 novel *Ragtime,* [he] plays it straight in *World's Fair;* all but one of his references to the Fair are historically verifiable."[18] We might pause to ask why including historically verifiable facts would mean that a novelist is "playing it straight"; after all, weaving such facts together into a fictional narrative is a hallmark of postmodern fiction. Doctorow himself has described *World's Fair* as a novel meant to confound generic expectations: the book, he said at the time of its publication, gives "the illusion of memoir."[19] This illusion is crafted in part by the temporality of the narrative voice. Written in the past tense and in the first-person, readers are at first inclined to believe that this is an adult Edgar (Doctorow himself?) reflecting on his childhood experiences. But this retrospective quality is never flagged as such, and the novel instead feels as if it unfolds in the present of a child's point of view moving forward through a sequence of events. Christopher Morris has argued that a hallmark of Doctorow's fiction is the way that it makes it impossible to say who narrates the work. The same can be said about *World's Fair,* despite its autobiographical and historical elements. A blurb by Anne Tyler on the back cover of the 2007 Random House trade-paperback edition declares that "*World's Fair* is better than a time capsule; it's an actual slice of a long-ago world."[20] Tyler's praise captures the most common assessment of the novel as a realistic, if nostalgic, testament to a lost way of life.

This misreading stems from the way that Doctorow uses a child's perspective not to tell a wholly sentimental or nostalgic tale, but to reckon with the fair's fragility and to explore what the fair's monumental transience might reveal about American object relations in the second half of the twentieth century. The child's perspective allows Doctorow to play with the fair's impressive scale: does the pop-up city underscore the structured permanence of American urban life to an immigrant family or reinforce the dazzling whirl of modernity by distilling its essential ephemerality? Doctorow thus troubles the expectation readers have for the fair to serve as a stable backdrop in a recognizable, perhaps even generic, coming-of-age crisis. The "world of tomorrow" indeed propels Edgar into *his* future, not by serving as a foil to his anxieties, but by mirroring them. The fair's objects cannot cure the impermanence of Edgar's childhood world; its transience invades the buildings and displays that Doctorow's novel depicts. Even as the novel seems a straightforward bildungsroman set against the 1939 fair, Doctorow's irony lies in his refusal to let Edgar offload his worries onto the objects around him. The novel, in other words, resists a palliative transfer of the subject's crisis onto objects. Edgar looks on the fair much as the young poet in Freud's "On Transience" gazes at the countryside so that readers come to see that the human values invested in the fair's objects include human vulnerability and mortality. Transience, after all, is the thing that links human and nonhuman material, not the thing that separates subject and object.

The fair of the novel's title looms throughout, beckoning Edgar and his family with its amazing vision of American automation and prosperity. But it announces itself to Edgar on a smaller scale, in a parade of small objects that proliferate like tokens of life on a different planet. At his father's music store near Radio City Music Hall, Edgar notes the fair's growing material presence:

> We had not yet been to the World's Fair but all around us were signs that it was going on. Kazoos and ocarinas in their cards had World's Fair emblems. Next door was a souvenir shop where Trylon and Perisphere pins were on sale, and banners with pictures of them painted on the cloth. (193)

The proliferation of souvenirs such as these, even miles away from Flushing Meadows, heightens Edgar's concern that he will miss the fair, that before he arrives at the "world of tomorrow," it will already be a thing of the past. His family has fallen into financial trouble and Edgar worries that his parents cannot afford to take him to the fair. The souvenirs thus have the effect of inciting Edgar's apprehension, in part because he understands that the mementos are necessary because the fair is short-lived. Despite his concern, Edgar admits:

> I did not pester my parents, I knew we would go eventually. Everyone was busy. Besides, the truth was I had misgivings about it, it seemed so vast, such an enormous place, with so many things going on simultaneously, shows and exhibits and people from foreign countries, that I did not know where I wanted to go first. It was difficult to visualize. I was not even there yet but had fallen into the habit when I thought about the World's Fair of worrying

> that I would miss the best things. I didn't know why I felt that way. (193)

Edgar's worry arises in part from the tension mounting between his parents. His father's music store has entered a state of steady decline and the fair stands as a painful contrast: all promise and plenitude next to his family's strain and austerity.

The souvenirs also make Edgar uneasy because they reflect the overwhelming scale of the "world of tomorrow." Neil Harris writes: "[The fair] lived on crowds; [it] was busy, energetic, crammed with people, merchandise, and exotic experiences. Profusion was its hallmark."[21] Such profusion would understandably threaten a child who confesses early on to having "difficulty with the proportions of things" and feeling the urge to make "reasonable spaces for [him]self in what was otherwise and unfairly giganticized home" (7). When he does finally make it to the fair with his friend Meg, whose mother works there, he repeats this strategy. He navigates the fairgrounds by collapsing their expanses into a more manageable scale. We will see a similar strategy in Chabon's novel, but for now I want to focus on the way that Edgar's negotiation reduces the fair from the monumental to the mundane, the projected future into the recent past. Edgar is initially awed by its awesome proportions, especially by the Trylon and Persiphere, spectacular and spectacularly deracinated, "white in the sun, white spire, white globe" (250). He quickly comes to think of the structures as "friends" that make him "incredibly happy" (250). Thanks to his encounters with reproductions of the dazzling white structures, Edgar can diminish their imposing, alien quality.

His negotiations suggest that, contrary to Simmel's trade-show argument, the fair is not scaled to sort out modernity; Edgar cannot simply take in the data of the fair, but must navigate it by collapsing its proportions into smaller, manageable images. He describes the General Motors Pavilion, a "great streamlined building of rounded corners and windowless walls," as "the kind of structure I would make by turning over a pail of wet sand at the beach and pounding the bottom of the pail and lifting it off the sand mold" (251). This association transforms the streamform architecture from an emblem of modernity to the ephemeral handicraft of a child at the beach. Likewise, when Edgar visits the Futurama exhibit, with its model city of the future, he says that looking at the miniature world with its "small moving parts, all the lights and shadows, the animation is like looking at the largest most complicated toy ever made!" (253). He draws out the comparison:

> In fact this is what I realized and that no one had mentioned to me. It was a toy that any child in the world would want to own. You could play with it forever. The little cars made me think of my toy cars when I was small, the ones I held between my thumb and forefinger, the little coupes and sedans of gunmetal whose wheels spun on axels no thicker than a needle as I drove them along the colored tracks of my plaid carriage blanket. (253)

Edgar's comparison has a curious effect. Rather than moving forward into the exhibit's near-future world of gleaming spires and high-speed motorways, Edgar regresses into nostalgic reverie. The future furnished by this miniature world becomes a wellspring of Edgar's past. Navigating the fair this way, attending closely to its many objects, the novels reveal that the appeal of the future may come in no small part from its ability to play upon idyllic memories. This nostalgic comfort makes sense given the fair's historical backdrop. Just before his first visit to the fair, Edgar learns that his father has lost his music store on the same morning that France falls to Hitler's forces. As knowledge of the horrors abroad and the threat of war creep into Edgar's consciousness, he finds pleasure in the fair's visions of the future by converting them into the comforts of his past.

By contrast, the historical realities of 1939 feel most present in the novel when the fair's diversions seem themselves passé. James Gilbert and Neil Harris have described the way that most world's fairs had fringe amusement areas whose erotic and exotic entertainments seemed at odds with the central fairgrounds. The 1893 Columbian Exposition, for instance, included the carnivalesque midway that the fair's architects tried so desperately to separate from their pristine White City.[22] The 1939 fair's official guidebook declared: "In many respects, [the Amusement Zone] is the most comprehensive collection of thrilling, laughable, and picturesque diversions ever assembled from the far-flung corners of the earth for the enjoyment of the peoples of the world."[23] This "collection" included trained animal acts, water ballets, sideshows of nature's "freaks," live babies in incubators and nude women swimming with fake sea creatures in a show called "Dream of Venus," designed by Salvador Dalí. Powers succinctly but vividly notes the contrast of such exhibits to the main fairgrounds in *Prisoner's Dilemma*:

> For all its elevating vision of the promise of tomorrow, something terribly wrong with the 1939 World's Fair escapes Bud. A tremendous gulf splits it down the middle. It epitomizes all we have done well. It is the abyss of insipidness. It is urgent, high-toned, and aware—the most magnificent civil-engineering project ever, transforming an ash dump into the hues of the fair's color-coded "zones," the place degenerates into a nudie show where near-naked girls tussle with octopi.[24]

In Doctorow's novel, Edgar finds the amusement zone disturbing, even grotesque. As he makes his way through the clumsy peep show in which his friend's mother swims with "Oscar the Amorous Octopus" and the "terrible-looking poor beasts" in the Odditorium, Edgar wishes he was back among the streamform buildings. He pities the beings he encounters, such as a "half-bearded man/lady wearing half of a bathing suit on one flank and half of a dress suit on the other; something that had fur all over its body; male Siamese twins joined at the hip; a man with enormous webbed feet," and notes that they look "worse for wear than the animals in Jungleland" (263). These people, held in a kind of captivity and offered up as entertainment, testify to the human frailty that the rest of the fair seems engineered to obscure or even obliterate. Edgar's description of their dehumanization evokes the specter of the concentration camp, a specter that becomes more palpable toward the novel's conclusion.

A few months after his mostly happy trip to the fair with Meg, Edgar learns that the essay he submitted for a world's fair contest has received an honorable mention, and therefore won his family a "free day at the fair with privileged access to all exhibits and events and free admission to all shows and rides" (278). Edgar's essay on the theme of "the typical American boy" reads, in part: "The typical American Boy is not fearful of Dangers, . . . If he is Jewish he should say so. . . . He should always hate Hitler. . . . He is kind. He cooperates with his parents. He knows the value of a dollar. He looks death in the face" (244). Edgar's personal essay contrasts with the clichés of the actual winning entry from 1940, which the novel reprints in full. Written by twelve-year-old Alfred Roberts Jr., the essay, which appeared in *The*

New York Times on September 29, 1940, repeats the insipidly patriotic rhetoric that the fair's sponsors endorse:

> The typical American boy should possess the same qualities as those of the early American pioneers. He should be handy, dependable, courageous, and loyal to his beliefs. . . . He is usually busy at some handicraft or hobby and is always thinking up something new to do or make. That is why America still has a future. (277–28)[25]

Edgar smarts upon reading this: "He had pioneers. Why hadn't I thought of that? And he had brought in the future of America. He was right—the typical American boy mentions America" (278). Doctorow uses the essay contest to satirize the hollow nationalism of the "typical American boy" and the fair itself. Edgar's essay, on the other hand, underscores troubling aspects of his life: anti-Semitism, health scares, and dwindling family finances. So, even as the novel presents Edgar's essay as a triumph, it begins moving toward a more ironic treatment of the fair. There is irony as well in Doctorow's unmarked choice to reprint the actual essay in full as a counterpoint to Edgar's fictional one. Playing the bemused archivist, Doctorow uses the novel as a medium to reproduce and revise history. Which essay, Doctorow asks, is more authentic: the real one culled from *The New York Times* or Edgar's fictional piece that captures something of the anxiety of what it meant to be Jewish-American on the eve of World War II?

This anxiety seems to permeate the fairgrounds on Edgar's second visit, when he realizes that the "world of tomorrow" is already fading and obsolete. The fair has lost much of its magic: "With fewer people in their dress-up clothes the fair wasn't as clean-looking or as shiny. I could see everywhere signs of decay. The officials who ran the exhibits seemed less attentive to the visitors, their uniforms not quite as crisp. Now the tractor-train horn playing 'The Sidewalks of New York' seemed plaintive" (282). This portrait of the fair's fading splendor creates a strong impression of an innovative world picture passing into ruin. The distracted fair officials and the plaintive cries of the tractor-train also gesture to the historical events unfolding beyond New York. Here, at the end of the novel, in the final days of the second season, September 1940, World War II has left its mark on Flushing Meadows. In Doctorow's novel, the painful contrast between the "world of tomorrow" and the world of 1940 is immediately and intimately connected with Edgar's Jewish identity. His mother, Rose, wants to see the Jewish Palestine Pavilion because, she says, it shows that "Jews can be like everyone else." Edgar's father visits the pavilions of the Netherlands and Czechoslovakia in order to "pay his respects to these nations now lost" (285–86). The fair's fleeting objects become, at this moment in the novel, historical markers: the intrusion of the war into the dream world of the fair connects ephemera to the tremendous losses beyond Edgar's immediate view.

Doctorow concludes the novel with an explicit reflection on what can and should be preserved of the fair's utopian visions, given our hindsight about the horrors of the Holocaust and the war. What does the fair leave in its wake? How might a Jewish American child and a novel about that child preserve something of the fair without fetishizing the future it falsely promised? Doctorow shows Edgar appropriating one of the fair's own strategies for self-preservation. Just as the fair closes its gates for good, Edgar goes to Claremont Park to bury his own time capsule, constructed from aluminum foil and a cardboard mailing tube. The fair's official Westinghouse time capsule contained a cache of objects meant to represent American life at the end of the 1930s, including a U.S. silver dollar, a Sears Roebuck catalog, a pack of Camel cigarettes, lots of microfilm, and elaborate plans to help finders from the appointed, wildly distant year of 6939 understand the contents. In *The Book of Record of the Time Capsule of Cupaloy,* distributed widely to museums and libraries, an anonymous text declares: "We choose to believe that men will solve the problems of the world, that the human race will triumph over its limitations and its adversities, that the future will be glorious."[26] While *The Book of Record* repeats the fair's rhetoric of a dazzling future close at hand, the capsule itself stages something more ambivalent. As Paul Saint-Amour writes of the time capsule, rather than attesting to a utopian future, it raises the specter of total annihilation. The "comprehensive archive" is "made necessary by the prospect of apocalypse."[27] On this point, along with an English-language dictionary, Aesop's fable "The North Wind and Sun," and copies of the Lord's Prayer, microfilm included in the capsule also contained much darker written messages from "important men of the time." Two of these three men were Albert Einstein and Thomas Mann, who by then had both fled fascist Germany for the United States. The remarkable messages by Einstein and Mann attest to the dissonance between the fair's future visions and the actual conditions of global politics. Einstein's message explicitly links the material practices celebrated by the fair with the brutality of war. He wrote:

> The production and distribution of commodities is entirely unorganized so that everybody must live in fear of being eliminated from the economic cycle, in this way suffering for the want of everything. Furthermore, people living in different countries kill each other at irregular time intervals, so that also for this reason any one who thinks about the future must live in fear and terror.[28]

Embedded with the capsule's record of plenitude (cigarettes, a credit card, and "one of the singular clothing creations of our time, a woman's hat") Einstein's words testify to the violent underpinnings of the consumer logics and militarized capitalism propelling the fair.[29] Thomas Mann likewise contradicts the fair's official, optimistic language with his blunt assertion: "We know now that the idea of the future as a 'better world' was a fallacy of the doctrine of progress."[30]

At least officially, the Westinghouse capsule celebrates the present while also positing a future so advanced that its people would view the contents as antiquated relics from a bygone era. But it also leaves readers to make sense of the competing language contained within; there are no instructions in the *Book of Record* as to how the beings from 6939 should reconcile Einstein's message, for instance, with the triumphal rhetoric that dominates the rest of the text. Is the Westinghouse capsule evidence of a techno-futurist dream or an apocalyptic nightmare? Does it contain precious artifacts or the leftovers of a civilization in decline? Are its contents random bits or do they make up a representative sample? Doctorow uses Edgar's time capsule, filled with explicitly transient materials, to draw out these contradictions and suggest that *they* might contain the truth of what 1939 meant to many Americans. When readers liken *World's Fair* to a time capsule, they do not usually mean that the novel evokes such conflicting messages. But it would be wrong to dismiss the novel as counter to the time capsule; rather, it is precisely the feeling of the capsule's antithetical dispatches into an unknown future that Doctorow's novel summons. In *World's Fair*, the fair itself is a time capsule, filled with the debris of an American past and its futures that we know in hindsight never came to fruition. Edgar's cardboard tube thus contains what is clearly meant to be the debris of his childhood: a broken Tom Mix decoder badge, a toy rocket ship with worn paint, and a torn silk stocking of his mother's as a sample textile. As Edgar buries it and trudges off across Claremont Park, "the wind stinging [his] cheeks and bringing a film of water to [his] eyes," we understand the image as one marking the end of his childhood and of the fair's dazzling optimism (288). Doctorow leaves readers with an image of the fair itself as an archive of emergent ideas made instantly residual. Doctorow's evocation of grief—for the passing of the fair's future visions, for wartime losses, for Edgar's childhood—is especially pertinent to the fair's actual ending. On October 27, 1940, at the fair's closing ceremony, a lone trumpeter stood atop the Helicline (the elevated walkway between the Trylon and Perisphere) and played "Taps."[31] The military dirge marked the end of the fair, but also its reincarnation. The Trylon and Perisphere, stripped of their gypsum surfaces, were turned into forty thousand tons of steel that went into ships, shell casings, and gun forgings for the American war effort. This, we might say, is the true afterlife of the fair, one that becomes historically visible only when we see that it was always vanishing.

CHABON'S MATERIAL MASS CULTURE

Michael Chabon's 2000 novel *The Amazing Adventures of Kavalier and Clay* begins, in some sense, where Doctorow's novel leaves off. With the help of Bernard Kornblum, "an *Ausbrecher,* a performing illusionist who specialized in tricks with straitjackets and handcuffs," the young Josef Kavalier flees to New York from a Reich-beset Prague in a coffin containing the city's golem.[32] Josef has witnessed the horrors of the war first-hand, and in this regard, he is more like Einstein and Mann than he is like Edgar. Where Doctorow's novel shows how the fair's transience evokes the perpetual war machine that its visions were meant to conceal, Chabon is more interested in the forms of mass entertainment and popular art that sprang up in response to the war. Hillary Chute, writing about the novel in relation to Doctorow's *Ragtime,* notes that "Doctorow is a strong influence on Chabon, and their respective novels . . . are both about the ascendance of popular culture in America, featuring immigrant heroes crafting that culture."[33] The immigrant heroes in this case are Josef, who is an artist, and his cousin, Brooklyn-born writer Sam Clay (né Klayman). The cousins team up and become major figures in the comics industry with their creation of an antifascist superhero called, fittingly, the Escapist. Chabon chronicles their personal struggles against a colorful backdrop of the New York comics industry, from its nascent years into its "golden age." In the course of the 636-page novel, Clay's father, a vaudeville strongman called the Mighty Molecule, neglects his family, Kavalier has an affair and fathers a child with the artist Rosa Saks, Clay explores his sexuality but ultimately marries Rosa, helps raise her child while Kavalier is stationed as a serviceman in Antarctica after his younger brother dies at sea trying to escape Europe, and the cousins are eventually reunited in New York City.

The 1939 fair's appearance in *Kavalier and Clay* is brief but crucial to the novel. It echoes Doctorow's emphasis on miniaturization, the disillusionment of the narrator's childhood dreams, and the darkening of rosy future visions by the storm clouds of war. Chabon's treatment of the fair also contemplates what it means if the fair, like the comic books that occupy the heart of his novel, is ephemeral. Chute and Andrew Hoberek have both written about the novel's preoccupation with the form of comic books. Hoberek notes that "the novel's thematic interest in mass culture . . . allows Chabon to include a number of expository digressions about (real or lightly fictionalized) comic book history."[34] Chute elaborates on the historical aim of these digressions, arguing that the novel "is about the articulation of history in popular, duplicable forms, whether those forms are repeatable performances of escape or mass-reproduced comics," and that it "presents a trajectory, showing us how its creative cartoonist protagonists embrace and adopt various comic book methodologies for the project of representing history."[35] Hoberek and Chute help situate the fair in a specific mass-cultural moment, as well as in a media-historical one. Though comics and fairs are part of a similar mass-cultural moment, the novel suggests that comics might oppose the monumental ambitions of the world's fair. *Kavalier and Clay* thus seems to vindicate an immigrant- and Jewish-built entertainment infrastructure that takes escapism seriously. Comics, in the novel, are not a childhood or childish genre, but rather an ephemeral form that draws upon the fears and dreams of America's ethnic outsiders. But, even as he celebrates the golden age of comic books and the pleasures of mass culture, Chabon is wary of lapsing into the nostalgia comics and fairs can preserve or the past they imagine. Because his characters encounter the fair only as a dying thing, it shapes the novel's orientation toward transience.

Chabon immediately calls attention to the fair as a way for the nation to distract itself from the kind of apocalyptic fears that we have seen paradoxically activated by the time capsule. The world's fair is first mentioned as an "outburst of gaudy hopefulness," a way for Americans to ignore the grim fact that "the rest of the world was busy feeding itself, country by country, to the furnace" (340). But in an especially poignant scene, Sam articulates what Edgar also came to realize: despite its best attempts at presenting the "world of tomorrow" as a present-day reality, the fair was never more than a mirage made material. Sneaking with his lover over the high fence around the fairgrounds just after the exposition has ended, Sam discovers a specter of the better world in which he had once believed. He sees that the Trylon and Perisphere are made of plaster of Paris, covered in scaffolding and in the process of being disassembled. The narrator marvels that these structures, which for "two years had been ubiquitous throughout the country, working their way onto restaurant menus, clock faces, matchbooks, neckties, handkerchiefs, playing cards, girls' sweaters, cocktail shakers, scarves, lighters, radio cabinets, et cetera," had disappeared "as suddenly as they had flourished, like the totems of some discredited Millerite cult that briefly thrills then bitterly disappoints its adherents with grand and terrible prophecies" (375). But the scene itself contests this sudden disappearance, giving readers instead a longer arc, a slower dissolve.

In a lengthy passage that attenuates the scene of the fair's disappearance, Chabon describes Sam's encounter with the ghost town that Flushing Meadows has become:

> It made his heart ache to look around the vast expanse of the fairground that, not very long ago, had swarmed with flags and women's hats and people being whizzed around in jitneys, and see only a vista of mud and tarpaulins and blowing newspaper, broken up here and there by the spindly stump of a capped stanchion, a fire hydrant, or the bare trees that flanked the empty avenues and promenades. The candy-colored pavilions and exhibit halls, fitted out with Saturn rings, lightning bolts, sharks' fins, golden grilles, and honeycombs, the Italian pavilion with its entire façade dissolving in a perpetual cascade of water, the gigantic cash register, the austere and sinuous temples of the Detroit Gods, the fountains, the pylons and sundials, the statues of George Washington

> and Freedom of Speech and Truth Showing the Way to Freedom had been peeled, stripped, prized apart, knocked down, bulldozed into piles, loaded onto truck beds, dumped into barges, towed out past the mouth of the harbor, and sent to the bottom of the sea. It made him sad . . . because he had so loved the Fair, and seeing it this way, he felt in his heart what he had known all along, that, like childhood, the Fair was over, and he would never be able to visit again. (376–77)

This scene establishes fairs as a special class of object: always temporary and vanishing while pointing toward a future and evoking eternal values. The abandoned icons of scientific progress and consumerism and American democracy are ruins that expose the fair's untenable promises and confirm the end of Sam's youth. But this collection also insists on the fair's remains, suggesting that it has in some sense simply entered another phase of the fleeting market ecosystem it always was. Sam's experience asks readers to face the transience of industrial production without imagining that it might be possible to reverse time, to resurrect the past that has been sent to the bottom of the sea.

Sam and Tracy Bacon, his lover, find their way into the Perisphere, right onto the terrain of Futurama, which the narrator calls "the *dernier cri* of the art and ancient principles of clockwork machinery in the final ticking moments of the computerless world" (378). This strange narrative perspective, infused with the knowledge of hindsight, suspends the fair's objects in a perpetual state not of instant and total loss, but one that is partial and ongoing. Chabon's detailed, lyric catalogs emphasize this peculiar aspect of the fair that no single artifact or archive can capture. As Sam treads across the artificial moss of Futurama's landscape and occasionally, despite his caution, steps on a model farmhouse or hospital, we see the fair's dreams crushed under the weight of history. If the fair is meant to screen out the history that motivates Chabon's plot—war, genocide, immigration, and ethnic outsiderism—the novel's characters, *because* they are Jewish, understand the fair as presenting an American mythology that tries to wish away the damage of history with the promises of tomorrowland. And so do its readers. But Chabon tempers this awareness, sustaining an ambivalence about the fair's end so that the scene cannot be read in a purely melancholic mode. Lying down in the model city, Sam loses "himself in the illusion of the model" and finds that it is "a perfect day in a perfect city" (380). This perfection is achieved only after the fair has closed and its promises have waned; no longer a gleaming monument to national progress, Futurama becomes the backdrop for Sam's erotic encounter, for the possibility of a future not represented by the model, but arising out of its ruins. Chabon suggests that the fair's future, already obsolete at the time of its staging, might give way to another future, one predicated precisely on this obsolescence. In the passing of the "world of tomorrow," the novel locates a different utopian possibility. Chabon concludes the scene at the fair with a moment of unironic tenderness: "They lay there for a few seconds, in the dark, in the future, with Sammy's sore fingertips in Tracy Bacon's mouth, listening to the fabulous clockwork of their hearts and lungs, and loving each other" (380). The future in which the two men lie together is Futurama, but it is also the time after Futurama, unfurling in darkness, unknown and unknowable. The carefully curated, collective future of the fair is replaced here by a personal, intimate one. Chabon's treatment of the world's fair raises the question as to whether utopia can only ever exist on this individual scale. His focus on the miniature proportions of Futurama already flags the impossibility of realizing utopia at scale. The novel suggests that such efforts are destined to fail, but that in their failing, individuals might locate strategies for living in a world of dying things.

DIGITIZING THE WORLD OF TOMORROW

Writing from an explicitly Jewish American perspective, Doctorow and Chabon do more than lyricize the ordinary management of time passing. Their attention to ephemera instead acknowledges how the fair's dreams of the future recede into the past at the very moment of their emergence. Rather than a romance about a lost way of life, then, the novels help us feel the anxiety that adheres to a future vision proven obsolete from the beginning. This type of temporal disjunction is not just a feature of their novels' contents, but a part of their place and predicament in American literary history. They are not quite contemporary novels, but they establish significant historical distance from the mid-twentieth century and the broken promises of modernism and modernity; we might once have called them postmodern. But what, we might ask, is the utility of this label today? Now that we have post-postmodernism, hypermodernism, metamodernism, and digimodernism, postmodernism has been declared a historical relic, dead and buried. The impulse to declare postmodernism a thing of the past is bound up with the desire to identify something new: a new type of author, a new period, a new style, a new politics. But what my reading of world's fairs suggests is that fascination with the future often obscures the forms of history and nostalgia that inhere in the new. In the case of our current literary historical moment, this includes the formal continuities between postmodern and contemporary texts, the global networks consolidated during the postmodern period (and long before), and the economic and consumer practices that may have changed in degree but not in kind since the beginning of the twenty-first century. As critics herald the arrival of a new period, and one that feels increasingly immaterial, vanishing objects and the postmodern texts in which they appear can help us make sense of this new period: they give us an important prehistory rooted in the material conditions of American modernity. A recent example demonstrates how research in material cultural studies, particularly on ephemeral objects and the history of exhibitions, remains relevant in our increasingly digital era.

In May 2011, the New York Public Library released its first iPad app, designed to appeal to a new audience. Created by The Potion Design Studio, the endeavor goes by the name of *Biblion: The Boundless Library.* The first release of Boundless Library was the World's Fair app, an interactive trove of over seven hundred items from the library's 1939–40 New York World's Fair collection (Figure 7). In a promotional video released by the library, an explanatory narration plays over footage of the app in use. I quote this narration at length because its rhetorical moves speak to the concerns that have been the subject of this chapter. As images of archival boxes and documents from the library's collection flit across the screen, the voice-over intones:

> What if you could hold in your hands countless one-of-a-kind treasures held within the legendary stacks of the New York Public Library. What if you could turn over, zoom in, flip through, and explore more than seven hundred items and even access rare film and sound archives? Biblion, the Boundless Library, lets you do all this within a chartered world or infoscape, of the vast collections of the library: the stacks. This launch edition showcases one of the largest and most used collections: the 1939–1940 World's Fair, the World of Tomorrow, contained here in twenty-five hundred

> boxes. New visual pathways into the stacks now lead to infinite narratives and unexpected connections. An exhibition wall is your entry point into storylines that emerge when original sources are given shape. Now you can see how the world's fair, like the library, has something for everyone. You'll find a world dealing with economic crises and war, to starlets, to pop culture, and technological innovation. So enter the World of Tomorrow and see a *real* visualization of the items that make up stories, ranging from text-based essays to galleries.[36]

After going through some specific instances of what users can find on the app, the video concludes with a last example and a broad appeal:

> Another interstory connection might lead you to art at the Fair and the making of Augustus Savage's uplifting work "The Harp." You might call it multilinear reading. With over seven hundred items to experience through myriad pathways, those yellow links taking you from stack to stack, story to story, this edition of Biblion is designed for you to come back to, again and again. Our goal: to provide you with countless serendipitous moments of discovery while you explore this world of information and inspiration, the World of Tomorrow.

The video makes a promise that app users will have an experience exactly like that of being in the stacks: inviting you to "hold in your hand" the "one-of-a-kind treasures" from the library's collection, offering you an oxymoronic "real visualization" of the items, as well as a "guided tour through the stacks." But at the same time, the video promises a brand new experience, one so innovative that it can be described only with new words: by entering the "infoscape," you will discover "new visual pathways that now lead to infinite narratives and unexpected, interstory connections," through a process that the video says "you might call multilinear reading." Yoking printed media to digital forms, literary narrative to visual links, Biblion promises to give users "the real artifact" *and* something more: a boundless library that preserves materials and joins them together in dazzling networks.

That the library's first foray into the realm of apps centers on the 1939 world's fair is no coincidence. There are practical reasons for this choice of course, as the archive is large but well organized, reasonably

FIGURE 7. Image from The New York Public Library's Biblion, The Boundless Library's World's Fair app promotional video. Published to YouTube May 16, 2011.

popular, and all about New York. But more than this, as a topic, the fair speaks to both aims of the app: to grant access to archival materials and to expand the shape of the archive itself. The library mobilizes the fair's own blend of nostalgia and futurity to give the app its appeal as we are offered a look at the past: the fashion, the architecture, the food; but also at the past of our media history in handwritten letters, telegrams, and typewritten documents. At the same time, the dynamic visuals of touch-screen technology and three-dimensional graphics are meant to awe us. In *this* narrative, the Trylon and Perisphere culminate not in metal for bullets but in the pristine surface of an Apple tablet. The video ends with an invitation to "enter the World of Tomorrow," as if the iPad is not a device allowing us to swipe through a curated, digital exhibit, but a portal leading directly into the future-past. The app thus plays upon a double fantasy: first, that everything of the fair (and the experience of library-going) would be lost without it and, second, that everything is preserved by it.

The Biblion app raises one of the central questions facing many scholars today, especially those trying to manage archives that are increasingly accessible digitally but can therefore seem increasingly ephemeral. The fact that the internet seems to preserve transient objects long past their "natural lives" leads us to wonder if ephemerality itself is an outmoded concept. If everything can be stored on the web, in the cloud, or on a server that we access through the evocatively named "wayback machine," is loss even possible anymore? And do we still need the actual artifact, the real thing? These are questions that I will take up at the end of this book, but for now, I want to linger with one lesson of ephemerality already learned. That lesson—think back to Edgar's time capsule—is that fictions of preservation have long underwritten our ideas of loss. In other words, loss as a concept depends upon the desire for things to endure. This is a dialectic that remains hidden but seems obvious the minute it is uncovered. The technologies and tools we create for preserving ephemera (from the time capsule to the digital infoscape) are therefore intimately related to the grief and anxiety that literature about ephemera captures. Chabon's and Doctorow's fictions help reveal the deep ambivalences of our relations to things. Like the app, their novels re-create the fair in vivid detail. But they do so with a crucial difference: insisting on the ephemeral, they help us see the fair's legacy as one of not only material or narrative presence, but absence. Literature then, it bears repeating, is a special kind of archive we can turn to even as "the archive" shifts around us, or even vanishes.

As we have seen, novels can also invoke the past futures that inhere in the present. Writing of the 1939 New York World's Fair, Doctorow and Chabon resurrect the past to show how its vision of the future paradoxically mobilized nostalgia: to move its visitors, it relied on the past, or more precisely, the *passing*. Their novels reveal that the past's futures so colorfully on display at world's fairs were always dying, and that that dying may still be with us today. Saint-Amour astutely describes this work that novels can do when he says of the archive that it "is also a repository for dissident temporalities." Drawing upon the work of the German historian Reinhart Koselleck, Saint-Amour adds that archives "stockpile" what Koselleck calls "futures past," "the traces of a past moment's orientation to the not-yet, to the nonexperienced, to that which is to be revealed."[37]

This is the temporal screw that transience turns, and world's fairs, with their ephemeral cities housing ephemeral goods, dramatize it at expanded scale. Fredric Jameson, who has dubbed Doctorow "the epic poet of the disappearance of the radical past," explains that science fiction futures of technological automation, like those celebrated at the 1939 fair, appeared in a brief window of time. Jameson writes: "These visions are now historical and dated—streamlined cities of the future on peeling murals. . . . That particular Utopian future has in other words turned out to have been merely the future of one moment of what is now our past."[38] It is telling that Jameson relies on the metaphor of the mural to describe the temporal status of past futures. Although the image of the mural vanishes as it peels, the metaphor also emphasizes the mural's enduring quality: thinking through an object here makes it easier to understand that discarded utopias never vanish completely. Moreover, the metaphor of cities on murals suggests that utopian futures play out on larger stages, not in the museum exhibit or store window but in the fair's infrastructure that awes with its massive proportions.

World's fairs, though hardly the kind of conventional objects that readers might expect to encounter early in a book on ephemera, are a useful starting point precisely because their hyperbolic scale illuminates the stakes that can attach to transience. We commonly associate souvenirs and memorabilia with personal memories and individual character; the exaggerated objects of the fair show the operations of collective longing and national identity. To riff on Raymond Williams, literature about world's fairs helps us see infrastructures of feeling, the material supports for shared, often murky experiences of social relations unfolding in time. Infrastructure may seem like an unlikely source of longing or lament, but as a part of the material matrix that joins people in a given space, it shapes and holds experience in powerful ways. Michael Sahlins argues this point in his essay "Infrastructuralism": "Rather than a discontinuity, temporal as well as ontological, wherein culture appears as the symbolic afterthought of a material practice that has its own rationality," he suggests, "what is entailed in infrastructuralism is the realization of encompassing conceptual schemes in the particular material function of provisioning the society."[39] These novels about world's fairs remind us of the many ways in which myth and infrastructure can be imbricated. Ironically, the temporary structures of the Trylon and Perisphere form a sort of scaffolding for the chapters that follow. They help us recognize the centrality of transience to our objects, our cities, our futures, and our selves. Chabon and Doctorow insist that such recognition need not lead to perpetual mourning or exuberant distraction. Instead, their novels invite us to look back at the "world of tomorrow" so that we can inhabit, even as it vanishes, the world in which we live today.

2

Counterhistory, Counterfact, Counterobject

PHILIP K. DICK, PHILIP ROTH, AND THE SECOND WORLD WAR

SPECULATIVE NOVELS AND SPECULATIVE MATERIALISM

Upon exiting Futurama, the model of a glorious, near-future America on display at the 1939 New York World's Fair, visitors received a small blue and white button that declared: "I Have Seen the Future." But had visitors actually been able to look into the future, past Bel Geddes's magic motorways and flying machines, they would have seen instead a glimpse of the unthinkable tragedies unfolding overseas. Not far from Futurama, across Constitution Mall and the Lagoon of Nations, the Czechoslovakia Pavilion had already begun to register a different future. A motto added to the side of the building after German annexation of the country read: "After the tempest of wrath has passed, the rule of thy country will return to thee O Czech people" (Figure 8). As Europe's present encroached on the American fair, the plaster castles and space-age gadgets were revealed as relics of a shiny technodream that the barbarism of war threatened to imperil, turning a progressive fantasy into a shimmering counterfactual. This last term, of course, evokes the literary genre that doesn't so much imagine the future as reimagine the past. Counterfactual fiction, or the subgenre that Catherine Gallagher has called the "alternate-history novel," returns to the past, sometimes distant and sometimes recent, to ask what could have happened differently.[1] Such novels invite readers to speculate on an altered history, one that we know didn't happen but find compelling or instructive nonetheless. Instead of seeing the future, then, counterfactual novels ask us to re-see the past. What are the contents of a revised past? What familiar things does it contain? What new and alien ones might it hold? In this chapter, I consider two counterfactual novels about the Second World War whose dense object worlds are

FIGURE 8. Exterior view of the Czechoslovakia Pavilion at the New York World's Fair, 1939. The opening of the pavilion took place on May 30, 1939, with the Czech flag blowing at half-mast, as a sign of mourning on the occasion of German troops attacking the country. Sueddeutsche Zeitung Photo / Alamy Stock Photo.

populated by transient artifacts. These objects trouble our understanding of "factual" history as well as our sense of how the genre of counterfactual fiction works using "factual" historical objects.

Philip K. Dick's *The Man in the High Castle* (1962) and Philip Roth's *The Plot Against America* (2005) depict counterfactual worlds filled with representations of factual objects. Like Chabon and Doctorow, who draw on the "real" history of the world's fair to ground their novels in a particular historical moment and material culture, Dick and Roth depict and describe real objects to give their alternative worlds historical weight and texture. We know that authors describe objects to make their texts more realist; we also understand that these descriptions situate texts in specific historical contexts. Plenty of scholars have done excellent work on this latter point: Bill Brown's discussion of Mrs. Blackett's sewing chair in Sarah Orne Jewett's *The Country of the Pointed Firs,* Elaine Freedgood's reading of the "Negro Head" tobacco in *Great Expectations,* John Plotz's treatment of jewelry in Anthony Trollope's *The Eustace Diamonds,* and more recently, Matthew Mullins's study of Coke bottles in Leslie Marmon Silko's *Ceremony* are just a few instances of scholars demonstrating the way objects make legible the regionalism, colonialism, imperialism, and racism that circulate in and around literary texts.[2] But the appearance of "real" objects in counterfactual novels seems to do something more than tether an imagined world to a real place and time. The factual artifact vibrates curiously in the counterfactual narrative: it jars the reader with its familiarity while the rest of the plot says "this never happened" in real time and space. Rather than attempting a seamless realism of a new world, the appearance of objects in counterfactual narrative insists that the imagined reality and the present one were the same up until the "nexus" at which "the ATL, or the Alternate Timeline, in contradistinction to OTL, or Our Timeline" diverge.[3]

But things get still more complicated. The objects in *Man in the High Castle* and *Plot Against America* never simply testify to the "actual" world as a knowable, static entity. As we have seen, Freud's work on transience, like Chabon's and Doctorow's novels, emphasizes the way that war often intensifies the human relationship to objects. Freud's poet refuses to find beauty in the countryside because he fears it will vanish; Doctorow's Edgar buries a time capsule out of a similar fear that life as he has known it will cease to exist. In both cases, the personal, affective object relation bespeaks a collective destiny. In Freud's case, there is an implicit question about how the artist who draws inspiration from the idylls of European nature continues to create art once it has been sullied by war. In Edgar's case, his time capsule raises the question of how America will see itself if it recognizes that its cycles of production fail to stop war, and perhaps even cause it. The examples I have considered thus far illustrate the many ways we turn to objects, especially in times of fear and grief. We preserve what is fleeting, collect what is scarce, and turn to objects to ward off the human fragility and mortality that war brings closer to home. This is true of the characters in *Man in the High Castle* and *Plot Against America,* who attempt to preserve objects in the form of the collection. Despite these efforts, the collections that aim to rescue ephemera from the ravages of war are shown to be *ephemeral*: the struggle against impermanence is vexed and central to these counterfactual novels.

Ultimately, Dick and Roth undermine the logics of collecting, what Jean Baudrillard calls "a triumphant unconscious discourse," with its drive toward possession, order, and totality.[4] The novels stress the ephemeral qualities of the most prized possessions, so that even the things their characters fervently try to save retain traces of extinction and disappearance. As a result, these objects become poignant symbols of the uncertainty and contingency that counterfactual history intends to record. These two postwar American texts use objects to do the work that the counterfactual genre does more broadly. Dick and Roth populate their novels with transient objects and partial ones, with counterfeit objects that turn out to be authentic in crucial ways and authentic artifacts that reveal the inauthenticity of existing histories. If counterfactual novels are time- and history-bending, then what of their objects? As Gallagher says of alternate-history novels, they "attempt to create a complete alternative reality, presenting in detail the social, cultural, technological, psychological, and emotional totalities that result from the alteration, which is why they are often called 'alternate *world* novels.' The historical alteration in the novels permeates to the level of commonplace individual lives, where habits of thought, modes of speech, and routines of daily life are registered."[5] More than just material corollaries of the novels' temporal twists, transient objects attest to the contingency of history, the possibility that our narratives about "what really happened" may conceal a reality more fragile than we imagine. The appearance of "real" objects in the "fake" worlds of these novels is puzzling for the reader, who must consider the realism of Dick's and Roth's alternative histories. And the transience of the objects causes a further shock: if the "real" objects are fleeting and fake, then so too is the history attached to them. Instead of performing an exercise in what could have happened, the novels ask readers to consider the possibility that the stories they tell relay a deeper truth about what did happen.

The sense that these counterfactual novels tell readers something about history as it really is has perhaps grown since the time of their publication. Certainly these novels make powerful and perpetually relevant critiques of American exceptionalism by collapsing the distance between America and Americana and then exposing Americana—stamps, comic books, memorabilia of various kinds—as serial, counterfeit, and ephemeral. If the objects we use to prop up our national identity and ideals are shown to be mere props, we are forced to reckon with the fantasy and fallacy of American democracy. But revisiting the novels today, their dystopic imaginings of a United States gripped by fascism feels newly urgent. Indeed, after the Trump election, *Plot Against America* saw a resurgence in sales and in headlines. *The New Yorker* ran an article in February 2017 about the novel's relevance, quoting Roth:

> Lindbergh, despite his Nazi sympathies and racist proclivities, was a great aviation hero who had displayed tremendous physical courage and aeronautical genius in crossing the Atlantic in 1927. He had character and he had substance and, along with Henry Ford, was, worldwide, the most famous American of his day. Trump is just a con artist. The relevant book about Trump's American forebear is Herman Melville's *The Confidence-Man,* the darkly pessimistic, daringly inventive novel—Melville's last—that could just as well have been called *The Art of the Scam.*[6]

Roth's insistence that Melville's novel from 1857, not *Plot Against America,* allegorizes the current political moment shows how literature can remind us that what seems new quite often is not. We can draw this lesson as well from the fact that, upon its publication, many read *Plot Against America* as a veiled allegory of George W. Bush in the years immediately following 9/11. But in a prepublication essay, Roth rebuffed this interpretation as well:

> Some readers are going to want to take this book as a roman à clef to the present moment in America. That would be a mistake. I set out to do exactly what I've done: reconstruct the years 1940–1942 as they might have been if Lindbergh, instead of Roosevelt, had been elected president in the 1940 election. . . . My every imaginative effort was directed toward making the effect of that reality as strong as I could, and not so as to illuminate the present through the past but to illuminate the past through the past.[7]

Despite Roth's assertion that his book accomplishes the single goal of illuminating the past, the recurrent relevance of the novel (after 9/11 and again after Trump) gives us a good reason to revisit his novel and its strategy for illuminating "the past through the past."

A television adaption of *Plot Against America by* David Simon, the creator of *The Wire,* aired in Spring 2020; it ran just after the third and final season of *The Man in the High Castle,* which premiered in January 2015 on Amazon's streaming platform. If the repopularization and remediation of the two novels is not proof enough of their contemporary relevance, it's worth noting that "Resistance Radio," released by Amazon as a companion program for *The Man in the High Castle,* enraged Trump supporters who thought that the prerecorded radio program in which people discuss the evils of the Third Reich was a real forum promoting a "liberal agenda."[8] Because the counterfactual genre works by blurring the line between fact and fiction so promiscuously, it illuminates the way that line has long been shifting and porous. And by populating their novels with fraudulent and fleeting objects, Dick and Roth expose the fragility of our institutions, our susceptibility to counterfeit and transient object worlds. Their counterfactual histories depict the ephemeralization of things often assumed to define the material bedrock of American history. Because they are so closely linked, destabilizing national narratives of infrastructure and industry can undermine the nation's myths and its democratic ideals.

At the same time that political tides swept these novels into new popularity, interest on the part of literary scholars in counterfactuals took off. A 2007 forum in *Representations* on "counterfactual realities" mentions the wide application of counterfactual methods: "in theoretical speculations in physics, political movements for redress, innovations in statistical analysis, military training, legal proceedings, historical regret, digital technology, and literary experimentation."[9] The broad relevance of counterfactual methods has certainly contributed to the burgeoning interest in speculative fiction and speculation itself as a conceptual frame among scholars of literature.

This most recent wave of widespread interest on the part of literary critics in speculative fiction has its counterpart in philosophy as well. Quentin Meillassoux's *After Finitude,* published in 2008 to much fanfare, argues that "speculative materialism" offers us a way of engaging with concepts not given to human thought.[10] But in addition to drawing on scientific discovery as a way to contest the correlationism (between thinking and being) that he sees as regnant in modern philosophy, Meillassoux also gives us a term that can illuminate the work objects perform in counterfactual fiction. I find that "speculative materialism," rather than "speculative realism," which Meillassoux uses less frequently, better diagnoses the paradoxical role of historical objects in alternate, fictional worlds. The concept of speculative materialism emphasizes the inscrutable, excessive nature of the object world: despite its appearance of fixity, the physical world insists that "the same cause may actually bring about 'a hundred different events' (and even many more)."[11] If the speculative nature of Dick's and Roth's fictions asks us to imagine some of these different courses of events and outcomes to the Second World War, the novels' materialism testifies to the truth content of these alternate realities. Describing the aim of science fiction, Ursula K. Le Guin mentions *Man in the High Castle* as evidence of her well-known claim that "science fiction is not predictive; it is descriptive."[12] A conventional reading of alternate history holds that the counterfactual world shows the reader what could have been but returns her to reality, often with some sense of relief that the nightmare imagined on the page has not, in fact, come to pass. In this reading, the "real" objects embedded in the novels subtend fake history. But these objects can also have the opposite effect: the presence of "real" historical objects show us that we are always trapped in the legacy of our past. Because the objects that Dick and Roth depict turn out to be transient, fake, partial, and forged, it would seem that they return readers to that sense of a comforting reality; these real objects aren't so real after all, and thus the alternate world they populate remains a fiction. The complicating twist of the transient objects, however, is that they subvert both readings: they thwart not only the preservationist reading that claims an unbroken line of progress and freedom but also a fantasy of absolute loss in which we can escape history. The novels' factual, impermanent objects challenge any safe landing, reminding readers that we don't own history the way we might imagine—that we never did. The attempt by characters in *Man in the High Castle* and *Plot Against America* to recapture the past, to re-create it, to assemble and fix it in collections is shown to be a futile pursuit. The fake or transient object thus makes real meaning; it makes the factual world unrecognizable. In counterfactual novels, such objects show the nation itself to be a dubious article of faith, one whose history cannot be authenticated. Dick's and Roth's novels do not simply explore ephemera in America; they offer chilling portraits of America *as ephemeral.*

Man in the High Castle and *Plot Against America* have both been the subject of astute readings. But these readings do not fully account for the central role that objects play in the novels' discomfiting relationship to reality. In the factual but vanishing objects of counterfactual literature, we see the residual alternatives of unchartered histories. The genre allows us to consider whether these alternatives are entirely lost or, like ephemera themselves, still flicker against the screen of our present. While the world's fair time capsule projects the present world into the future, the transient objects of counterfactual fiction recast the present as a past always slipping through our hands. Fredric Jameson writes that Dick feels "nostalgia for the present, something that can only be achieved when the present is transformed into a distant past by a future perspective whose true function and reason for being is merely and precisely to be the operator of just such a shift in tense perspectives."[13] A central strategy Dick uses to create that nostalgia is turning objects of the present into artifacts of the past. Read with an eye toward the transience that Dick writes into his object world, *Man in the High Castle* is a study in temporal and material enjambment, imagining collisions between real and fake, presence and absence, as well as between then and now. Like Roth's, Dick's novel catalogs ephemera and draws upon ephemeral dynamics to suggest that reimagining America's wartime past shows us the many ways we still live there today.

PHILIP K. DICK'S COUNTERFEITS

Among science fiction writers, Philip K. Dick looms large in popular culture and in literary criticism. Of his 44 published novels and more than 120 short stories, several have been made into films, including *Blade Runner* (1982), *Total Recall* (adapted twice, in 1990 and 2012), *Minority Report* (2002), *A Scanner Darkly* (2006), and *The Adjustment Bureau* (2011). In 2018, Amazon Video released *Philip K. Dick's Electric Dreams,* a series of ten episodes based on Dick's short stories. His fiction has been the subject of two special issues of *Science Fiction Studies,* several academic monographs, and countless journal articles.[14] His canonization seemed complete when, in 2007, Dick became the first science fiction writer to be included in The Library of America series. *The Man in the High Castle,* Dick's ninth published novel, appeared in 1962 when he was thirty-three and earned him early acclaim, including a Hugo Award for Best Novel.[15] Jameson, who has called Dick the "Shakespeare of Science Fiction," lauds the novel for its "capacity to render history" in what Jameson sees as a present devoid of "a sense of the historical past and historical futures."[16]

The history Dick renders in *High Castle* is an alternate outcome to the Second World War. It is 1963, and victorious Germany and Japan have divided up the Unites States. The Pacific States of America (PSA) are ruled by Japan, the East Coast is under German rule, and the Rocky Mountain States (RSA) compose a rough, neutral buffer zone in between. While the Japanese have adapted a capitalist economy, a Daoist ethos, and a passion for prewar American artifacts in the PSA, the Nazi regime is thriving, continuing its exploits around the world: committing genocide in Africa as part of its racial purification program, draining the Mediterranean Sea as part of "Project Farmland" to create tillable land through the use of atomic power, and sending troops into space to colonize the moon and Mars in the name of the Reich. Although Germany and Japan parceled out the world peacefully, a cold war between the two superpowers is well underway at the time of the novel.

Against this backdrop, Dick threads together five different plots. The main plot follows the journey of Rudolf Wegener, a high-ranking anti-Nazi German officer who travels via commuter rocket to the PSA to warn Japanese officials about Nazi plans to launch a nuclear attack on the Japanese islands. Despite numerous setbacks, Wegener successfully carries out his mission with the help of Nobusuke Tagomi, a bureaucrat in the PSA who shoots the Nazi assassins sent to kill Wegener. The shooting is no easy task for Tagomi, a pacifist and devotee of the *I Ching,* an ancient Chinese divination manual. In the other plot lines, we meet the obsequious Robert Childan, the owner of an antique shop in San Francisco who sells Americana to Japanese customers who covet "genuine" American artifacts. Frank Frink (né Fink) is a Jewish American Pacific War veteran who works for the Wyndham-Matson Corporation in San Francisco, which specializes in reproducing exactly the kind of Americana Childan sells. Frank's ex-wife, Juliana, lives in the RSA state of Colorado, where she works as a judo instructor. She begins an affair with Joe Cinnadella, a Swiss assassin posing as an Italian truck driver. Joe involves Juliana in his plot to kill Hawthorne Abendsen, the eponymous "man in the high castle" who has written a controversial alternate history novel called *The Grasshopper Lies Heavy.* When Juliana discovers Joe's real identity, she kills him and visits Abendsen alone to warn him and to learn the strange truth about his novel. At the end of *High Castle,* Tagomi enters an alternate reality that is San Francisco "as it really was" in 1962 and then returns to the world of the novel to retaliate against local Nazi authorities by saving Frank, who has been arrested for his acts of forgery and is bound for deportation to a concentration camp.

With the exception of Juliana's story and her visit to Abendsen's "castle," the entirety of the novel takes place in the Japanese-occupied PSA, where issues of transience and imitation are thrown into stark relief. In Dick's PSA, the Japanese residents have Anglicized names, speak English, and fetishize the kinds of objects that Childan sells at American Artistic Handcrafts. Bill Brown describes Childan's shop as "the site through which the story of things . . . begins to unfold, thanks to the Japanese collecting habit, prompted by the impulse to make some contact with a lost culture that has come to seem idyllic."[17] In the early 1960s, when Dick was writing *High Castle,* Japan had already undergone a significant social reform brought about by the British Commonwealth Occupation Force, as well as a dramatic economic reconstruction. Beyond these changes, mass popular culture was exploding: metropolitan Japan absorbed American television, music, comics, and fashion. This ongoing "Westernization" of Japan is one of the novel's historical referents, and Dick is especially interested in what it means for people to mimic the cultural tastes and habits of their aggressors or, equally, to idealize and fetishize the pasts of those they conquer. At the level of plot, Dick reverses the postwar conqueror–conquered relations between the United States and Japan. But what critics have yet to remark on, and what shapes the novel's object world, is that, alongside this political reversal, Dick has kept familiar consumer relations intact. They are, however, complicated by the way that objects in the novel turn out to be imitations, forgeries, and fakes. Dick uses a series of mass-culture objects to encode the novel's contingent and conflicting histories in material form.

Even when the forgeries in Dick's novel are not strictly ephemeral—guns or zippo lighters instead of playing cards or matchbooks—they nonetheless encode the drama of durability and disappearance that is the hallmark of ephemera. The post-American world of *High Castle* contains objects of the past that have survived because they have been deemed valuable; the ephemera in Childan's store have evaded ephemerality because Japanese buyers have lent them market value. Dick's novel discloses the dynamics of projecting that value through authentication: a document attesting to an object's provenance, a personal anecdote about how it was used, or an expert's appraisal. In Dick's hands, this process is the stuff of an alternate reality, but it remains very much the stuff of our contemporary reality. Contemporary auction houses often deal exclusively in ephemera, reminding potential buyers that such objects offer them a chance "to own a piece of history," and that an ephemera auction opens up "a treasure trove of memories embodied in delicate items that were never meant to last."[18]

Childan's store indeed seems at first like a treasure trove of magical residua. At the novel's outset, Childan remembers the provenance of his goods: "the pre-war days, the other times. Franklin D. Roosevelt and the World's Fair; the former, better world."[19] It is not long, though, before this nostalgic view is deflated and the novel exposes that these mass-culture artifacts are unworthy of the reverence they receive. If the political lines of the novel represent a world order that is truly different from our own, the novel's objects become darkly ironic reminders that the narrative of a "former, better" America has always been a fiction. Whereas other parts of the novel feel deeply earnest, Dick channels his satirical energy through the artifacts in Childan's store. Childan's sense of gravitas and his reverence for "American traditional ethnic art objects" appears absurd given the schlocky nature of his most coveted merchandise (11). When Paul and Betty Kasouras, an elegant Japanese couple, enter the shop, Childan touts his rustic antiques: a wood-pegged New England table, a mirror from the War of 1812, and a group of handmade goat-hair rugs. But the young man mentions that he prefers "the art of the cities," and Childan is soon rattling off a list of desirable "urban" artifacts: a mural from the WPA (Works Progress Administration) post-office period, a Victrola cabinet from 1920 refashioned into a liquor cabinet, and most impressive, a "framed, signed picture of Jean Harlow" (12). This whimsical list reveals the arbitrary nature of what represents "real" America for the Japanese colonizers in the PSA.

Childan comes to represent (if not recognize) something paradoxical about the objects he sells and the America he lauds. On a visit to Paul and Betty's house, Childan simultaneously admires and abhors their obsession with American culture. As he sits down to a dinner of T-bone steak and listens to the "authentic American folk jazz" that Paul favors, his resentment boils over in an inner monologue:

> Pilfer customs right and left, wear, eat, talk, walk, as for instance consuming with gusto baked potato served with sour cream and chives, old-fashioned American dish added to their haul. But nobody fooled, I can tell you; me least of all. . . . What they say is true: your powers of imitation are immense. Apple pie, Coca-Cola, stroll after the movie, Glenn Miller, . . . you could paste

> together out of tin and rice paper a complete artificial America. Rice-paper Mom in the kitchen, rice-paper Dad reading the newspaper. Rice-paper pup at his feet. Everything. (112–13)

Childan not only speaks but thinks about Japanese mimicry in "Japanesed English." As he condemns the Japanese parasitism that he exploits for his own gain, he dreams of being their social equal in the PSA, and of seducing Betty. Who imitates whom? What is being imitated? The list that Childan lays out ("Apple pie, Coca-Cola," and so on) turns American identity into a repeatable formula of mainstream consumerism. If the original is devoid of content, then what is left to imitate? Childan's interior monologue betrays his fear that America itself may have always been a "complete artificial" construct, and the expert imitation, made of tin and rice paper, might in some ways be better or more authentic than the "real thing."[20]

The "real thing" also frequently encodes the nation's foundational violence, sullying the fantasy of a once-innocent, democratic America. Instead of giving the Kasourases a pop-culture or mass-consumerist object as a gift, he presents the couple with a scrimshaw: "No single thing could have summed up old U.S. culture more," he thinks (106). The scrimshaw is another peculiar item, recalling not just the heyday of New England whaling during the mid-nineteenth century, but its extinction. The romance of the scrimshaw is bound up with the disappearance of the culture that produced it. A similar point is made by the buffalo head hanging on Tagomi's wall, which he says "is nothing less than the creature which sustained the aboriginal in bygone days" (72). The sense of loss that inheres in the buffalo head and in the scrimshaw abuts the Kasouras's feverish preservation of all things American. These objects are not only melancholy in the way that Peter Schwenger describes in *The Tears of Things*: they don't just elude total possession, but in fact mark the violent extermination foundational to American history and to the war that the novel fictionalizes. The scrimshaw ironizes Childan's sense that the war taints all the objects in the house: "It's everywhere, in a book I happen to pick up or a record collection, in these bone napkin rings—loot piled up by the conquerors. Pillage from my people" (112). "His people," of course, pillaged their objects from indigenous people and earlier settlers. So, while the objects that Childan sells and the Kasourases consume are reminders of the defeat that the United States has suffered in Dick's alternate history, they also attest to the nation's real genocidal past.

As Cassie Carter explains in her essay on "metacolonization" in the novel, "the PSA represents an America occupied and oppressed by a simulation of itself."[21] I would add that objects like the scrimshaw reveal that the notion of an authentic, and authentically democratic, America has been a simulation all along. Though Childan finds it mysterious that cheap, mass-produced objects are now coveted as singular, exemplary relics of a vanishing America, the novel wryly suggests that these objects—a Mickey Mouse watch, comic books, celebrity paraphernalia—capture America's "authentic" nature as a juvenile nation of imitators and mass-culture consumers. The habit of collecting itself comes under scrutiny in the novel as an indulgent pastime, one that reflects a childish impulse to accumulate meaningless objects. One of Childan's clients, Major Ito Humo, admits that he finds his own addiction to "the collecting of old magazines dealing with U.S. brass buttons, as well as the buttons themselves" baffling. "It was of the order of coin or stamp collection; no rational explanation could ever be given" (31). The novel suggests that what is irrational about the desire to collect is, in fact, that the collected objects can never represent the innocence and optimism of an America that never existed. For instance, when Tagomi presents Wegener with a 1938 Mickey Mouse wristwatch that he solemnly describes as "most authentic of dying old U.S. culture, a rare retained artifact carrying flavor of bygone halcyon days," America is doubly indicted. If this watch is indeed a meaningful artifact, how trivial is the nation's legacy? And if the scene is meant to demonstrate an absurd understanding of the past on Tagomi's part, then we must also ask what, if anything, is left of the America he now occupies?

Dick turns to objects, especially the pop-culture kitsch now revered in the PSA, to do this work, precisely because they have always embodied a perverse blend of childishness and bloodlust. He chooses objects that accomplish a double undoing: they empty prewar American history of its meaning and undermine the dubious fantasy that America was benign before its current occupation by the Axis powers. Before he selects the Mickey Mouse watch, for instance, Tagomi considers an array of possible gifts for Wegener. One is "an almost mint copy of Volume One, Number One of *Tip Top Comics,*" which Childan declares "a choice piece of Americana" (27). The first issue of *Tip Top*

Comics, printed in April 1936, has a cover that shows Tarzan in a boxing match with Li'l Abner (Figure 9). Dick's choice to include this particular comic is hardly arbitrary in a novel about America's defeat and colonization. Tarzan, an archetypal feral child raised in the African jungle by primates, fights Li'l Abner, a muscular "hillbilly boy" whose naiveté makes him an unlikely hero in a cynical world populated with villains. This bit of ephemera, lost to all but the most dedicated collector, gestures toward America's ambivalence about its own heroes: Tarzan is a dubiously racialized other who nonetheless embodies independence and masculinity; Li'l Abner is a low-class, uneducated southerner who represents the myth of the American "heartland" and fights against the elite. Each "factual" object that Dick selects encodes the irreconcilable contradictions in the country's narratives of freedom and democracy.

In addition to the comics, we also learn from Major Humo about his friend who collects "Horrors of War" cards, a series of 288 full-color cards produced by a Philadelphia-based company, Gum Inc., in 1938. The cards, valuable collector's items to this day, show scenes of torture, bloody battlefields, and children under attack on the front. The backs offer detailed descriptions of the scenes from the Spanish Civil War, the Ethiopian War, and the Chinese–Japanese War (Figure 10). The final forty-eight cards, released as a supplement to the original series, include three depicting Adolf Hitler (Figure 11).[22] Childan explains to Major Humo how he and his friends used the cards:

> "Flip cards," Childan had said suddenly.
>
> "Sir?"
>
> "We flipped them. There was a head and a tail side on each card." He had been about eight years old. "Each of us had a pack of flip cards. We stood, two of us, facing each other. Each of us dropped a card so that it flipped in the air. The boy whose card landed with the head side up, the side with the picture, won both cards." How enjoyable to recall those good days, those early happy days of his childhood.
>
> Considering, Major Humo had said, "I have heard my friend discuss his 'Horrors of War' cards, and he has never mentioned this. It is my opinion that he does not know how these cards actually were put to use."
>
> Eventually, the major's friend had shown up at the store to hear

FIGURE 9. *Tip Top Comics,* issue no. 1, 1936. Published by United Feature Syndicate.

> Childan's historically firsthand account. That man, also a retired officer of the Imperial Army, had been fascinated. (32)

The cards, in reality and in Dick's novel, represent the familiar but nonetheless perverse way that violence can be repackaged into child's play. Although the creators claimed the cards were pacifist and each card included the motto, "To know the HORRORS OF WAR is to want PEACE," children nicknamed the popular series "War Gum" (Figure 12). Like the children's game "Cowboys and Indians," the cards remind readers that violence is entrenched in the American mythos that Childan remembers as good and peaceable, "those early happy days." But without Childan's "historically firsthand account," the cards are denuded of their former "use value" and become more like the meaningless brass buttons that Major Humo collects. The fact that these cards were used in a game of chance is precisely what makes them most meaningful in the context of Dick's novel. The flip of the card represents the precariousness of history, its predication on a series of accidents and chance outcomes. Does it really matter which side the card lands on? Is political destiny any different than absurdist fate?

This last question is posed most vividly through yet another set of objects: the guns that structure the second half of the novel's plot. Like the flip cards, the guns with which the characters commit acts of violence blur the line between agency and accident, as well as between deliberate or authentic acts and mere performance. In the PSA, there exists "an unlimited market for small arms of the American Civil War and Frontier period" (51). The robust market for antique guns is symptomatic of the desire for objects that can connect their owners to the romantic past of the nation they have "inherited." Of course, this narrative that guns are fundamental to the "American story" as

FIGURE 10. 1938 Horrors of War Cards set. Published by Gum, Inc. Photograph provided by Small Traditions, Inc.

FIGURE 11. 1938 Horrors of War Cards #283–85 and 277, featuring Adolph Hitler and Nazi forces. Published by Gum, Inc. Photograph provided by Small Traditions, Inc.

FIGURE 12. 1938 Horrors of War Cards, back side of cards #283–85 and 277, featuring Adolph Hitler and Nazi forces. Published by Gum, Inc. Photograph provided by Small Traditions, Inc.

emblematic of the frontiersman, brave revolutionary, and Civil War solider remains potent today. Perhaps the frontier period and Civil War hold special relevance for the Japanese living in the PSA, who find themselves struggling to maintain sovereignty in their recently acquired territory. The demand for these antique weapons is so high that it has given rise to the manufacture of forgeries, which are "cautiously but expertly fed into the wholesale art object market, to join the genuine objects collected throughout the continent" (51). Again, Dick's irony scrambles the status of the guns: are the "genuine" guns really "art objects?" Or is it the fakes that are art, reproduced with expert craftsmanship? Throughout the novel, the guns demonstrate a point Umberto Eco makes about simulacra: "The American imagination demands the real thing, and to attain it, must fabricate the absolute fake."[23] But Dick wants to do more than indict American consumerism and the desires that necessitate endless mimicry. As the plot of the novel begins to contract around these forged guns, Dick's broader interrogation of reality and history gathers force. Frank blackmails Childan with the knowledge that his store sells forgeries and Tagomi uses his imitation Colt .44 to shoot two men from the Gestapo who barge into his office to kill Wegener. Tagomi's fake gun does real damage: "With record-eclipsing speed he fanned the hammer of the single-action Colt, firing it again and again." The two Germans lie dead on his office floor, and Tagomi, anticipating more assailants, channels John Wayne and stoically utters, "Now we will mow them down" (192). Tagomi performs the part of American hero with a fake gun, but the "bits of bone, flesh, shreds of tooth" that cover his office are nonetheless real (192).

Does violence authenticate the object? After all, even if Tagomi is only impersonating John Wayne (who was only impersonating cowboys and cavalrymen), his actions do foil the assassination plot. While the "real" objects like the flip cards and comic book that Dick writes into his story have the effect of making readers recognize America's history in his alternate world, the emphasis on fakes seems to contradict this move, instead casting the real as fraudulent. But Dick makes the additional move of contemplating how fakes can become real, either in their function or, more paradoxically, through an awareness of the objects' inauthenticity. In an oft-cited scene, Mr. Wyndam-Matson, who owns the fabrication business where Frank reproduces antique guns, explains the counterfeiting business to a woman named Rita. He sets two lighters on the coffee table in front of her: "Look at these. Look the same, don't they? Well listen, one has historicity in it" (65). She asks what he means by "historicity" and he replies:

> "When a thing has history in it. Listen. One of those two Zippo lighters was in Franklin D. Roosevelt's pocket when he was assas-

> sinated. And one wasn't. One has historicity, a hell of a lot of it. As much as any object ever had. And one has nothing. Can you feel it?" He nudged her. "You can't. You can't tell which is which. There's no 'mythical plasmic presence,' no 'aura' around it." (66)

Rita is uninterested in Wyndam-Matson's theory of historicity. She thinks instead about F. D. R.'s assassination and wonders what might have happened had he lived. Dick uses the objects here to weave an intricate web: the lighter records the counterfactual history that is "real" only for the characters in the novel, not its readers. But it also raises the specter of "real" history, the version of events in which F. D. R. lived and steered the United States to an Allied victory in World War II. Wyndam-Matson's final comment on the lighters effaces any distinction between real and fake objects and real and alternate history. Of the lighter's authenticity, he tells Rita: "I'd have to prove it to you with some sort of document. A paper of authenticity. And so it's all a fake, a mass delusion. The paper proves its worth, not the object itself!" (66). Even the syntax here doubles back on itself and further unravels the notion of aura: in the end, the paper proves only its own worth.

The entire plot of *High Castle* hinges on imitation, fakery, and false belief. Frank poses as a gentile while he makes fake guns; Childan mimics Japanese speech patterns as he sells fake objects; Wegener pretends to be a Swede to divulge the Nazis' secrets; and Cinnadella, the Italian truck driver with whom Juliana has an affair, turns out to be a Swiss assassin on a mission to murder the man in the high castle. Amidst this sea of dissimilation, critics have pointed to one moment, or rather one object, that seems to offer authenticity, an antidote to the proliferation of fake identities and fake artifacts. Toward the end of the novel, Frank quits his job producing sham antiques to make jewelry. He defies the "Nazi idea that Jews can't create, that they can only imitate," and pours his efforts into creating original, abstract forms (52). His "pieces were abstract, whirls of wire, loops, designs which to some extent the molten metals had taken on their own. Some had a spider-web delicacy, an airiness; others had a massive, powerful, almost barbaric heaviness" (131). The jewelry winds up at American Artistic Handicrafts, where Childan assents to displaying the pieces because he realizes that "with these, there's no problem of authenticity" (145). Frank's original forms seem to escape the problem of historicity altogether.

Jameson and Brown have both focused on the way Dick valorizes handicraft. Jameson claims that Dick's work often draws "utopian force from the nostalgia for handicraft itself and as such," and Brown expands on this insight and addresses the abstraction of Frank's jewelry, arguing that "handicraft in the fiction of Philip K. Dick can in fact be understood as 'modernism,' with all its utopian longing."[24] Frank's jewelry indeed seems, for some time, like a kind of utopian object, a foil to the serialized Americana that has been the novel's focus up until this point. When Tagomi appears at Childan's shop to return the Colt .44 that he has used to commit two murders, Childan refuses the gun but asks Tagomi to examine the jewelry. Childan explains the effect that jewelry has already had on him: "This is the new life of my country, sir. The beginning in the form of tiny imperishable seeds. Of beauty" (217). Tagomi leaves with a small silver pin and sits on a bench in Portsmouth Square to contemplate his purchase. In a scene that the television series captured vividly as the conclusion of the first season, he studies the object intently, hoping that the silver triangle will "cough up arcane secret" (220). Eventually, the pin seems "not heavy, weary, but pulsing with life" (221). In the metallic form, he sees a "corpse turned to fiery display; the past has yielded to the future" (221). The meditation triggers a temporal shift whereby Tagomi is briefly thrown into a world that resembles the reader's own reality, the reality of the still-mysterious novel-within-the-novel, *The Grasshopper Lies Heavy,* in which the Allied forces have won the war. In this moment, Tagomi finds himself in contemporary San Francisco: white people do not defer to Japanese people and are even openly racist to them, the Embarcadero Freeway runs through downtown, and the entire city has a "dull, smoky, tomb-world cast" (223). The creative labor that Frank has invested in the pin disrupts the characters' attachment to the past and their illusions of the present. By honoring his own ideas, Frank Frink has invested his jewelry with *Wu,* a kind of enlightenment or "inner truth" strong enough to unmoor Tagomi and push him "out of [his] world, [his] space and time" (224).

Even as the jewelry offers Tagomi an opening into a different world, the objects up until this point in the novel have worked to remind readers that this different world is not utopian: it is the compromised reality that Dick has critiqued through comic books and the Colt .44. Ultimately the novel refuses to satisfy the longing for utopia that both Jameson and Brown cannot entirely dispense with. The jewelry might exist, for a brief moment, outside commodity logic. But Dick's novel does not settle on a claim that a given object—even a handmade, abstract one—is simply bad or good; it is rather always both. If the jewelry carries the residuum of the world as it once was or as it "actually" is, we know by the end of the novel that what was and is cannot rightly be called utopian. The jewelry is another object that accrues history *and* its mutability, as is evidenced by the fact that Tagomi seems to "awake" from this experience of an alternate America and no further explanation of the transporting effect of the pin is given. The jewelry itself is not ephemeral, but it points to the possibility that historical worldedness might itself be temporary and transient.

While Tagomi encounters the reality that is counterfactual to the world of the novel, Juliana also learns that the war might have had a different outcome from the one she knows. After discovering Joe's plan to kill Abendsen, she slices his neck with a razor blade and flees the hotel room where he lies bleeding on the floor. She arrives at the "high castle," a heavily guarded home where Abendsen lives. Juliana asks him about his book: she suggests that *The Grasshopper Lies Heavy* tells a true story of an Allied victory and shows "that there's a way out" (244).[25] Abendsen confesses to Juliana that he used the *I Ching* to write the book, basing his plot decisions on its hexagrams. To understand why the *I Ching* would write *this* book, and not another, they turn to the source: "Oracle, why did you write *The Grasshopper Lies Heavy*? What are we supposed to learn?" The answer confirms her suspicions:

> "It's Chung Fu," Juliana said. "Inner Truth. I know without using the chart, too. And I know what it means."
>
> Raising his head, Hawthorne scrutinized her. He had now an almost savage expression. "It means, does it, that my book is true?"
>
> "Yes," she said.
>
> With anger, he said, "Germany and Japan lost the war?"
>
> "Yes." (247)

The scene presents a palimpsest of interpretative options: we read about characters in an alternate reality reading the *I Ching* to discover that a novel they have read may be true. If Juliana's interpretation is correct, the Axis powers have lost but people still somehow live under the illusion that they have won. Is the novel's world, even for the characters, just a hoax? An initial reading of Tagomi's and Juliana's revelations would understand the conclusion of the novel as undoing the counterfactual scenario it has created: in a kind of antitwist, it turns out that the fictional world has been a fiction all along. In this reading, characters and readers alike can feel a sense of relief upon returning to history "as we know it."

But like the objects that cannot be stabilized as entirely fake or wholly real, history's course cannot be so easily pinned down. The plot of *The Grasshopper Lies Heavy,* importantly, does not reproduce "real" postwar history. In Abendsen's novel, F. D. R. survives assassination and is succeeded in 1941 by Rexford Tugwell, who presides over the defeat of Axis powers and the subsequent division of the world between the United States and Great Britain. Paul K. Saint-Amour writes of this decision as representing "Dick's refusal to diagram historical possibility using a scant number of switches."[26] Without the familiar switches, many readers have found themselves lost in the metaphysical eddies of the novel's multiple paths. It is tempting, especially in light of Dick's own interest in Taoism, his use of the *I Ching* while writing *High Castle,* and his well-documented drug use, to read the novel as ending in a space of total chaos where truth is unknowable.[27] Might all reality be, to borrow Wyndam-Matson's phrase, "a mass delusion?" N. Katherine Hayles gestures toward this kind of fully deconstructionist reading when she argues that, "when we realize that the world of *Grasshopper* is not ours either, we are forced to recognize that we may too be fictions."[28] But to conclude that the novel evacuates history of any truth content is, I think, a mistake. The lack of neat closure in the novel is not a gesture toward complete chaos, but rather an insistence on the way that history is inescapable, and so too is change: we cannot alter the past, nor can we hold onto it completely. The *I Ching,* as Dick represents it in this novel, is itself an object, a set of oracular statements embodied in coins and hexagram lines.[29] Eastern philosophy, like Childan's artifacts, Abendsen's novel, and even Dick's, cannot offer a "way out." We are left instead with multiple contaminated possibilities: The Allies won the war, and the novel has been an exercise in imagining otherwise, or alternatively, the Axis powers won but the characters' arrival at a different, inner truth at the end of the novel suggests the triumph of humanism. What the novel's treatment of objects reveals, though, is that "the truth" lies somewhere in between these fantasies of preservation and loss. A reading of the novel framed by Dick's speculative materialism, by his interest in the liminal, in-between state of objects, insists that, although the Axis powers have lost, the ugly reality of a fascist America persists. This means that, regardless of who "won" the Second World War, the spirit of fascism was not defeated; the international corporations that supported the Nazis remain powerful, and racism, violent militarism, and blatant disregard for the earth continue. Gallagher argues that, while the United States and the Soviet Union technically won the war, they lost peace by devoting the majority of their economic, technological, and cultural energies to waging the Cold War.[30] As Kim Stanley Robinson poetically says of the novel, "by constructing scene after scene . . . in which the real world and the fictional world interpenetrate one another Dick brings us to that quintessentially science fictional moment of cognitive estrangement, wherein we stare at a strange face in a window full of wonder, and then realize the window is a mirror."[31] This estrangement, I would insist, depends upon the stuff of Dick's fictional world: its windows and mirrors are guns and cards and comic books that refract the world as it might have been to show us better how it really is.

PHILIP ROTH'S COUNTERFACTUAL COLLECTION

Compared to *Man in the High Castle,* with its time- and mind-bending, unresolved storylines, Philip Roth's *The Plot Against America* seems, as far as counterfactual novels go, a straightforward affair. But Roth's novel, published forty-two years after Dick's, also stockpiles real objects that chillingly suggest that the alternate version of events in the novel, in fact, accurately diagnoses history. The autobiographical elements of *Plot Against America* contribute to the reader's sense that Roth is writing an account of the past as he experienced it, even if that account is to some degree untrue. The novel's generic styling thus links it to Doctorow's *World's Fair,* another fictionalized memoir in which the boy protagonist tries to make sense of anti-Semitism at home and war overseas. This is an instructive comparison, not only because it raises questions about how we might situate Roth in relation to other postwar authors, but also because it illuminates the special role that counterfactual thinking plays for Jewish Americans writing after the war. Michael Chabon's 2007 detective novel, *The Yiddish Policemen's Union,* for instance, depicts an alternate history in which a temporary settlement for Jewish refugees was established in Sitka, Alaska, during the Second World War and is, by the present day of the novel, a large, Yiddish-speaking metropolis. Whereas Dick's novel asks what could have happened, novels like Chabon's and Roth's appear to ask a more personal version of that same question: "what could have happened to me?" This form of the question marks the particular religious-ethnic dimension of Roth's work, placing him in conversation with other Jewish writers who have grappled with the same query. Nathan Englander's recent short story "What We Talk about When We Talk about Anne Frank" offers a searing portrait of two Jewish couples, one American and one Israeli, asking this question.[32] What would happen to me if the Holocaust began here, now? Who among my loved ones would hide me from the Nazis? Though Englander's short story is a darkly comic meditation on the bonds of marriage—and the form of the short story, as the title's riff on Raymond Carver's 1981 story makes clear—it stands as a contemporary reminder that counterfactual thinking about the Second World War is the terrain of more than just military strategists. In Englander's account, and I'd argue in Roth's, this kind of speculative thought is seen as a hallmark of postwar Jewish existence. Those fortunate enough to have been born after the war process this privilege, the trauma of their ancestors, and the collective Jewish relationship to the Holocaust through counterfactual thinking.

The other Roth novel that might rightly be called counterfactual is *The Ghost Writer* (1979). In the novel, it is 1956 and a young Nathan Zuckerman pays a visit to an eminent Jewish writer, E. I. Lonoff, who lives with his wife in the country. There he meets Amy Bellette, a former student of Lonoff, who Zuckerman comes to suspect is Anne Frank. In a section that ruptures the novel's narrative time, Zuckerman continues the story of Anne Frank as Amy Bellette. He recounts her survival of Auschwitz and Belsen and adoption of Amy Bellette's identity after emerging from a coma. Zuckerman also narrates her reactions to reading her own diary in its Dutch edition and her breakdown after seeing it dramatized on Broadway. This counterfactual excursus is a way for Roth to consider the obligation Jewish authors feel when reckoning with the Holocaust. It is difficult to touch on these issues without diving fully into the veritable sea of scholarship that exists about Roth's Judaism and status as a Jewish author.[33] My point here is that, for Roth, the counterfactual genre affords the chance to meditate on what it means to be a Jew in America, and perhaps more importantly, what of America is uniquely visible to its Jews. Hana Wirth-Nesher asserts that the real story of *Plot Against America* is "the making of the Jew," that the novel responds "to the global rise of anti-Semitism in recent years" by "bringing a version of . . . tragic European Jewish life to the shores of the United States." The result, Wirth-Nesher continues, is that "the American-Jewish experience rejoins a version of Jewish history whose distinguishing feature is persecution as a minority."[34] Alternatively, Timothy Parrish writes, "the idea that Roth would portray American culture as a kind of anti-Semitic conspiracy contradicts Roth's familiar and frequent defense of his right to think of himself as American first and Jewish second."[35] Both these readings inadvertently position the "American-Jewish" experience as distinct from the "American" one. Although *Plot Against America* is clearly interested in anti-Semitism as it exists and persists in the United States, the novel is more keenly interested in interrogating the mythic version of history that America narrates for itself. If there is a strain of counterfactual thinking that could be called uniquely Jewish, Roth's work uses it less to illuminate ethnic identity and more to investigate twentieth-century America.

We have seen how Doctorow's and Chabon's novels use an outsider's perspective on the world's fair to note peeling paint instead of progress, decay and disrepair among the promises of an invincible future. The fair's ephemerality evokes the horrible fact that lurks just offstage and off the page in these novels: that Jews in Europe are disappearing and that all of America's exuberant and self-aggrandizing displays are a duplicitous diversion. Roth's novel, however, brings the truth of Jewish extermination closer to home, and objects perform the dual role of temporarily masking this fearful reality and ultimately disclosing it vividly to the novel's characters. In this way, Roth, like Dick and Doctorow and Chabon, approaches national myth through the details and disappearance of ephemeral objects. The objects in Roth's novel contribute to the way that counterfactual thinking becomes a kaleidoscope that scatters familiar historical narratives, rearranging them into new patterns. This way of thinking is immediately evident in the intervention made by the novel's title, which insists, after all, that a plot against Jews is a plot against America.

That plot begins when Charles Lindbergh, the aviation hero and Nazi sympathizer, is elected President in 1940, which leads to the persecution of Jews in the Unites States. Shortly after Lindbergh takes office, federal policies are implemented to send Jews from urban areas into the American "heartland." Philip's father, Herman, is a staunch opponent of Lindbergh; Philip's brother, Sandy, becomes an enthusiast for farm life among Gentiles after he is sent to rural Kentucky for a summer; his older cousin, Alvin, joins the Canadian army to fight with the British; and Philip's aunt marries a collaborationist rabbi who helps her ascend social ranks until she is dining at Lindbergh's state dinner with Nazi foreign ministers. As the novel unfolds and anti-Semitic forces gather, neighbors make plans to emigrate, the leading critic of Lindbergh, gossip columnist Walter Winchell, is assassinated, and American anti-Semites launch pogroms that include the destruction of stores and synagogues and, ultimately, murder. The objects in this story, like those in Dick's, link the protagonist's personal story to a larger, national critique.

The pivotal objects in *Plot Against America* are stamps, which are mentioned on the novel's first page. In his essay about the novel, Roth mentions the narrator's treasured stamp collection: "Whereas his father struggles with his America falling apart and the terrible invasion of history, the boy is still living in the heroic America of his stamp collection."[36] Collecting stamps is, for the young Philip, a hobby that links him to his "heroic America." Describing his family in 1940, the narrator says "My brother, Sandy, a seventh-grader with a prodigy's talent for drawing was twelve and I, a third-grader a term ahead of himself—and an embryonic stamp collector inspired like millions of kids by the country's foremost philatelist, President Roosevelt—was seven."[37] The novel introduces its central object, then, as a decidedly national one. Philip's hobby is an American pastime, one that F. D. R. has given a patriotic air and sense of grandeur. The stamps that Philip collects commemorate America's heroes, celebrate its monuments and pastoral beauty, and mark scientific achievements. Susan Stewart's claim that the collection creates "a fiction of the individual life, a time of the individual subject both transcendent to and parallel to historical time," helps us understand that Philip's collection is his way of asserting and managing his relationship to the nation.[38]

Though the collection affords Philip a measure of symbolic containment and control, it has a different effect on the reader. Like Dick, Roth fills the collection with "real" stamps, describing the artifacts in meticulous detail. On the one hand, this lends the text the historical accuracy that Roth says he was aiming for in reconstructing his childhood. This reading is one that emphasizes Roth's realism, something Debra Shostak finds characteristic of his writing. "Even when Roth is most engaged in the play of postmodern narrative form and epistemologies of identity," she claims, "he clearly strives for verisimilitude."[39] But as in *Man in the High Castle,* the presence of these "real" objects does not simply produce a heightened sense of reality; rather, it attests to the intersections of the counterfactual world with the factual one. Moreover, Roth transforms the stamps in a number of ways, using them to embody the contortions and convulsions of history that are the subject of his novel. The stamps, like Dick's forged guns, are factual documents in a counterfactual narrative that reveal the counterfactual possibilities latent in all history. Stamps are strangely doubled objects; they are appealing collectibles in part because they are ephemeral—subject to alteration, decay, and disposal. In Roth's novel, this doubleness plays out as the stamps go from undergirding Philip's heroic America to undoing it.

The first extensive discussion of a stamp foregrounds the dual role they play in the novel as artifacts of real history and arbiters of that history's fictive nature. Sandy's drawing skills win him first place in an Arbor Day poster contest with a design he has "based on a red two-cent stamp in Philip's collection that commemorates the sixtieth anniversary of Arbor Day" (21). Roth describes the stamp at length:

> The stamp seemed to me especially beautiful because visible within each of its narrow, vertical white borders was a slender tree whose branches arched at the top to meet and form an arbor—and until the stamp became mine and I was able to examine through my magnifying glass its distinguishing marks, the meaning of "arbor" had been swallowed up in the familiar name of the holiday. (21)

These details correspond to the real stamp on which Roth appears to have based his description (Figure 13). The protective, pastoral image is first presented as a token of Philip's heroic America. He explains that "the appeal of the Arbor Day commemorative stamp was greatly enhanced by its representing a human activity as opposed to a famous person's portrait or picture of an important place—an activity, what's more, being performed by children" (22). To win the contest, though, Sandy adapts the stamp. His fictional changes ironically highlight the very real racial inequality plaguing the United States in the 1940s.

FIGURE 13. Two-cent Arbor Day stamp. Issued by the U.S. Postal Service on April 22, 1932, to celebrate the sixtieth anniversary of the establishment of Arbor Day. Author's photograph.

At his mother's urging, Sandy adds a third child to the scene. Philip, in his best school knickers and high socks, poses for Sandy and becomes the model for the new figure. But Sandy makes an important adjustment: "The third child planting the tree was a Negro, and what encouraged my mother to suggest including him—aside from the desire to instill in her children the civic virtue of tolerance—was another stamp of mine, a brand-new ten-cent issue in the 'educators' group'" (23). Philip explains that the stamp in the educators group features "Booker T. Washington, the first Negro to appear on an American stamp" (23). While this fact, alongside Mrs. Roth's efforts to teach her children tolerance, might indicate a national expansion of tolerance and equality, Roth is quick to mine the scene for its darker implications. The narrator remembers asking his mother, "Do you think there'll ever be a Jew on a stamp?" Despite her optimistic reply, we are told, "in fact, another twenty-six years had to pass, and it took Einstein to do it" (23).[40] In this moment, Roth links his narrative of American anti-Semitism to the true history of American racism against blacks in order to remind readers that the idyllic America of Philip's Arbor Day stamp has always been illusory. Walter Benn Michaels chafes at the line Roth draws between anti-Semitism and anti-black racism. He laments that Roth's counterfactual history "did happen here, only not to the Jews": "It happened to black people, almost never to Jews."[41] Benn Michaels asks: "Why should we be outraged by what didn't happen rather than outraged by what did?"[42]

It seems clear to me that Roth's goal here is not to occlude one history with another, or to add gravitas to his counterfactual history of anti-Semitism in America by joining it to a very real history of racism. Rather, the episode testifies to history's omissions and elisions, reminding readers that the construction of mythic history as factual depends on excision and exclusion. Anti-Semitic violence is easy to imagine precisely because white supremacy was (and is) a pervasive ideology in the United States. Because the stamps that Roth references are real, the history encapsulated in the stamp is not counterfactual; it is our own. The anecdote also suggests that, as in *Man in the High Castle,* the "truth" of historical change can be encountered only obliquely, on a smaller, material scale.

Since the novel immediately establishes Philip's hobby as a means through which he forms connections to his country and its government, it makes sense that the erosion of his national ideals begins on the pages of his cherished stamp album. Indeed, while the nightmare of Lindbergh's administration escalates toward its fever pitch, the stamp collection serves as Philip's principle means of shoring himself up against terror and uncertainty. He distracts himself from the growing distress around him by dreaming about the stamps he'd like to own:

> What I would have asked for from a genie were the most coveted of all American stamps: first, the celebrated 1918 twenty-four-cent airmail, a stamp said to be worth $3,400, where the plane pictured at the center, the Army's Flying Jenny, is inverted; and after that, the three famous stamps in the Pan-American Exposition issue of 1901 that had also been mistakenly printed with inverted centers and were worth over a thousand dollars a piece. (23)

Philip wants these stamps because they are rare and therefore valuable. But the two stamps also function as apt emblems of the counterfactual genre. In miniature, ephemeral form, they attest to what should not have been. This is true, first of all, on a literal level. The first stamp, from 1918, was issued to inaugurate the new regular airmail service route between Washington, D.C., Philadelphia, and New York City (Figure 14). As the postal service rushed to complete the design and printing of the new stamp, one sheet of one hundred stamps was misfed during the two-color printing process, thereby producing the inverted image.[43] The stamp, though intended to commemorate a technological breakthrough in America, is a defective marker of progress (and a testimony to operator error). What's more, the Curtiss "Jenny" (JN-4) that the stamp depicts evokes the war that looms on Philip's horizon. The airplane was produced as a training aircraft for the U.S. Army during the First World War and subsequently became central to American postwar civil aviation.[44] The second stamp similarly troubles nationalist myths of progress. As part of the Pan-American Exposition held in Buffalo in 1901, the U.S. Post Office issued a series of six commemorative stamps. The stamps have ornately colored frames that enclose a black-and-white image of a ship, locomotive, or stagecoach. The two-color process produced the same kind of mistake seen in the "Inverted Jenny": the one-cent, two-cent, and four-cent stamps were printed on sheets in which the center vignette was inverted relative to the frame (Figure 15).[45] The inverted vehicles hang suspended from the stamps' upper borders like pendulums ironizing the expo's message of perfection and progress. The real stamp that Roth describes here thus evokes those same paradoxical feelings conveyed by Doctorow and Chabon in the previous chapter. Given that the 1901 Pan-American Exposition is most remembered as the location of President William McKinley's assassination, the stamp further gestures toward the violence that inheres in historical ephemera.

The violence congealed in the stamps becomes more apparent as Lindbergh mounts his presidential campaign against F. D. R. and Philip learns from Sandy that a victory by his aviation hero would result in America "going fascist" (26). It turns out that the enemy himself lurks in the collection. Philip confesses, "the oldest U.S. postage stamp I owned—which I couldn't possibly tear up and throw away—was a ten-cent airmail issued in 1927 to commemorate Lindbergh's transatlantic flight" (26). Philip is ashamed that he cannot bring himself to get rid of the stamp and nervous that his parents will discover it. He loves the stamps, but begins to see in his collection the adhesion of his fantasy and his fears. Like the counterfactual genre, the stamp collection conveys the impossibility of an untainted, "good" America, even

FIGURE 14. Twenty-four-cent “Inverted Jenny” stamp. Issued by the U.S. Postal Service on May 10, 1918.

FIGURE 15. Pan-American Exposition commemorative stamp with invert. Issued by the U.S. Postal Service on May 1, 1901. Reprint from 2001. Author’s photograph.

an imagined one. Once again, Roth devotes ample narrative space to a description of the stamp, asking readers to contemplate the meaning of the image alongside his novel's protagonist. The narrator recalls:

> It was a blue stamp, about twice as long as it was high, . . . [with] a picture of the *Spirit of St. Louis* flying eastward over the ocean. . . . Adjacent to the white border at the left of the stamp is the coastline of North America, with the words "New York" jutting out into the Atlantic, and adjacent to the border at the right the coastlines of Ireland, Great Britain, and France, with the word "Paris" at the end of a dotted arc that charts the flight path between the two cities. At the top of the stamp, directly beneath the white letters that boldly spell out UNITED STATES POSTAGE are the words LINDBERGH-AIR MAIL in slightly smaller type but large enough certainly to be read by a seven-year-old with perfect vision. The stamp was already valued at twenty cents by Scott's *Standard Postage Stamp Catalogue,* and what I immediately realized was that its worth would only continue increasing (and so rapidly as to become my single most valuable possession) if Alvin was right and the worst happened. (27)

Why give over so much time to the description of a stamp? What is it about this actual stamp that captures Roth's fictional aims so well? The stamp, which resembles a miniature blue dollar bill, depicts the airplane Lindbergh flew in the first successful solo non-stop transatlantic flight (Figure 16). Aside from commemorating the historic flight that propelled Lindbergh to instant celebrity, the stamp brings Philip's home in disconcerting proximity with the war abroad. The description of the stamp places New York and Europe within the same small frame and even joins the two continents with the dotted line representing Lindbergh's flight. The image contrasts with Lindbergh's isolationist policies and instead suggests the terrifying ease with which the aviator could bridge the distance between America and Europe. Philip's shame is compounded by the realization that he stands to gain from "the worst" happening. Philip speculates about what the stamp might mean in the future; readers speculate about what it might have meant in the past.

Thus far, Roth's treatment of stamps seems relatively straightforward: he shows how real stamps themselves promote and throw

FIGURE 16. Ten-cent "Spirit of St. Louis" stamp honoring Charles Lindbergh. Issued by the U.S. Postal Service on June 18, 1927. Author's photograph.

into ironic relief a counterfactual version of American history. Drawing attention to the stamps, to their idiosyncrasies and their omissions, Roth uses the stamps as indices of the nation's ills that wartime obscured. But this is only part of the story, and as the novel continues, the stamps register the full force of Philip's terror. They become a psychic screen for the novel's protagonist, one that captures the fear he feels in the face of transience. In a nightmare, Philip dreams that his stamp collection has been perverted. He recalls that, in the dream, "the design on two sets of my stamps had changed in a dreadful way without my knowing when or how" (41). He opens his album to a horrifying sight:

> When I opened to my 1932 Washington Bicentennials—twelve stamps ranging in denomination from the half-cent dark brown to the ten-cent yellows—I was stunned. Washington wasn't on the stamps anymore. Unchanged at the top of each stamp . . . was the legend "United States Postage," . . . but instead of a different portrait of Washington on each of the twelve stamps, the portraits were now the same and no longer of Washington but of Hitler. (43)

The metaphor is heavy-handed: Washington replaced by Hitler, an icon of American democracy stamped out by the fascist *Führer.* But Roth's elaborate description allows readers to envision the nightmarish stamps, and his insistence that the Washington bicentennials remain the same except for the figure depicted in their center has a curious effect (Figure 17). The dream stresses the interchangeability of Hitler and Washington, and Roth's description therefore hints at the substitution being less of an aberration than we might assume. The changes to the stamps in the dream mimic the workings of counterfactual history: an imagined change to real events initiates a domino effect into the future. But, in Philip's dream, the counterfactual events of Lindbergh's victory and America's descent into anti-Semitism also taint the past, reaching backward to tarnish stamps from 1932 depicting a president born in 1732. The stamps thus gesture simultaneously toward the past and the future.

FIGURE 17. Half-cent, one-cent, one-and-a-half-cent, and two-cent Washington bicentennial stamps from a set of twelve. Issued by the U.S. Postal Service in 1932. Author's photograph.

Like Tagomi's vision of contemporary San Francisco in *Man in the High Castle,* the dream sequence offers Roth a way to juxtapose fact and counterfact, reality and something imagined. And, in the rest of the nightmare, the Nazi threat captures not only time but space. After the Washington bicentennials, his 1934 national-parks stamps are afflicted. Before revealing what has happened to the stamps, the narrator offers a lengthy description of the them, a catalog of America's natural treasures:

> Yosemite in California, Grand Canyon in Arizona, Mesa Verde in Colorado, Crater Lake in Oregon, Acadia in Maine, Mount Rainier in Washington, Yellowstone in Wyoming, Zion in Utah, Glacier in Montana, the Great Smoky Mountains in Tennessee—and across the face of each, across the cliffs, the woods, the rivers, the peaks, the geyser, the gorges, the granite coastline, across the deep blue water and the high waterfalls, across everything in America that was the bluest and greenest and the whitest and to be preserved forever in these pristine reservations, was printed a black swastika. (43)

Roth's lyrical prose here celebrates the national parks in a familiar patriotic mode, but the list of sites and natural features creates suspense so that the terminal swastika lands indelibly for the reader, even after Philip wakes up on the floor, screaming. This is curiously reinforced by the cover of the book itself. Almost every edition of *Plot Against America* has a cover featuring an image from the nightmare (Figure 18). Embossed on the cover, the green one-cent Yosemite stamp shows a landscape that is almost entirely obscured by the thick black swastika superimposed across its center. On the one hand, the cover design simply reproduces one of the novel's most vivid images. But it also makes Philip's nightmare "real," turning the novel that the reader holds into an ersatz stamp album. The relay here between the narrative and the physical book, achieved through an object, is one more way that the novel troubles easy distinctions between counterfactual and factual history: our nightmare is Philip's.

The nightmare and the cover design also play on the vexed temporality of stamps, one reason why Roth (and Thomas Pynchon, as I'll discuss later in this book) turns to philately as a central trope in the novel. Stamps are collected because they are serial, portable, and

FIGURE 18. Cover of *The Plot Against America* by Philip Roth (Boston: HMH, 2004).

most of all ephemeral. Individual stamps like the ones in Roth's novel depict monumental figures, events, and locations. But they condense the monumental into a miniature, fragile form. They mark both the transience of paper correspondence and the fluctuating economics of postal service. The paradoxical "forever stamp" speaks to the strange work that these banal objects do.[46] The stamp collection, like the time capsule in Doctorow's novel, calls attention to the impermanence it means to ward off. This conflict comes to a head in *Plot Against America* when Philip loses his album in an ill-fated attempt to run away from home. While the government's "Homestead 42" program threatens to relocate the Roths to Kentucky, Philip hatches his escape plan. He decides to run away from home disguised as a neighbor boy and present himself to the nearby Catholic orphanage as an orphan. His plan fails when he is kicked in the head by a horse on the orphanage grounds and saved only because the neighbor boy has followed him. In the chaos of this episode, Philip loses his stamp album, which he has brought with him because, as he says, "it was intolerable to think of my album ever being broken up or thrown out, or worst of all, given away wholly intact to another boy" (233). But, when he returns home from the hospital and realizes the album is gone, he is inconsolable: "I envisioned a horde of orphans spotting the album in the woods and tearing it apart with their filthy hands. I saw them pulling out the stamps and eating them and stomping on them and flushing them by the handful down the toilet in their terrible bathroom" (236). If the album is, or has been, representative of Philip's "heroic America," its imagined destruction in the hands of children who "hated the album because it wasn't theirs" allegorizes Philip's sense that fascist brutes have seized his America while also attesting to his own xenophobia.

How does the loss of the album contribute to the novel's historiographic project? Jason Siegel notes: "If Philip's stamp collection represents a naïve sense of history as an assembly of two-dimensional icons, then Philip's loss of the collection and simultaneous realization of his vulnerability in a Christian America advances the novel's argument that historical truth is never as simple as it seems."[47] But the stamps, I have suggested, always complicated the naïve sense of history that Philip himself had. If historical truth is "never as simple as it seems," its complexity inheres in the stamps from the beginning. As in Dick's novel, the ephemeral object here is always already idealized and degraded. Each stamp is a literary object that condenses the novel's double history into a single material instant. The collection's loss thus asks readers to reflect on what, if anything, vanishes from the record. The collection entails the preservation of "real" transient objects; although Philip loses it, it endures in the form of the counterfactual novel. The terror of loss, then, is less about the specific objects, which Roth has gone to great lengths to depict as inherently compromised, than about whether it is possible to preserve things at all, in any medium or genre. Philip himself expresses this concern obliquely when he reflects with regret on his actions: "Perhaps if I could have been sure that it would have been *preserved undisturbed* after I was gone, I wouldn't, at the last moment, on the way out of my bedroom, have stopped to open my dresser drawer and, as quietly as I could, lifted it from where it was stored beneath my socks and my underclothes" (233; emphasis mine). The irony is that Roth has already used the stamps in Philip's collection to show that nothing can be "preserved undisturbed."

The presence of the stamps in a collection in fact reveals their figurative absence—the way they can never represent the kind of mythic America Philip wishes they could—and the loss of the album comes to represent that even things that "have vanished into thin air" in fact leave traces (236). The most important of these traces comes in the form of an association Philip makes. He compares the loss of the album to the traumatic loss he has seen first-hand: the leg that his older cousin Alvin lost fighting in the war. Alvin comes home a broken man: angry, depressed, and suffering from his amputated limb, which is in terrible shape. When Philip finally works up the courage to examine Alvin's leg, he sees "what the word 'stump' describes": "the blunt remnant of something whole that belonged there and once had been there" (136). Philip makes the comparison to his own loss when he says: "The biggest thing I had ever owned was gone. Gone and irreplaceable. Like—and utterly unlike—losing a leg" (235). The loss of the album is like the loss of a leg in that the collection has been a part of Philip, something that has given him a sense of wholeness. Roth emphasizes the link between amputation and Philip's collection more than once, also connecting the stamps to Little Robert, who begs on the sidewalk by Herman Roth's downtown office, a "man who began at the hips and was himself no more than a stump" (127). Once Philip learns that Alvin will convalesce in his family's home, he lies awake at night drawing out the connections between disfigured men and his disfigured stamps. "I would involuntarily envision Robert on his platform and wearing his work gloves whenever I lay stiffly in the dark trying to force myself asleep: first my stamps covered with swastikas, then Little Robert, the living stump" (128).

So, the stamps are like stumps, a far cry from the emblem of a heroic America that Philip described with rapture at the beginning of the novel. The novel reminds readers that the body, like the stamps, can be altered, disfigured, and lost. Saint-Amour argues that the amputation "gives *The Plot Against America* its master-tropes, which, despite its title, are neither plots nor plotting nor unplotted roads-not-taken but, instead, phantom-limb syndrome and the prosthesis." The novel's counterfactual anatomy figures a timeline we know as a whole limb that is "amputated" along with Roosevelt's presidency yet continues to transmit sensation even in its absence, even as it is replaced by an alternative, prosthetic history. Saint-Amour adds that the "novel banishes its 'true chronology' of the early twentieth-century to a postscript, resignifying what was to have been history's unpruned body as another prosthesis, a paratextual apparatus."[48] As such, the "true chronology" related hastily at the end of the novel cannot offer, after our journey through Roth's counterfactual world, a comforting resolution. In principle, the genre prohibits it; history as we know it always becomes a prosthesis, haunted even after the close of the novel by the story of what could have been. As Philip puts it: "Turned wrong way round, the relentless unforeseen was what we school children studied as 'History,' harmless history, where everything unexpected in its own time is chronicled on the page as inevitable. The terror of the unforeseen is what the science of history hides, turning disaster into the epic" (113–14). While "History" elides the contingent nature of reality as it strives for epic heights and monumental depths, the small, ephemeral objects expose it from the novel's outset. Roth's transient objects do not simply inject his counterfactual novel with realism meant to shock the reader with the recognition of her own history; they expose that history for its fictiveness, its unreality, and its impermanence. *Plot Against America* works to convince readers that its version of events is as plausible as what actually transpired from 1940 to 1942; its transient objects convey the disturbing message that we can never own history, that it always contains its own counterfactuals. The contingency of history, "the terror of the unforeseen" echoes Einstein's message in the time capsule that "anyone who thinks about the future must live in fear and terror." The way Roth's objects shuttle readers between the real and the imaginary enforces this point even as his novel returns readers to a known history. Roth's dying things, like Dick's, do not comfort us, but instead suggest that the desire to collect, to consume, and to counterfeit stems from the wish to make objects hold what history cannot.

BOOK COUNTERHISTORY

Collections, like counterfactual novels, present us with multiple timelines. If collecting, to return to Baudrillard, is itself an alternative discourse that attempts to ward off impermanence and give the collector "the sense that from now on he can live out his life uninterruptedly and in a cyclical mode, and thereby symbolically transcend the realities of an existence before whose irreversibility and contingency he remains powerless," then these novels expose the fallacy of such thinking.[49] Things, even when they are collected and preserved, as Roth's and Dick's novels show readers, die at different speeds. Novels on world's fairs made it clear that the ephemeral plays out at different scales, and here we see that the temporality of vanishing is not always the same. In *Man in the High Castle,* objects linger and fade over time; in *Plot Against America,* they vanish suddenly, the victims of punctual disasters like elections, wars, and violent blows. Given the way counterfactuals frequently rely on nexus points at which history "as we know it" suddenly hurdles down a different course, it makes sense that the objects in such novels might meet sudden fates. The speed at which a given object vanishes makes for a different experience of that vanishing. These two counterfactual novels thus seem uniquely poised to help us see what happens when the tethers of objects unravel at different velocities. We have, of course, already encountered the "slow fade" of objects in world's fair fiction: the sadness and even repulsion that Doctorow's protagonist Edgar feels when he sees the fair's buildings peeling and crumbling is not the same as the sudden shock and disorientation one might experience upon returning to the fairgrounds only to discover all of the structures vanished and gone.

It is hard to say which is "easier" to mourn, an object that fades slowly or one that vanishes quickly. Is a protracted disappearance more painful than a rapid one? Can we grieve only when an object is dead, not when it is dying? Dick's and Roth's novels offer answers to such questions, contemplating the fading object in the antique store and the abruptly absented stamp collection, allowing us to feel alongside the characters who confront such loss. But these novels suggest that, while the speed of disappearance may produce different affective responses, it does not change the fact that vanished things leave traces, transmit pain, and make meaning. Even when objects vanish "at speed" in counterfactual novels due to sudden, traumatic events, they enact the Freudian ambivalence of things never fully owned and never fully surrendered. Roth's discussion of Alvin's phantom-limb pain in *Plot Against America* materializes this ambivalence through a different metaphor.

In closing, I want to return to an aspect of Roth's novel that affords another way to think about the temporality of ephemera, another perspective on what novels can tell us about the time of vanishing. I have already discussed the cover of Roth's novel adorned with an image of the swastika-imprinted stamp from Philip's nightmare. In light of the temporal concerns I am tracing, the cover not only blurs the line between factual and fictional objects; it also foregrounds the tension between the novel as an object and the objects it represents. For all the sudden vanishing of Philip's stamps in Roth's novel, the novel itself, with its stamped cover, remains. While Philip's collection entails removing the stamps from circulation so that they can be classified and organized according to his own desires, the book stays in circulation, and even increased circulation, to which my earlier anecdotes about contemporary demand and relevance for the novel attest.[50] This contrast renders the book a durable object, the lasting and mobile container of ephemera preserved by the stories it tells. Though this certainly adheres to conventional notions that books endure and make authors and ideas immortal, such claims feel tenuous given current, anxious debates about the status of the printed book. I take up these debates at greater length in my coda, but for now, I want to linger with the way Roth's novel—and Dick's too, through Abendsen's fictional text—provokes readers to consider the potential ephemerality of the book they are reading.

In addition to drawing analogies between the novel and the stamp collection, or Dick's novel and Abendsen's, readers are invited to reflect on what kind of enduring object a book can be in the aftermath of political upheaval and collective trauma. Counterfactual novels play a particular role in this question of aftermath because they are self-reflexive, commenting on the power of fiction to represent history anew while pointing out the fragility of historical narratives. The genre makes an implicit claim about the need for different forms to record different losses; we need more than a timeline of events, and we cannot reconstruct the record if we arrive after the fact. Roth's and Dick's novels insist that we try to imagine and narrate the experience of loss, even at a distance or personal remove from it. Such fiction can animate loss, its uneven process and its unequal distribution. In this reading, the object of the book looks less like an enduring monument and more like a collector's album: an idiosyncratic, affectively charged assemblage that condenses national history and its counterfactual possibilities into something personal and portable. These novels are, in this additional sense, not monumentalizing, but ephemeralizing. Dick's use of science fiction conceits and Roth's use of a confessional, autofictional mode torque the counterfactual genre so that its treatment of large-scale history feels local, even intimate. The multiple genres of the novel allow stamps and flip cards to tell meaningful, diachronic stories of disappearance without insisting that their stories are definitive of a singular or sustainable history. In the next chapter, genre does similar work in a very different context, allowing midcentury black writers to represent the uncanny contortions of urban change that cannot be captured by the conventions of realism.

3

Zoned Out

CHESTER HIMES, RALPH ELLISON, AND URBAN INFRASTRUCTURE

THINKING INFRASTRUCTURALLY

In his 1948 essay "The Harlem Ghetto," first published in *Commentary,* James Baldwin laments the grim constancy of the city where he was born: "Harlem, physically at least, has changed very little in my parents' lifetime or in mine. Now as then the buildings are old and dirty, there are too many human beings per square block."[1] Baldwin describes how "all of Harlem is pervaded by a sense of congestion, rather like the insistent, maddening, claustrophobic pounding in the skull that comes from trying to breathe in a very small room with all the windows shut."[2] He paints Harlem's crushing density with characteristic eloquence, but he leaves the opening disclaimer that Harlem is unchanged, "physically at least," unexplained. Baldwin is thinking structurally, as it were, about racism in midcentury America by thinking structurally about the buildings and streets of his hometown. In the enigmatic turn of an adverbial phrase, "physically at least," he alludes to the multiple and intersecting factors that give a city or a neighborhood its character. But what, exactly, does Baldwin mean? What changes in a city, if not its physical structure?

Twelve years later, Baldwin struck a different note about Harlem in "Fifth Avenue, Uptown," an essay published in the July 1960 issue of *Esquire* magazine:

> There is a housing project standing now where the house in which we grew up once stood, and one of those stunted city trees is snarling where our doorway used to be. This is on the rehabilitated side of the avenue. The other side of the avenue—for progress takes time—has not been rehabilitated yet and it looks exactly as it looked in the days when we sat with our noses pressed against the windowpane, longing to be allowed to go "across the street."[3]

The piece seems at first like a negative image of the earlier essay: this time Baldwin takes the city's transformation as his starting point. With bitter irony, he describes the effects of "rehabilitation": a menacing tree stands in front of the looming housing project, which Baldwin later calls a "monument to the folly, and the cowardice, of good intentions."[4] Visible changes to Harlem's infrastructure do not conceal the deeply entrenched racism that is the subject of Baldwin's essay. His tensed syntax captures a crisis of representation generated by urban change. In these sentences, transformation is not only spatial, but temporal: it takes time, it happens unevenly, it layers past and present. Baldwin's essay also reveals that, because the built environment is thought to be permanent and because its large scale challenges immediate perception and direct representation, infrastructural change is made visible through discrete objects: a tree, a doorway, a windowpane.

When objects like these command Baldwin's (and our) attention, they register what we now call "gentrification" as an enduring process that never entirely erases the infrastructure of urban life-worlds. Nor does gentrification fully transform the social relations that lie underneath. Its vexed temporal contours, though at times hard to read at the level of buildings and city blocks, become legible in the object worlds of midcentury black writers. Signs, storefronts, and an array of other transient objects serve as proxies for an urban environment undergoing partial yet constant modernization. Literary objects encode the temporal paradox of urban change, allowing writers to represent in concrete form and manageable scale both the vulnerability and the persistence of cityscapes. They reveal the urban elements that vanish, but also the persistence of what should be ephemeral, the harmful systems and sentiments that endure, not unlike the grim artifacts in Philip K. Dick's 1962 *The Man in the High Castle* that have been carefully conserved, just on a larger scale. Attending to infrastructure and its surprising intersection with ephemerality opens up surprising new relays between authors usually separated by notions of literary genre and literary value. Ralph Ellison and Chester Himes, the two writers who are the subject of this chapter, shared a broader representational project localized in Harlem but definitive of the postwar black canon. While they so evidently differ in purpose and style, Ellison and Himes developed their narrative aesthetics in response to the same strange coupling of permanence and loss they saw shaping Harlem from the 1940s to the 1960s. What happens, they both ask, when neighborhoods experience a perennial unmaking, often at the expense of black lives and black communities? The strategies these two writers used to explore such questions recast the way we currently understand postwar urban history. Their novels show how infrastructure registers this change, congealing past and present. Like Baldwin (or, at an earlier moment, Ann Petry), Ellison and Himes made indelible fiction from the paradox of gentrification, depicting Harlem in the mid-twentieth century as a black space undergoing a process of constant transformation that is never complete.[5]

Once we understand gentrification through the logics of ephemera, it becomes more challenging to represent. What portraits can adequately show the duality of persistence and disappearance, the strange reality of things remaining although they are destined to vanish? The poignant reversals and contortions in Baldwin's prose point the way to a broader rereading of African American fiction's engagement with postwar urban terrain. In our current climate of polarized debate, it's especially hard to capture this kind of contradiction and nuance, to go beyond the political argument that gentrification is good because it "improves" neighborhoods or bad because it displaces minorities. Recognizing the long and contradictory history of urban development also shifts our conversation away from metanarratives of gentrification as "good" or "bad" featuring one-directional change over time. Instead we might consider, as a context for the midcentury African American novel, the political paradoxes of gentrification, paradoxes that defy both catastrophic and utopian narratives of modernization, and that therefore demand literary innovation and layered representation.[6] It would be easy to assimilate Ellison's and Himes's work to the conventional critique of gentrification in which white material gain means black loss. But even as Ellison and Himes, like Baldwin, retain the political freight of this point, they refute diagnoses of total erasure or total progress. Their novels insist that black communal life in Harlem and its modes of material engagement are not so easily erased. More broadly, their novels suggest that postwar fiction, with its focus on ephemera, can mediate between the discourses of urbanization as large-scale change and the daily practices of individual subjects who inhabit American cities.[7] Studies of urban life usually focus either on implacable structures and abstract forces or on individuals and their social agency. Infrastructure, however, lies between these two poles, and therefore becomes a logical site of inquiry for writers seeking to avoid an absolutist model of gentrification as liberal freedom or inert resignation, as total loss or redemptive persistence.[8] The term that I use here, "infrastructural racism," illuminates how racist social forms are embedded in the built environment. It suggests that racism is neither eternal nor gauzy and purely ideational; likewise, collective black life in the city, which both shapes and is shaped by the infrastructure of neighborhoods and urban spaces, is neither invincible in the face of economic threat nor altogether fragile. "Infrastructural racism" names this "in-betweenness," reminding us that historically contingent racism and resistance comingle in the same spaces.

It is precisely these complexities of historical process, localized in Harlem, that inspire Ellison's and Himes's most distinctive fictional projects, *Invisible Man* (1952) and the Harlem detective novels known collectively as the *Harlem Cycle* (1957–69). Ellison and Himes wrote in the era when "urban renewal" was generally used to describe the changes taking place in New York. Urban renewal denoted state-sponsored initiatives that involved tearing down older buildings and erecting new ones in their places. Major urban renewal projects in the United States took off during the postwar period, largely kick-started by the Housing Act of 1949, which allocated federal funding to cities to redevelop "slums."[9] Urban renewal aimed, as Myka Tucker-Abramson writes, "to clear vast sections of the city deemed to be 'blighted' in order to create new urban spaces in line with the principles of modern planning."[10] As Baldwin famously quipped in a 1963 interview with Kenneth Clark, "urban renewal . . . means negro removal."[11] "Gentrification," on the other hand, was coined in 1964 by sociologist Ruth Glass to describe the influx of middle-class people into working-class neighborhoods.[12] The term names a process that is rarely state-sponsored and supposedly happens at a slower pace, as lots and buildings in a "deteriorating" neighborhood are renovated to raise property values. Older housing stock may be torn down, smaller apartments combined into larger units, and rentals replaced with purchase-only properties. The liquor store becomes a coffee shop, which eventually becomes a high-end smoothie shop. Regardless of the actual demographics of property ownership, the term "gentrification" suggests the displacement of black, ethnic, and poor residents by upwardly mobile whites who "reclaim" urban landscapes blighted by neglect. While urban renewal stresses removal and replacement, gentrification emphasizes the repurposing of urban forms. "Gentrification" has now largely displaced "urban renewal" in discussions of changing cities. Both terms, however, encode the infrastructural racism that renders the built environment disproportionately hostile to non-white subjects over the long arc from the postwar past to the postindustrial present. If we now see gentrification as a privatized, neoliberal process, it is nonetheless useful to observe that, even as government initiatives gave way to corporate ones in the last decades of the twentieth century, gentrification continued the segregationist work once carried out under the banner of urban renewal.

Critics of gentrification frequently lament it as a form of destruction and erasure. Jane Jacobs, for instance, recalls Rudy Giuliani's Manhattan project: "The poor, evicted, or priced out by the higher costs of renovating, were victims."[13] Scholars of urban studies such as Mark Davis, David Harvey, and Saskia Sassen are among those who have shown how infrastructural planning (and the lack thereof) helps produce and sustain inequality by distributing access to services and goods unevenly.[14] More recently, literary critics have also begun theorizing infrastructure, exploring the ways in which literature makes infrastructure, and its absence, visible. In addition to Bruce Robbins's "The Smell of Infrastructure" (2007) and Michael Rubenstein's *Public Works* (2010), which began a conversation about literary representations of public utilities, Caroline Levine has suggested that fiction can help expose "the relations between structures such as racial hierarchies and infrastructures such as electrical grids."[15] And in their 2016 volume, *Race and Real Estate,* Adrienne Brown and Valerie Smith gather essays that reflect on literary representations of the vexed relationships between black subjects and the property they own, or are prohibited from owning. These scholars generally use the term "infrastructure" to denote "hard infrastructure," the physical networks necessary for the functioning of modern industry, such as roads, railways, and bridges. Kate Marshall has shown how such systems and facilities often function in novels as what N. Katherine Hayles calls "material metaphors," "a category of physical object that is both constructed by and functions through its metaphoric networks." For Marshall, infrastructure like corridors, furnaces, ducts, and pipes are media in novels because they are self-reflexive: "They embed the forms of self-reflection in a material object that also demonstrates a capacity to reflect upon itself."[16] This is certainly true in novels by Ellison and Himes, where infrastructure often throws into relief both the material conditions of midcentury black life and the temporality and possibilities of fiction itself. I thus use "infrastructure" to encompass the ephemeral objects that are a part of Ellison's and Himes's urban landscapes, such as signs and billboards but also storefronts and subway stations, all things that reveal to readers everything that persists amidst radical transience.

These objects are part and parcel of the built environment that can discriminate, and that is frequently designed to do so. In *Times Square Red, Times Square Blue,* Samuel Delany chronicles the cross-racial, cross-class contact that happened in pornographic movie theaters and its decimation by the "Baron Haussmann–like" rationalization of Times Square in the 1990s.[17] Because Delany insists on infrastructure's central role in urban life—"Infrastructure makes society go. Superstructure makes society go smoothly (or bumpily)"—he devotes significant attention to the buildings, streetlights, and food carts that form the topography of his sex-positive landscape.[18] Delany's writing suggests that Haussmannization (or Giulianization) cannot erase all the urban forms that it seeks to push to the margins. Gentrification entails racialized economic violence, but rhetorical emphasis on victimization and displacement can constitute another act of erasure. The narrative of utter disappearance obscures how much of an urban environment remains untransformed. In this sense, even stinging critiques of gentrification can participate in the very ideology of urban progress they intend to condemn.

Perhaps this mixed legacy of vulnerability and persistence can help account for Baldwin's temporally knotted prose with which I began and also offer new access to the ways that Ellison and Himes embed objects in changing black neighborhoods. Issues of access and affordability intersect to perpetuate in concrete form the racial inequality that Ellison and Himes confront in their fiction, especially in their treatment of material culture. Both depict objects whose transience points to the changes happening in the city at large by the way that they vanish, leave traces, become clues or debris; both call for an interpretive method that can address the way that time inheres in objects. If we think about the racial dimensions of the current infrastructural turn and integrate those insights with this book's methodological commitment to ephemera, we can see physical matter in Ellison and Himes as vital to the politics and aesthetics of *Invisible Man* and the Harlem Cycle. These novels encode the temporal contradictions of postwar black life in their object catalogs, elaborating the "changing same" logic that we have seen depicted by Baldwin and that was later codified by Amiri Baraka and Deborah McDowell. Objects in the Harlem of Ellison and Himes make concrete the pathos of changing infrastructure at a sensory scale that readers and historical subjects can more readily perceive. Woven into and out of the urban environment, these objects materialize the "changing same," and thus make visible the temporal paradox at the heart of urban development in the postwar United States. Himes and Ellison invest aesthetic and political value in the literary object that is always vanishing but never fully vanished. As we will see, their uncanny objects and the temporal paradoxes of urban history and black life that they encode define the revisionary work that Ellison and Himes performed on two very different genres: modernist psychological realism and sensational crime fiction.

UNREAL HARLEM

Ellison and Himes testify to Harlem's layered character in their novels, depicting a city that retains the traces of its pasts while pushing forward into the future. This view of Harlem as a dynamic archive, preserving some remnants of its history while discarding others, remains relevant in black life and black cultural studies. Debates over Harlem's fate are heated and ongoing. *The New York Times,* for instance, ran a splashy feature story in May 2016 declaring and dissecting "The End of Black Harlem." But even if its demographics have reached a tipping point and "Black Harlem" seems to name a historical site situated squarely in the twentieth century, Harlem still signifies lived and artistic blackness: what Alain Locke and others called the "black mecca" since the early twentieth century.[19] In a foundational text of the Harlem Renaissance, *Black Manhattan* (1930), James Weldon Johnson remarks that "the significance of the name Harlem has changed from Dutch to Irish to Jewish to Negro."[20] And Sara Blair points out that "the texture of this transformation—of its survivals and afterlives, its residual and palimpsestic effects—was even more variegated than Johnson suggests."[21] Black Harlem's particular social and artistic history has long made it a contradictory space of sporadic renaissance and recurrent decline. In 1930, Johnson celebrated Harlem as "the greatest Negro city in the world," "not a slum or a fringe" but "located in the heart of white Manhattan," occupying "one of the most beautiful healthful sections of the city."[22] But, as Cheryl Greenberg recounts in her history of Harlem during the Great Depression, segregation allowed white landlords to charge extortionist rents to black tenants who could not find housing elsewhere. Hemmed in by white neighborhoods that resisted integration, overcrowding in Harlem intensified and building owners let their buildings deteriorate. The economic devastation of the Great Depression exacerbated these conditions so much further that, by the end of the 1930s, Harlem had higher levels of crowding, greater poverty, fewer parks and public spaces, higher illness and death rates, and higher rents for poorer quality housing than any other area in New York City. As Myka Tucker-Abramson describes, the postwar period saw the ascendancy of discriminatory urban renewal policies, and it was during this period, Tucker-Abramson notes, that "the language of housing reform" was turned into "a tool for the uprooting and removal of largely black communities in the name of economic development."[23] Ellison's interest in this intersection of housing and race is well documented. In the late 1930s, he worked for the Federal Writers Project chronicling the impact of New York's segregated housing policies on Harlem residents. He famously described the psychological toll inflicted by the city's spatial forms upon black people in his 1948 essay, "Harlem Is Nowhere." Writing between the Harlem Renaissance and the Civil Rights Movement, Ellison and Himes reckoned with the fact that material change in Harlem did not necessarily mean progress. Their texts present racism not only as abstract and interpersonal, but as material and infrastructural, inscribed in the city's gridded matrix. Streets and stoops, diners and nightclubs, and even electrical grids occasion the racial conflicts in Ellison and Himes. Their novels consider what change really means when the fundamental—and fundamentally violent—conditions of discrimination remain untransformed.

The two authors pursue these themes in the same setting, but in fictional languages that have long seemed antithetical to each other. The pigeonholing of Himes as a writer of genre fiction has obscured his subtle treatment of Harlem, while Ellison has been credited for his attention to the psychological toll inflicted by the city's spatial forms. Scholarly work on Himes remains relatively scant (especially in comparison with the mountains written about Ellison), and it has been noted that Himes's pulp appeal puts him at odds with the politics of social protest and racial uplift seen in the African American novels traditionally favored by critics. As Christopher Breu puts it, Himes's "almost gleefully non-redemptive representations of the violent intersectionality of race, gender, and sexuality have, until recently, made his novels nearly impervious to critical recuperation for the African American canon."[24] It is true that Himes's hardboiled fiction is pulpy, featuring lurid crimes, prostitution, gambling, and small-scale robbery. But, as Breu points out, critics have indeed recently begun to reevaluate the politics of Himes's hard-boiled detective series; for instance, Clare Rolens has called attention to the surprising sentiment present even in his "criminal texts,"[25] and in his recent biography of Himes, Lawrence P. Jackson argues that, despite Himes's claiming that "he had dropped his concern with protesting against racial oppression or writing in a realistic style," what he really had done was "create sizzling exaggerations that amplified and telescoped his concerns."[26] Jackson opposes realist and genre impulses in Himes, an approach that makes biographical sense. At a different level of analysis, however, Himes's incorporation of detective plots and Ellison's of realist psychological drama invoke a similar logic of temporalized objects and a similar urban geography of the changing same.

Put differently, we might say that Harlem, rapidly transforming while remaining untransformed in crucial ways, was an uncanny place that posed a representational challenge for both Ellison and Himes. Neither author takes a documentary approach, despite the details they offer such as street names, the layout of shops and diners and apartment buildings, or the ebbs and flows of crowds. Ellison, who knew Harlem well, described it in "Harlem Is Nowhere" as masquerade, "a world so fluid and shifting that often within the mind the real and the unreal merge, and the marvelous beckons from behind the same sordid reality that denies its existence."[27] Himes, on the other hand, recalls in his 1976 autobiography how he wrote about Harlem from Paris: "I would sit in my room and become hysterical about the wild incredible story I was writing. And I thought I was writing realism. It never occurred to me that I was writing absurdity. Realism and absurdity are so similar in the lives of American blacks one cannot tell the difference."[28] Eve Dunbar deftly examines the problem of realism that Himes's novels pose for readers. She notes that, while Himes is "invested in re-creating an accurate verbal map of Harlem," ultimately he shuns realism, creating instead an "ethnography of the absurd that seeks to document not black life with any realism but black life under the arresting pressure and violence of white oppression."[29] To Dunbar's assessment, I would add that realism and accuracy are not necessarily equivalent. Himes's inaccuracies can produce a realist effect precisely because they reflect Harlem's inauthenticity and fluidity. Rather than dismissing the liberties Himes takes with urban geography and his liberal use of stereotype and hyperbole, I take Michael Denning's cue that Himes has written "topographies of this unreal city," giving readers a realistic glimpse into a Harlem de-realized through transience.[30] In short, Himes's *irrealism* and Ellison's *surrealism* are both formal strategies that address the strange palimpsests created by urban change and compressed into objects that persist even as they are scored by history.

HIMES'S PALIMPSESTS

The Harlem Cycle consists of the eight novels Himes wrote between 1957 and 1969 while living in Paris.[31] Their recurring characters are two black detectives who police Harlem, although they do not themselves live there: Coffin Ed Johnson and Grave Digger Jones. All of the novels contain vivid descriptions of the Harlem streets that the two detectives patrol: buildings, businesses, and swirling eddies of people. The novels often read like parodic riffs on narratives of the Harlem Renaissance. Raymond Nelson notes this lineage in his observation that "Himes . . . brightens his sordid criminal Harlem with the wild comedy, eccentricity of character, and exotic low-life that he inherited from the celebratory black writers of the twenties."[32] But the more striking connection is Himes's many mentions of iconic Harlem Renaissance sites. The street that Himes mentions more than any other is Lenox Avenue, the portion of 6th Avenue running north–south through Harlem from the Farmers' Gate at Central Park North (110th Street) to 147th Street. Himes's fictive maps of Harlem always feature Lenox Avenue as the address for storefront churches, illicit nightclubs, and new brick apartment buildings, a stretch of road to be patrolled by the detectives. In *The Real Cool Killers,* for example, a short 150-page novel, Himes includes twelve distinct references to Lenox Avenue; in *Blind Man with a Pistol,* ten. *The Real Cool Killers* opens with a clear evocation of the blues and jazz clubs that made Lenox Avenue famous during the Harlem Renaissance: the first words of the novel are the lyrics of a blues song, and the narrator relates that "the colored patrons of Harlem's Dew Drop Inn on 129th Street and Lenox Avenue were having the time of their lives that crisp October night."[33] But, of course, this is the late 1950s, not the 1920s, and Himes shatters the scene and its nostalgic glance backward with an eruption of spectacular violence. By referencing Harlem Renaissance hotspots frequently, not to laud them but to use them as the backdrop for violence, crime, and poverty, Himes's novels seem to evoke the legacy of the Harlem Renaissance in order to dismantle it. In this way, the Harlem Renaissance becomes another lost object, a literary past that Himes's novels simultaneously archive and attempt to erase.

Seven of the eight Harlem Cycle novels follow a relatively straightforward formula: a crime is committed, the detectives are put on the case, incredible mayhem ensues until a solution of some kind is reached. But the eighth novel, *Blind Man*, published in 1969, works differently. The main plot of the novel follows three interlocking but only vaguely related crime stories, but they are intercut by six "interludes," strange fragments that renarrate events from the other chapters and offer seemingly random impressions. Thomas Heise has argued that the novel's "formal incoherence" is "both an effect of the numerous and contesting tensions it seeks to negotiate and an integral part of the cultural work that *Blind Man* performs as it demystifies the powers that police inner-city black life and produce newly legible discursive racial formations."[34] I would add that the novel's "formal incoherence" is a reflection of the spatial transformations that can be neither neatly cataloged nor undone. From the outset of *Blind Man*, Himes insists that the city's material convulsions cannot be policed because they resist the ordering logic of detection.

In the first interlude, a floating narrative voice charts the novel's setting:

> *Where 125th Street crosses Seventh Avenue is the Mecca of Harlem, . . . Most of the commercial enterprises—stores, bars, restaurants, theaters, etc.—and real estate are owned by white people. But it is the Mecca of the black people just the same. The air and the heat and the voices and the laughter, the atmosphere and the drama and the melodrama, are theirs. Theirs are the hopes, the schemes, the prayers and the protest. They are the managers, the clerks, the cleaners, they drive the taxis and the buses, they are the clients, the customers, the audience: they work it, but the white man owns it. So it is natural that the white man is concerned with their behavior; it's his property. But it is the black people's to enjoy. The black people have the past and the present, and they hope to have the future.*[35]

It appears at first that the interlude will offer a familiar version of Harlem: its busy streets pulsing like arteries stretched in a connective matrix. But the passage takes an unexpected turn and quickly becomes an ambivalent meditation on urban transformation. This interlude makes a fraught claim about ownership: Harlem belongs to black people even if the property does not. Although the passage celebrates this claim, the evocation of slavery ("they work it, but the white man owns it") is unmistakable. The ambiguous referent of "it's his property" signals the history of black people themselves treated as property under chattel slavery. The passage highlights what has *not* changed despite the forward march of time. It transforms the experience of life on the streets—the air, the heat, the atmosphere—into goods that can be owned, while the infrastructure of the city continues to concretize racial discrimination. A sense of loss abuts the declaration of hope: even as the narration insists that black people own "the past and the present," this ownership is shown to be partial and elusive. The interlude, like the novel as a whole, registers the changing cityscape without lapsing into an exuberant optimism about the future or giving in to a wholly nostalgic view of the past. By attending to the layered histories in the built environment, Himes invokes the material consequences of change and the way that a narrative of progress can obscure what remains untransformed.

To enforce this point, Himes follows this interlude with a literal instance of layering in which gentrification rearranges the materials of the past. A shop sign on 125th Street illustrates how the past and present coexist, creating curious contradictions in the urban landscape. It reads: "*CHICKEN AUTO INSURANCE, Seymour Rosenblum.*" The narrator explains that "white motorists" assumed that this was a real product on offer, when in fact "the 'chicken' sign was left over from a restaurant that had gone bankrupt and closed months previously, and the "sign advertising auto insurance had been placed across the front of the closed shop afterwards."[36] More palimpsestic still, the store is actually a front for an activist organizing protests. The comingling of signs attests to the nature of change in Harlem: insurance replaces chicken and a Jewish name stands in for the displacement of black businesses by white ones. Here infrastructure enacts its curious temporality: the past abuts the present, which ironically entails a speculation on risk. The accretion of text, played for comic effect, testifies to the fact that neighborhood change may be paper-thin, while the racially stacked economies of American enterprise run deep.

A number of other objects also act as proxies for the built environment in the crimes Coffin Ed and Grave Digger must solve. Like the characters of *Man in the High Castle,* the detectives are forced to reckon with fakes, frauds, and rubbish, the kinds of objects that prolong mystery rather than unravel it. Things, in short, are rarely what they seem. When an object is evidence in the Harlem Cycle, it is evidence of the eddying current of postindustrial crisis that has thrown black life in Harlem into a state of both constant change and constant loss. While Coffin Ed and Grave Digger *do* solve crimes and put criminals in jail, the novels also frustrate readers' expectations of the genre. Since the "real crime," we might say, is the dispossession of black people and the systemic racism that allows it, the black detectives are always something like thwarted agents pursuing partial crimes. Take, for instance, the titular bale of cotton in *Cotton Comes to Harlem,* the seventh novel in the Harlem Cycle, published in 1965. The novel begins with a "Back to Africa" rally, in which "starry-eyed" Harlem residents pay $1,000 for reserved places on a ship that will take them to Africa. Masked hijackers crash the rally and steal the money that has been collected. While Coffin Ed and Grave Digger begin their investigation, a homeless junk collector discovers a bale of cotton lying at the corner of Lexington Avenue that has fallen off the hijackers' get-away truck. Between the homeless man's discovery of the cotton and the novel's ending, a game of pursuit and escape ensues. The bale zigzags through Harlem's underground economies, winding its way from a junk warehouse to an exotic dancer's stage, where it is incorporated into a flagrantly racialized "cotton dance." The dancer auctions the bale off to Colonel Robert Calhoun, a white southerner who has opened a storefront for his "Back to the Southland" movement in Harlem. The advertisements on the "B.T.S." storefront promise that the first families who sign up to move south and make a living picking cotton will receive $1,000 bonuses.

As it turns out, Calhoun arranged the original hijacking; he then opened the storefront to search for his money-stuffed cotton bale. A giant "white-painted, black-lettered banner" on the store window includes a small notice at the bottom that reads "Wanted, a bale of cotton."[37] By the time Coffin Ed and Grave Digger unravel the mystery of the original theft, the money is no longer in the bale because the homeless man has taken it for himself. The two detectives make a deal with the Colonel: he'll hand over $87,000 to pay back the money stolen from the Black Harlemites and the detectives will look the other way while he leaves New York. The bale of cotton is hardly standard detective fare. The bale and the money hidden inside it become largely irrelevant by the novel's end. If it is immaterial to the resolution of the novel's plot, then what *is* the point of the bale? The cotton works to critique the racist iconography of the American South and its plantation labor, and both the schemes in the novel raise the issue of relocation: if Harlem is no longer home, where could home be? The South? Africa? A speaker at the Back to Africa rally draws on the reality of gentrification and its drive toward racialized displacement to convince listeners:

> "See that sign," Reverend O'Malley shouted, pointing to a large wooden sign against the wire fence which proclaimed that the low-rent housing development to be erected on that site would be completed within two and one half years, and listed the prices on the apartments, which no family among those assembled there could afford to pay. "Two years you have to wait to move into some boxes—if you can get in, and if you can pay the high rent after you get in."[38]

Seen in this light of this larger narrative, the cotton and the missing money are epiphenomenal, props in minor street crimes that are set against a much larger infrastructural backdrop that retains traces of the historical crimes of enslavement and displacement. The bale might be seen as an artifact of slavery's "ghost infrastructures" that haunt Himes's Harlem: it contains traces of black labor and white theft, a highly mobile compound that is always out of place in Himes's urban grid.

To elaborate on this point, I want to turn to another set of objects, these from the first novel in the Harlem Cycle, *A Rage in Harlem,* published in 1957. The novel deals obsessively with the issue of fake objects. This preoccupation with fraud and forgery, one shared by *Man in the High Castle,* further troubles the status of objects as evidence. But like Dick, who I have suggested uses fake objects to disrupt stable narratives of the nation, Himes also turns to fakes to challenge tidy, linear conceptions of gentrification.[39] The novel follows an innocent man who is caught up in a counterfeiting scheme involving a trunk of fake gold. The man, Jackson, "borrows" his boss's car to transport the trunk. Since Jackson works for an undertaker, that car is a hearse. The hearse, like the cotton bale, is a kind of fake object or empty-set representative of the urban environment:

> When [Jackson] turned to climb into the driver's seat he noticed that the back of the hearse was loaded with funeral paraphernalia. It was a 1947 Cadillac that had first seen service as an ambulance. Now it was used mainly to pick up the bodies for embalming, and to do double duty as a truck. The coffin rack was half hidden beneath a pile of black bunting used to drape the rostrum during a funeral, plaster pedestals for lights and flowers, wreaths of artificial flowers, and a bucket half-filled with dirty motor-oil changed from one of the limousines.[40]

The ambulance, once part of the city's infrastructure for saving lives, has been repurposed into a hearse dedicated to hauling those who have lost theirs, signaling desuetude even more than death. The objects inside are a vulgar affront to a sentimental or redemptive view of death: who wants to know that funerary objects are recycled? The trappings used to mark the passing of a loved one mingle in a heap with dirty car oil. Jonathan Eburne has noted the way that this scene grafts horror and humor together to form a "vernacular collage," but the hearse also speaks to gentrification.[41] It reveals the horror of the partially transformed, how it signals the uncomfortable fact that renewal does not make things entirely new. Instead, as the passage stresses, objects do "double duty": half-hidden, half-filled, only ever half-transformed. The objects in the hearse reflect the darkest side of the infrastructural racism that Himes describes. Especially later in the novel, when Jackson's brother is murdered and winds up among the hearse's cargo, "rammed . . . feet first into the funeral paraphernalia underneath the trunk," the objects highlight the human cost of the changes happening in Harlem under the banner of gentrification.[42]

The objects in the hearse, like the cotton bale, raise the specter of authenticity, pointing as they do to the finality of death and the horrors of plantation slavery. But as it turns out, the hearse is also a get-away car in a botched crime involving fake gold, and the cotton a fake prop in a long con. These objects aren't exactly red herrings or MacGuffins; they are instead strange emblems of the changing material world that Himes wants to capture. The fakes, the decoys, and the debris circulate in an imagined Harlem that is marked by the paradox of constant change *and* persistent forms. Despite their role in Himes's detective stories, the many objects can hardly be called evidence: even if they can "prove" something, they do so in the context of crimes that prove senseless. Instead, these objects echo the contradictions of the postwar urban space that simple narratives of gentrification flatten out. As remnants of ghost infrastructures, these things are both agile signifiers and encrusted matter, dwelling between the life and language of the new black city and the historical specters of death and displacement.

The layering of signs, the emptiness of evidence, and the partially transformed matter in Himes's novels also point the way to a new understanding of *Invisible Man*. Though Himes's first novel, *If He Hollers Let Him Go* (1945), has been compared to *Invisible Man* by Richard Yarborough because it features a protagonist who is disillusioned in his search for economic and social mobility, it is the Harlem Cycle that shares its setting and its object world with Ellison's text. Himes's detective novels thus prime readers to consider the ways that Ellison's narrator is embedded in an infrastructural space being reshaped by urban change, confronting objects that are receding but never gone.

ELLISON'S EPHEMERA

Ralph Ellison's invisible man is not a detective. But he is an urban explorer of sorts, and like Coffin Ed and Grave Digger, his "beat" is Harlem. For all of the novel's early interest in the figuratively underground spaces of the South and its conclusion set in Harlem's literal underground, the narrator's first glimpse of the "city-within-a-city" is pure surface: light and noise and motion, the chaos of swirling stuff. When the narrator finally arrives in Harlem after being expelled from his school in the South and "regurgitated" from the crowded subway train onto the street, he is amazed by the "bombardment of impressions":

> I had never seen so many black people against a background of brick buildings, neon signs, plate glass, and roaring traffic—not even on trips I had made with the debating team to New Orleans, Dallas or Birmingham. They were everywhere. So many, and moving along with so much tension and noise that I wasn't sure whether they were about to celebrate a holiday or join in a street fight. . . . Sure I had heard of it, but this was *real*. My courage

> returned. This really was Harlem, and now all the stories which I had heard of the city-within-a-city leaped alive in my mind.[43]

The threat of violence is palpable to the narrator from his first moments in Harlem and indeed, he wanders immediately into a volatile gathering that he quickly flees, not wanting to "see a riot flare" (161). The premonition of violence fits with the city's frenetic tenor, its mercurial moods and unknowable plans. As the novel progresses, the relentless pace of change becomes menacing, bound up with Harlem's housing crisis and the broader conditions of racism that the narrator confronts. Though Ellison's aesthetic register may be very different, we can see already that he is charting many of the same social and spatial problems as Himes.

An early encounter in Harlem emphasizes the fungibility of the built environment. Walking through Harlem and gazing at Manhattan, the invisible man admires the way "the skyscrapers rose tall and mysterious in the thin, pastel haze" (172). His reverie is interrupted by the sight of a "man pushing a cart piled high with rolls of blue paper" and singing blues songs. Although the man's songs remind the invisible man of "times [he] had heard such singing as home," his cart full of blue paper in fact marks him as a man of Harlem, and of the moment. It turns out that the cart is full of blueprints. When the narrator asks what for, the man responds:

> "Damn if I know—everything. Cities, towns, country clubs. Some just buildings and houses. I got damn near enough to build me a house if I could live in a paper house like they do in Japan. I guess somebody done changed their plans," he added with a laugh. "I asked the man why they getting rid of all this stuff and he said they get in the way so every once in a while they have to throw 'em out to make place for the new plans. Plenty of these ain't never been used, you know. . . . Folks is always making plans and changing 'em." (175)

Although the invisible man perceives the stranger as a kind of folk figure from "down South," the man's speech casts him as knowing and even cosmopolitan. His material cargo here speaks loudly: the blueprints testify to the rapidity of structural transformations occurring in Harlem. The image of cast aside plans is of course a comment on the invisible man's own plans that will soon be derailed, but it also bespeaks the dizzying logics of urban renewal. The plans are still good, but crowding makes them superfluous, turning them into waste that winds up in the man's shopping cart. In this sense, the plans are paper witnesses to the spatial unrest and racialized displacement that the novel chronicles.

Despite the shelves of excellent scholarship on *Invisible Man* and Ellison, these blueprints, like the novel's other objects, have been largely overlooked.[44] Critics have focused on Ellison's urbanism and his engagement with space, but little has been said about his use of objects to encode the dynamics of that space, to represent at reduced scale the very environments they fill. Ellison addresses the infrastructural level of black experience by compacting it into the novel's material and imagistic substrate; it is there he presents the layering of change and the persistence of social forms. The blueprints in the narrator's "gleaming calfskin brief case," for example, and the items he encounters on the street during an eviction are generally taken as props in his encounters with history or in his psychological development (32). But like the blueprints illuminating Harlem's swirling currents, the objects in *Invisible Man* often mediate between abstract, external forces—history, environment, politics—and the subject's interior life. Attention to these objects reveals their transitive power, their piercing ontic energy that inflects narrator and narrative with the material conditions that readers might otherwise be tempted to dismiss as mere setting. Sianne Ngai has illuminated one of the meaningful relays between subject and object in the novel with an incisive reading of the infamous black Sambo doll animated by a Harlem activist. And, in *Other Things,* Bill Brown reads the narrator's repulsion by the Sambo puppet as an emblem of the anachronistic South, much like Himes's cotton bale. "Black life in the south," Brown writes, "is the static life of a windup toy; life in New York provides a kinesthetic alternative."[45] Both readings stress animation, kinetics, motion: a hint that objects in *Invisible Man* harbor and reflect the larger-scale changes shaping Harlem in the novel.

Nowhere is the centrality of infrastructure made more visible or more material than in the scene of eviction that spurs the invisible man into political speech and ultimately into the Brotherhood. The narrator stumbles on an elderly black couple being put out onto the street with their belongings by a group of white men. Overwhelmed by the emotions that the couple's plight causes him, the invisible man turns aside and looks "at the clutter of household objects" that are accumulating on the sidewalk. In an astonishing passage that I can only excerpt here, he describes the items he sees in exhaustive detail:

> My eyes fell upon a pair of crudely carved and polished bones, "knocking bones," used to accompany music at country dances, used in black-face minstrels; the flat ribs of a cow, a steer or sheep, flat bones that gave off a sound, when struck, like heavy castanets (had he been a minstrel?) or the wooden block of a set of drums. Pots and pots of green plants were lined in the dirty snow, certain to die of the cold; ivy, canna, a tomato plant. And in a basket I saw a straightening comb, switches of false hair, a curling iron, a card with silvery letters against a background of dark red velvet, reading "God Bless Our Home"; and scattered across the top of a chiffonier were nuggets of High John the Conqueror, the lucky stone; and as I watched the white men put down a basket in which I saw a whiskey bottle filled with rock candy and camphor, a small Ethiopian flag, a faded tintype of Abraham Lincoln, and the smiling image of a Hollywood Star torn from a magazine. And on a pillow several badly cracked pieces of delicate china, a commemorative plate celebrating the St. Louis World's Fair. . . . I stood in a kind of daze, looking at an old folded lace fan studded with jet and mother-of-pearl. (271)

Why this avalanche of *stuff*? Why do the evicted couple's belongings command so much more of the narrator's attention than the couple themselves or the building they must leave behind? Certainly the objects thrust into view the history that the invisible man had hoped to escape by coming to Harlem. The objects cycle back through the twentieth century: Marcus Garvey's deportation in 1927 and the St. Louis World's Fair of 1904 lead back even earlier, to the "knocking bones" that evoke the horror of minstrel shows that the narrator will revisit later in his encounter with Clifton and the Sambo doll. The couple's objects revivify the history that the invisible man would prefer to forget. But, in attending to the way that the "artifacts of blackface are stubbornly durable," as Julia Sun-Joo Lee does, critics and readers may overlook the way that the relics of the past comingle with emblems of a contemporary urban existence: magazine and newspaper clippings, a curling iron and straightening comb.[46] The passage, like Himes's interludes, disrupts time not just by bringing the past close but by revealing that the present entails only a partial transformation of that past; the present is literally of a piece with the history it disavows.

Though we tend to think of long lists as stopping or slowing narrative time, the inventory here is frenetic, even propulsive.[47] Ellison's description evokes the paradox of gentrification by insisting on a social backdrop that remains static while the material and infrastructural foreground undergoes rapid change. The objects mark so many past moments and as they pile up in the text and on the sidewalk, they accumulate the kinetic speed that the invisible man finds everywhere he looks in Harlem. The invisible man tries desperately to bring some order to the collection by replacing the jumble of objects into the cap-sized drawer. But the list resists order as it jumps between spatial, affective, and temporal registers. Blair describes how the objects "testify not to social fact but to the mysterious alchemy by which lived experience, including [the narrator's] own, becomes the stuff—traumatic, unspeakable, irresistible—of history."[48] I think it is important to note that what is "mysterious" about the "alchemy" Blair describes is that it does not produce an ordered whole. The list's uncanny juxtapositions are mirrored by the invisible man's efforts to return the objects to their rightful places. The pathos of the scene derives from the narrator's awareness that, because the couple is being removed from their home, their belongings no longer have a place to which they belong. Collateral damage of gentrification, the couple's most personal things have been violently relocated from a private space to a public one. The list reaches its painful conclusion with a discovery by the invisible man, one that explicitly links the issue of private property and housing with slavery. He discovers, in "the dirty snow," a "fragile paper, coming apart with age, written in black ink grown yellow." With growing horror, the invisible man reads: "FREE PAPERS. *Be it known to all men that my negro, Primus Provo, has been freed by me this sixth day of August, 1859. Signed: John Samuels. Macon . . .*" (272). Despite the document's signs of aging, it is painful evidence of slavery's proximity to the invisible man's present. He is terrified, shaking and gasping as if he had "come upon a coiled snake in a busy street" (272).

The objects here form a record of the infrastructural racism that gentrification tries to push to the margins. The invisible man asks the gathered crowd "where did [Provo's] labor go?" The answer, for the invisible man, is that the Provos' years of labor reside in their possessions and in their home, which is why seeing "everything tossed out like junk whirled eighty-seven years in a cyclone" is intolerable (278). This step in the invisible man's political awakening, spurred on by the paper and tin and hair and velvet in the Provos' jumbled belongings, entails an awareness of the relationship between property and dignity, object and subject. It is not only historical or class consciousness that the narrator confronts in this scene, but a realization about the crucial role that material objects and infrastructure, which are both in a constant state of change, play in shaping lives. This is why the invisible man seizes on the concept of dispossession. "That's a good word, 'Dispossessed'!" he shouts while urging the crowd to help bring the Provos' things back into their building (279). When stopped by a police officer, the narrator mocks the language of urban renewal, calling his actions "a clean-up campaign," designed to help clear the streets (283). Heise notes that the scene brings attention to the hidden fact of evictions that were "an occurrence that unfolded daily throughout Harlem."[49] It also prefigures the conclusion of Himes's *Blind Man,* in which displaced residents lament the demolition of "slum buildings in the block on the north side of 125th Street between Lenox and Seventh Avenues."[50] "One angry sister," Himes writes, calls out loudly, "They calls this *Urban Renewal,* I calls it poor folks removal!"[51] Like the Provos, Himes's dispossessed "had been forced to live . . . in all the filth and degradation, until their lives had been warped to fit, and now they were being thrown out."[52]

In their Harlem fictions, Himes and Ellison emphasize the particular violence of gentrification by which the private is made public. The sheer length and detail of Ellison's list puts readers in the position of the transfixed narrator, shocked by objects he (and we) are not *meant* to see. This is why the invisible man calls to the crowd helping him repatriate the objects that they must: "Hide it, hide their shame! Hide *our* shame!" (281). The shame is the truth of enslavement and minstrelsy, but it is also the shame that the narrator feels because he realizes that even the objects that are *supposed* to have profound meaning are simply tossed among the other debris, repurposed for banal use, and cast about in the dizzying jumble of history. In this way, the Provos' belongings evoke the bank that the invisible man discovers earlier at the house of Mary Rambo, a woman who takes him in after an explosion injures him at the Liberty Paint factory. The invisible man is enraged that Mary owns the bank, a "cast-iron figure of a very black, red-lipped and wide-mouthed Negro" (319). The protagonist is aghast, enraged by the fact that Mary can "keep such a self-mocking image around" (319). What is the meaning of this sordid little figure that reduces painful history into racist kitsch? The bank, the Sambo doll, and the Provos' many belongings all testify to the persistence of history and its transformation into an unlikely, chaotic archive. They become vehicles for the violence and pathos of infrastructural change, coded as uncanny, even surrealist objects that bob to the surface of modern Harlem from the nightmare of history papered over.

When, much later in the novel, the invisible man falls into an uncovered manhole in Harlem and begins his journey to the underground lair from which he narrates the beginning and end of the novel, he claims to be leaving this aboveground world with its tragic Provos and its swirling stuff. Many scholars have accepted the narrator's claims that the hole he inhabits is, in some figurative sense, outside of history. But reading the novel's material engagements with gentrification suggests instead that the invisible man's behavior underground is in line with his actions above ground. His fall into the manhole is not an escape from history, but a short trip into the very infrastructure that has conditioned his journey. The dark space of the utility grid encodes the lost time of subaltern history, underscoring the protagonist's immersion in a potentially endless struggle for justice. The invisible man drops down the manhole in the chaos of a riot during which he helps the Brotherhood set fire to a tenement building near Lenox Avenue, thus completing an arc that began with the blueprints he saw when he arrived in Harlem. When the narrator expresses hesitation and asks, "where will you live?," a member of the Brotherhood replies: "You call *this* living?" (545). Instead of waiting for the building's inevitable tear-down, the Brotherhood takes matters into their own hands. Blair, Heise, Barbara Foley, and Kenneth Warren all consider the scene in relation to the Harlem riots of 1935 and 1943, the first of which Ellison criticized openly in an article for *The New York Times*.[53] I am especially interested in how the scene of the tenement's burning once again emphasizes the unjust property relations that the eviction scene has already made visible. The parade of objects looted from during the destruction of the tenement—flashlights, zinc buckets, dress coats, dummy rifles from an Army and Navy store, linked sausages, quarts of milk, and even a pound of butter that goes skidding across the street—reminds readers that the riot is a protest against the material relations that buttress white supremacy. The tenement presents the invisible man with a difficult question: how much does he want to see Harlem gentrified? The dire conditions in the tenement building are inhumane, but so too is the building's violent decimation. As the narrator moves through the building slopping kerosene on the floor, he hears "the occasional prayerful protest of some old one being forced to leave" (547). How can he reconcile the Brotherhood's methods with the indignity he felt at the Provos' eviction? If the underlying conditions in Harlem do not change, what kind of infrastructural transformation is desirable?

It would seem that, because he cannot answer these questions, all the invisible man can do is retreat. But the fire follows him into his subterranean escape route, implying at the outset that there is meaningful continuity above and belowground. Groping through the dark of the underground tunnels, the narrator opens his briefcase and sets fire to its contents that he has loyally carried and fiercely protected for the entire novel. Robert Stepto argues that this act reveals the invisible man's hard-earned knowledge that the objects he thought could protect him are in fact useless: his high school diploma, the letters from Bledsoe, the name of a contact from the Brotherhood. As Stepto phrases it, once these documents are "*usefully* destroyed (here, burned to light his way)—he is ready to begin his life and tale again, or rather to *prepare* to begin again."[54] But this action, seen in the light of the menacing fire that immediately precedes it, feels less redemptive. It is surprising that critics rarely draw a connection between the burning tenement building and these burning documents, preferring instead to read the latter as a symbolic clearing of the invisible man's past that readies him for his reflective state of hibernation. Similarly, scholars tend to accept the narrator's own claims that the hole in which he lives is outside of history, "away from it all" (573).[55] But it is precisely here that Ellison brings objects and environments together: stuff and structure, paper blaze and building fire, are subject to the same historical logic at two different scales. Reading the novel in light of its vexed infrastructural engagements, we must reckon with the fact that the invisible man replaces his collected objects with new ones: 1,369 filament light bulbs that cover "every inch" of his basement habitat (7). These lights are also usually read symbolically: as figurative power that the invisible man claims for himself, as an antidote to his invisibility, as illumination that his tale affords the reader.[56] But a shift in focus from the narrator's interiority to the novel's insistence on exteriority casts the epilogue in a new light. Marshall aptly points out the importance of the lights as infrastructure when she writes, "The narrator's description of a self-reflexive, *formal* and formed subject depends on his sometimes gleeful, sometimes rueful theft of energy from Monopolated Light & Power. That theft, while exempting him from one aspect of urban social bureaucracy, also counteracts his enforced isolation from the world above."[57] Tapping the power line tethers the invisible man to the world above; it reminds readers that, despite his best efforts to find a space where he can listen undisturbed to the "invisible music of [his] isolation," there is nowhere outside the material environment (7). The lights are the tie to the built city that cannot be effaced or evaded.[58] The last memory that the invisible man recalls before concluding his narration also marks this persistent connection to the physical city. On the subway platform, a much older and very lost Mr. Norton approaches the invisible man to ask him for directions. The narrator begins to give directions to Centre Street, but Mr. Norton has become so rattled that he instead hops onto the first train that approaches, an express that presumably leads deeper into Harlem. The subway vignette is another incursion into the narrator's supposed isolation insofar as it marks subterranean Harlem as already colonized, excavated and populated for the needs of the above-ground urban inhabitants.

Ellison's attention to infrastructure amounts to a poignant comment on the gentrification that the narrator has confronted throughout *Invisible Man.* The inescapability of the urban matrix illustrated here at the end of Ellison's novel returns us to the world of Himes's Harlem Cycle. In the works of both authors, we see repeatedly that, even as the city is transformed, the past remains present. The persistence of old forms and old ways of life belies the tidy narrative of gentrification that posits one thing replaced by another. Materiality in these novels encodes the conflicted reality of postwar Harlem that is often occluded by the false twin narratives of civic progress or racist destruction. Lest this seem too pessimistic a reading of *Invisible Man,* let me return briefly to the broader logics of my book. Gentrification in Ellison's novel mimics the dynamics of the ephemeral: the city, like the other things that are the object of this study, is never permanent, but also not wholly transient. The invisible man lingers at the level of infrastructure, *infra* not only as below or underground, but also as between, the connective tissue between space and subject. His hibernation is not so much an act of isolation as it is a means of embedding himself (quite literally) in the city whose contortions the novel has charted. To hover here, to hibernate in the in between, with the knowledge that the city can be neither entirely preserved nor entirely lost, that the narratives of nostalgia and of progress are both inadequate, is to be prepared. It is a way of keeping "a steel helmet handy" (6). To see the rapidity of change *and* the persistence of forms is to be prepared for the history that moves like a boomerang.

GENRES OF TRANSIENCE

Coffin Ed and Grave Digger Johnson are also underground men; their names evoke violence as well as the subterranean spaces of the cemetery. Despite the fact that they are detectives in action-packed novels, Coffin Ed and Grave Digger are also *stuck*. At one point in *Blind Man*, the narrator pauses to review their careers: "Their careers as cops had been one long period of turmoil." Unlike their colleagues and superiors, neither has "taken a dime in bribes," and neither has been promoted despite twelve years of service. Their houses and cars, "bought on credit" are still unpaid.[59] The detectives are, as the phrase "Harlem Cycle" reminds us, stuck in a loop. The serial form of the novels enforces what the detectives experience: an endless variation on the theme of violence and murder. The twelve years of service named here are the same twelve years between the publication of the first and last novels of the Harlem Cycle. In genre fiction that appears to prioritize action and the fast pace of urban life, this moment directs readers' attention to the racial injustice that doesn't change, to the non-resolution of Himes's fiction that thwarts the detective novel's usual narrative momentum and generic resolution.

Ellison and Himes share an interest in their characters' stasis, and that illuminates the paradox of gentrification at the core of their apparently different fictional projects. Lawrence Jackson's biography of Himes brings the two writers back into close contact at last, detailing their contentious relationship as friends and rivals. As scholars more regularly and forcefully assert genre fiction's centrality to literary production and study, authors of so-called literary fiction have also been experimenting with popular formulae. Paul Beatty, Nnedi Okorafor, and Colson Whitehead are just a few of the black writers whose recent work in the genres of satire, science fiction, and apocalypse novels has garnered critical acclaim.[60] Reading across genre lines, in this case by focusing on the shared thematic and political concerns of Ellison and Himes, suggests that the taxonomies scholars have long used to classify the literature they study are ripe for reevaluation. Seen as chroniclers of the transient city, Ellison and Himes might be said to use the conventions of the novel as a backdrop against which they plot formal changes and social transformations that are surprisingly incomplete.

Once we see that Ellison and Himes were experimenting with realist conventions—and accordingly with the transient object world that defines infrastructural space—in order to grapple with the paradoxical effects of urban transformation, we can return to Baldwin's prose. He describes the Harlem that remained untransformed despite the mutation of space around him. With mixed feelings, Baldwin describes a mixed medium of urban transience, emphasizing in his own way the persistence of a dense African American object world, one that holds black memory, black community, and black life within its infrastructural folds. This world could not be swept away easily by the merciless machinery of capitalist destruction, nor by the progressive promises of urban uplift. The scalpel of Baldwin's language, like the generic innovations and finely inventoried scenes of Ellison's and Himes's Harlem novels, refutes at once the fallacy of total progress as defined by proponents of gentrification and that of complete erasure bemoaned by its critics. This is the complex dynamic of gentrification that these two writers capture in their narratives: as long as structural racism endures, change will always mean progress *and* stasis. In relaying this paradox, Ellison and Himes reveal the structure of the world as it is while making space for the possibility that its infrastructures might be used differently.

4

Time, Stamped

THOMAS PYNCHON'S MEDIA SYSTEMS

THE REAL OF WATTS

In his autobiography, Chester Himes admits that it was with scant first-hand knowledge of the place that he invented the Harlem his novels depict. But his treatment of Los Angeles is a different story. Himes claimed that he worked twenty-three jobs in Los Angeles between 1941 and 1944, including one in a naval shipyard that inspired the setting for his first novel, *If He Hollers Let Him Go.*[1] In *The Quality of Hurt* from 1972, Himes offers a blistering account of Los Angeles:

> Los Angeles hurt me racially as much as any city I have ever known—much more than I can remember from the South. It was the lynching hypocrisy that hurt me. Black people were treated much the same as they were in an industrial city of the South. They were Jim-Crowed in housing, in employment, in public accommodations, such as hotels and restaurants. During the filming of *Cabin in the Sky* starring Esther Waters, Bill "Bojangles" Robinson, and Lena Horne, the black actors were refused service in the MGM commissary where everyone ate. The difference was that the white people of Los Angeles seemed to be saying "Nigger, ain't we good to you?" The only thing that surprised me about the race riots in Watts in 1965 was that they waited so long to happen. We are a very patient people.[2]

Himes's description of Jim Crow L.A. links it to the conditions he chronicles in the Harlem Cycle, such as to the institutional racism that leads to the riots at the end of *Blind Man with a Pistol.* It also links him to an unlikely interlocutor. In a nonfiction essay published on June 12, 1966, in *The New York Times,* Thomas Pynchon also set out to understand what had caused the riots in May of the previous year, or more precisely, to determine what the specific place, Watts, had to do with the racial conflict that Pynchon knew to be a national one.

The essay, "A Journey into the Mind of Watts," is a startling, heartbreaking affair. It uses a second-person address, calling on readers to occupy the position of the black people who face systemic racism and police violence: "With a cop it may get more dangerous, but at least it's honest. You understand each other. Both of you silently admitting that all the cop really has going for him is his gun."[3] Although there is certainly something discomfiting about Pynchon appropriating a black perspective, it is clear that he does so in an earnest attempt to make legible the racism that maintains what he calls "black impoverishment." Pynchon's use of the second person, his insistence that readers try to imagine themselves into the scenarios he describes, is intended as an antidote to the psychological segregation that physical segregation makes possible. As Pynchon points out, it occurs to very few white commuters who pass through Watts on the Harbor Freeway "to leave at the Imperial Highway exit for a change, go east instead of west only a few blocks, and take a look at Watts. A quick look. The simplest kind of beginning."[4] For Pynchon, the unreality of Watts is site-specific, not only because the infrastructural matrix of Los Angeles keeps Watts hidden from view, but also because the "white scene" surrounding Watts is so synthetic that it makes the material realities of racism almost impossible to fathom. What Pynchon encounters in Watts makes the rest of Los Angeles look "a little unreal, a little less than substantial." Los Angeles, he writes, "exists chiefly as images on a screen or TV tube, as four-color magazine photos, as old radio jokes, as new songs that survive only a matter of weeks. It is basically a white scene, and illusion is everywhere."[5] Once accustomed to the fantasy version of Los Angeles, with its endless sunshine and manicured lawns, it becomes ever harder to understand the entrenched brutality that the city in fact harbors.

Although we are accustomed to thinking of Pynchon as a writer of screens and surfaces, his essay on Watts attempts to locate what lies beneath the simulacrum of Los Angeles. Behind the illusion of white Los Angeles is the "real" of Watts: the site where the long history of violence enacted on raced bodies becomes visible. Like Ellison and Himes, Pynchon is interested in the way that infrastructural change can conceal the trenchant nature of U.S. race relations. While Ellison and Himes revealed the racist aims of urban renewal efforts in postwar

Harlem, Pynchon suggests that L.A.'s infrastructure, a network of freeways, interchanges, and overpasses, has effectively hidden the reality of race from white eyes, making such "renewal" efforts unnecessary. What remains invisible need not be displaced. In addition to L.A.'s architecture that makes it possible for Pynchon's readers to have ignored Watts, the sheen of newness that is the Hollywood-culture industry's hallmark ("new songs that survive only a matter of weeks") obscures persistent injustice. Although Pynchon disparages the inequality he sees in Watts, he also finds something positive about the neighborhood's contrast with the rest of Los Angeles: "Watts is tough; has been able to resist the unreal." Like Himes and Ellison then, Pynchon tries to name what isn't changing, even as so many other things are. He makes this clear by considering an "interesting question":

> Why is everybody worrying about another riot—haven't things in Watts improved any since the last one? A lot of white folks are wondering. Unhappily, the answer is no. The neighborhood may be seething with social workers, data collectors, VISTA volunteers and other assorted members of the humanitarian establishment, all of whose intentions are the purest in the world. But somehow nothing much has changed. There are still the poor, the defeated, the criminal, the desperate, all hanging in there with what must seem a terrible vitality.[6]

On one hand, Pynchon claims that racism, segregation, and the neighborhoods that these forces shape are unchanging and he wants to expose his readers to the "terrible vitality" that they try to ignore. On the other hand, though, the riot that occasions the essay does mark change, an eruption by people who refuse to submit to police violence and "L.A.'s racial sickness." Even if it has not yet produced material change, the riot has commanded the attention of white people who can no longer pretend quite so easily that Watts doesn't exist. What kind of change will the riot bring about? Pynchon leaves the question unanswered but not foreclosed. He concludes the essay by discussing a "Renaissance of the Arts" festival held in Watts during Easter week 1966. He describes a room full of sculptures "fashioned entirely from found objects—found, symbolically enough, and in the Simon Rodia tradition, among the wreckage the rioting had left": "Exploiting textures of charred wood, twisted metal, fused glass, many of the works were fine, honest rebirths."[7] Out of the wreckage, something is reborn: a new aesthetic, the possibility for self-expression, forms that can rupture the irreality Pynchon is known for diagnosing.

Here Pynchon turns to objects for the peculiar ways they hold history. In the fragments and debris left by the riots, Pynchon finds an enduring witness to what has happened in Watts and the raw materials out of which something new might be born. These objects, like many I have already discussed, have the unique capacity to mark what the riots have changed *and* what refuses to vanish. Seen alongside the object worlds of Pynchon's early fiction, the Watts essay gives us a view of Pynchon's historical logic, a logic that seeks to accurately capture what America's capitalist war machine has swept away and what it has left unchanged. The final image of the essay, an art piece in which a hollow television set houses a human skull "with scorched wiring threaded like electronic ivy among its crevices and sockets" is not so much a memorial for Watts as a macabre reminder that humans and their objects coexist in an ongoing state of loss and decay, but also of mutation and regeneration. It stands as an emblem of the real that exists in Watts, away from the media glare and surface sheen of Los Angeles. Pynchon's writing on Watts has the power to astonish us, even today, in part because it chafes against the notion of Los Angeles as a labyrinthine city lacking a center. Fredric Jameson's depiction of the Bonaventure hotel and the final chapters of Edward Soja's *Postmodern Geographies* have cemented the scholarly consensus that, if Los Angeles is recognizably any one thing, it is postmodern. Critics maintain it is a city built on "myth," "spectacle," "erasure," and "forgetting."[8] But Pynchon insists in his essay on Watts that many things cannot be so easily erased or forgotten, especially the record of real violence. If we agree to make the journey with Pynchon "into the mind of Watts," we will be shown that only by accepting the conditions of ongoing loss caused by white supremacy can we begin to remedy them. This instance of Pynchon's broader historical aims concludes with the found objects that allow him to write empathetically, even poetically, about the human suffering he sees in the overlooked neighborhoods of Los Angeles.[9]

In this chapter, I follow Pynchon's lead on the work that objects can do, from his treatment of Watts in 1966 to the landscapes of his first novels, *V.* (1963) and *The Crying of Lot 49* (1966). Reading Pynchon as a novelist deeply concerned with ephemera recasts his early works and revises the most common critical understanding of Pynchon as an endlessly ludic and thoroughly cynical writer. Pynchon's first two novels deploy objects as a means for understanding the jeopardized subjects who must navigate the ruins and remnants of postwar America. The ephemeral appears as a class of objects and a conceptual problem throughout these texts. *V.* and *The Crying of Lot 49* ask what happens to individuals when they reckon with this duality. The novels' protagonists, Stencil in *V.* and Oedipa in *Lot 49,* do their best to follow even the faintest reminders of ephemera; their efforts thus cast the novels as metaphysical detective fictions in which neither the trace nor the case may be real. Since Pynchon's mysteries cannot be neatly solved, his characters, like Ellison's and Himes's, remain in a state of suspension. But their encounters with the transient object world nonetheless disclose the kind of history that Pynchon narrates in his piece on Watts. Without the dual logic of ephemera, in which what disappears is never entirely gone and what we wish to preserve never fully endures, there would be no mystery for Pynchon's characters to solve, nor any sense that a history of the twentieth century might be recovered from what has gone missing.

The history that Pynchon narrates through ephemera differs from that described by earlier critics. In the 1980s and 1990s, Pynchon was enthroned as the reigning king of postmodernism. Brian McHale captures this phenomenon when he writes that, "without Pynchon's fiction, there might never have been such a pressing need to develop a theory of literary postmodernism in the first place."[10] In an impressively succinct summary of the critical "Pyndustry" that has developed since the publication of *V.* in 1963, Hanjo Berressem explains that Pynchon and postmodernism are ideal pairings under the larger umbrella of poststructuralist theory. The latter cast Pynchon as "a master deconstructionist whose immensely convoluted plots should make the reader aware of the futility of any search for order." In this vein of criticism, Berressem continues, "the texts were about the endless dissemination of meaning; vast, sprawling, metafictional games."[11] Reading Pynchon as a postmodernist whose central imperative is to deconstruct, decenter, and destabilize has certainly yielded a great deal of significant and nuanced criticism. But, in casting Pynchon as a master postmodernist whose radical agenda centers on ironic detachment and discursive play, critics have made the historical imperatives of Pynchon's work something of an afterthought. This earlier deconstructionist reading concludes that Pynchon views history as something that cannot be located, grasped, or represented. Pynchon's interest in science and technology has also been largely subsumed into this vein of criticism. His frequent references to machines, weapons, scientific inventions, and the raw materials that go into their making are seen as symptomatic of the author's fascination with a kind of technological sublime, one that overwhelms so that it cannot be traced or tracked in any meaningful way.[12]

More recently, a number of critics have begun to outline different perspectives on Pynchon's history and his objects. Although Amy J. Elias affirms Pynchon's commitment to "polyvocal postmodernist history," she implies that this history may be best understood not through sublime objects, but mundane ones:

> Perversely [Pynchon] asserts, with postmodern philosophers of history and literary theorists, that history is multi-voiced rather than monologic, chance and event rather than deterministic time, mythic rather than legalistic, openness and improvisation rather than a closed book of facts. History for Pynchon is a plot orchestrated by power. But this history is in dialectical relation with a "history from below," the unrecorded, accumulated force of preterite, everyday life.[13]

The force of everyday life becomes visible in Pynchon's novels precisely through the objects he depicts. Elias's insistence that Pynchon may be postmodernist without being posthistorical or a-historical has cleared the way for scholars looking to read Pynchon beyond the framework of deconstruction. These readings entail a shift of attention away from the technosublime of rockets and missiles and toward less flashy objects that irritate the high postmodernist arc into which Pynchon has been inscribed. In his book *Site Reading* from 2015, for instance, David Alworth argues that Pynchon's treatment of Malta's ruins in *V.* mediates his historiography. Alworth attends to the leveled streets and piles of rubble that reveal Pynchon's effort to "develop an original model for apprehending and narrating the past."[14] Mark Greif is also interested in what kind of past Pynchon's objects might disclose. In *The Age of the Crisis of Man,* Greif claims: "'Man' as a being and a concept is put into jeopardy for Pynchon, not first by high-technological machines or weapons but by use of ordinary materials and the creation of mundane objects—the changing status of the *parts* of men, and the insertion of inanimate *things* into their bodies and daily habits." Greif elaborates on these *things*: "The trouble with things, furthermore, is not that they are produced ephemerally and vanish in their use (as it was sometimes common to say in critiques of consumer society and consumer production from Pynchon's era). The trouble, rather, is that material objects *persist,* transferring neutrally from one time and place to another, while all values and intentions get stripped from them."[15] Greif and Alworth illustrate that history inheres in Pynchon's ruins and remainders; they help establish a new way of reading Pynchon and his objects that avoids rehashing the slogans of earlier critics.

While many objects persist in Pynchon's early novels, others *do* vanish, leaving behind vexing traces, or no traces at all. Disappearing objects do crucial conceptual and formal work in Pynchon's novels. They form part of the novels' infrastructures, both in the sense that disappearing objects are often bound up with Pynchon's portraits of communication technologies, such as broadcast radio in the case of *V.* and the postal system in *Lot 49,* and in the role they play in shaping the books' narratives. The urban infrastructure that we have seen in other novels works in Pynchon's to capture the transience of the built environment and to comment self-reflexively on the nature of narrative. The ephemeral messages transmitted, waylaid, misapprehended, and lost in the novels are crucial to their plots. They generate the mysteries that structure *V.* and *Lot 49*: Who is V.? Why has Inverarity named Oedipa his executor? Is Trystero real? The transience of the material world motivates these questions and the characters' attempt to answer them. But, in addition to advancing new readings of Pynchon's fiction, focusing on transience also tells us a great deal about the critical moment in which we currently find ourselves. A reading of Pynchon's ephemeral infrastructures and objects can reorient the thinking about agentic objects and posthumanism that continues to gather momentum in literary studies. For now, though, I want to stress that my reading reclaims Pynchon's fiction from the era of high postmodernism that is so often declared long dead.

To put it another way: in the 1980s and 1990s, scholars "needed" Pynchon to put their theoretical aims into literary form, to echo the important historical critiques that they were making by way of deconstruction. Today, scholars of contemporary literature preserve this idea of Pynchon in order to draw a hard line between the postmodern past and the present.[16] This seems to be one reason that the 2012 *Cambridge Companion to Thomas Pynchon* largely reproduces the familiar maxims about Pynchon inherited from the critics who helped canonize him. Is it possible to look at Pynchon with fresh eyes? My point is not that the established postmodern reading of Pynchon is wrong. On the contrary, what the logics of ephemera constantly recall is that whatever we think (or even want) to be wholly lost to us remains a part of our present. So, the Pynchon whom critics would like to relegate to history remains contemporary in ways yet to be fully explored, and the history that they have yet to read fully out of Pynchon's objects also complicates the place he has been assigned in our literary past. It is helpful here to recall Jameson's insight in *A Singular Modernity* that the borders between experimental aesthetic forms and realisms are always porous. Adapting his claim for the current context, we are reminded that "each successive realism can also be said to have been a [post]modernism in its own right."[17] The forms in Pynchon's early novels that were once coded as highly experimental (language games, lists, unresolved and multiple plots, digressions, exaggerations) look, by today's light, more like a realist response to the conditions of postwar America that Pynchon sought to describe, including the production norms that flooded markets with cheap and transient consumer goods. For all the games that Pynchon plays with form and language, he continually reaches for a literary form that can adequately represent the painful mess of history and its elision. His humor does not conceal the fact that his novels proclaim an urgent need for a new historical awareness, a real (but not new) sincerity about the plight of the lonely souls cast into the eddies of a consumerist America ignorant of its own past. As his essay on Watts demonstrates, Pynchon was always invested in more than just sheen and surface. The fleeting, fragmented, and broken objects in his fiction compose Pynchon's precisionist historical archive. By now, subjects have adjusted to the epistemological challenges of navigating the convoluted world we encounter in Pynchon's pages. It seems past time, then, for a reading of Pynchon that has also adjusted.

Reading Pynchon as I do, as a writer concerned with disappearing objects and infrastructures, emphasizes his commitment to rendering a human subject who can cope with the maddening currents of postwar America. To return to the lessons of Freud's "On Transience" and the central logics of this book, what emerges from this reading of Pynchon is neither a coherent subject nor a neatly legible history. But it is also not the absence of either of those things. Once again, in that troublesome space between the comfort of the subject and the allure of the object, we encounter the people who our things have demanded we become. This is, perhaps, an odd turn in a book on ephemera: my aim, ironically, is to recover the objects in Pynchon that have been lost to critics, and thus recover the forms of historical knowledge and narrative that his writing is said to have made obsolete. But things that die and disappear help us reflect on the scholarly need to relegate certain fictions themselves to the past. These objects also show us a Pynchon who is less committed to chaos and irony than to an empathetic, even ethical, view of a compromised world. What happens when people pursue the traces of vanished objects? What kind of conflicts and contracts arise between Pynchon's characters and his fleeting things? And where does all that stuff actually go?

OBJECTS IN HUMANS: *V.*

"Christmas Eve, 1955, Benny Profane, wearing black Levi's, suede jacket, sneakers, and a big cowboy hat, happened to pass through Norfolk, Virginia. Given to sentimental impulses, he thought he'd look in on the Sailor's Grave, his old tin can's tavern on Easy Main Street."[18] So begins the labyrinthine tale of Pynchon's first novel, *V.*, published in 1963. Like the opening of a familiar joke, Benny Profane, one of the novel's two protagonists, walks into a bar. But along with Benny, a self-proclaimed "schlemihl" (Yiddish slang for an unlucky simpleton), what walks into the bar are Benny's clothes, an amalgamation of drifter, cowboy, sailor, and all-American boy.[19] Already at the outset, Pynchon plays with the notion familiar from eighteenth- and nineteenth-century novels that clothing can define, taxonomize, and constitute characters. Benny is a protagonist in one of the two interrelated narratives that compose *V.* He is part of "The Whole Sick Crew," a group of amorous young people floundering in mid-1950s New York. In the other narrative, Herbert Stencil begins an obsessive search for the elusive V. who is mentioned in his father's journal. The search leads him on an imaginative tour of the past that takes readers to Alexandria, Florence, Paris, Namibia, and Malta between 1898 and 1943. The novel, with its vignettes and vivid set pieces, is "about" many things: twentieth-century decadence, the growing mechanization of modern culture, the possibilities and perils of artistic production, ruin, genocide, and the Second World War. But if there is a single theme woven through the many episodes of *V.*'s panorama, it might go by the name of "desire," and desire's persistent confusion of subject and object. Pynchon's treatment of desire allows him to comment on the imbrication of bodies and things, on the implication of bodies *as* things, and the kind of histories that inhere in such composites.

In *V.*, the entanglement of inanimate objects with (female) bodies and the regularity with which women serve as objects to be seen, handled, and manipulated scramble desire at every turn. Women are indeed objectified throughout the novel by the male characters: they are targets of sexual conquest, damsels in distress, and glittering fetishes. But the pervasive comingling of inanimate and animate complicates these vectors of desire. If women are, in various senses, *already* objects, can they be further objectified? In *The Four Fundamental Concepts of Psychoanalysis,* Lacan famously defines "desire" as a process circling interminably around an absence or void. For Lacan, desire regulates the movements of the subject, defining its broken and barred position in relation to both its own being and the world of objects.[20] The subject's desire is motivated by an impossible attempt to locate an object in the world that can fill or replenish the void that constitutes the subject in the first place. In *V.*, though, female characters often appear to have located objects that sate their desires precisely because they are inanimate. One of the first women to appear in the novel is Rachel Owlglass, who nearly runs over Profane in her beloved 1954 MG. After "being clipped in the rear end by the car's right fender," Profane reflects: "Here was another inanimate object that had nearly killed him. He was not sure whether he meant Rachel or the car" (17). As it turns out, if Rachel is "inanimate" to Profane, it is because the car—and her erotic relationship to it—allows her to refuse Profane's advances. Profane sees Rachel washing the car in the middle of the night, talking lovingly to the MG as she runs "the sponge caressingly over its front bumper" (22). Profane is "about to approach her" when he is rebuffed by the sight of Rachel fondling the car's gearshift. The scene is comic, of course, insofar as it exaggerates automotive erotics (the sexualized language used to talk about cars, as well as the cliché image of the pinup girl draped across a sports car) to absurd effect. One the one hand, it seems Rachel loves the car because she herself has been treated as an object and the MG is thus an appropriate "partner." On the other, the affair with the car represents a canny strategy on her part, one that makes her unavailable or at least resistant to the objectifying gaze of the men she encounters.

Objectification does not always name a condition of subjugation, nor is it always a condition foisted on an unwilling subject. As Anne Cheng has argued, agency and objectification often entwine in an intimate relationship, rather than an oppositional one.[21] Individuals may use their objectification in various ways: to go unnoticed, to retreat into a submerged interiority, to evade certain demands, to throw a wrench into things. Such strategies, Katherine Behar notes in the introduction to *Object-Oriented Feminism,* have long been practiced by the "humans (women, people of color, and the poor)" who have been treated as objects.[22] I don't mean to suggest that behind Pynchon's treatment of women as objects and with objects lies an uncovered, radical feminism. But his novels suggest that, in addition to *being* fetishized, women can also have fetish objects of their own. In fact, there is no character in *V.* who is not constituted by the objects that Pynchon describes. As a result, there is no character who is not constituted, to some degree, *as* an object. A few examples illustrate this point: the graphic, protracted description of Esther's nose job at the hands of a military-mechanic-turned-plastic-surgeon named Schoenmaker renders the female face an "operative terrain" alien to even the patient herself (105); a man named Fergus Mixolydian who claims to be the "laziest living being in Nueva York" embeds electrodes in his forearm so that he "became an extension of the TV set" (52); the physician Dudley Eigenvalue is defined by the special pair of dentures he has made for the unknown V. in a mahogany case, and their mere presence has transformed him into "Cinderella's prince," "still looking for the jaw to fit [the teeth]" (163). These examples, just three of many, convey the specific historical context for Pynchon's portrait of the compromised subject. Plastic surgery, televisual technology, and what the narrator refers to as "psychodontia," the combination of dentistry and psychoanalysis, are markers of the midcentury American culture that *V.* catalogs.

This historical specificity ultimately troubles the logic of the fetish by marking it so heavily with the stamp of time. Freud famously claimed that the fetish is both a "token of triumph over the threat of castration and a safeguard against it." We understand the fetish to be the recipient and bearer of human values displaced from one object onto another: the shoe, for instance, stands in for the woman whose genitals inspire a man's fear of castration.[23] The fetish is in this sense a "triumph" over the object of desire it displaces. But what happens when the fetish object is itself so clearly impermanent, subject to decay and disappearance? Because the material substrate of Pynchon's novel is undeniably marked by particular moments in history, it cannot work like the fetish that promises to keep desire, as Lacan puts it, "frozen in the permanent memorial."[24] Thus, *V.* asks what happens when every possible object of desire has been touched by historical time, and therefore evokes the kind of preemptive grief that Freud attempts to shield against in "On Transience." Desire is thus always part of *V.*'s historical matrix; more to the point, it is the feeling that leads Pynchon's characters to encounter history. The most obvious instance of this in *V.* is V. herself (itself? themselves?). V. is the object of Stencil's obsessive desire, and the mystery of her identity drives much of the novel's plot. In an early chapter, Stencil discloses that he has been reading his father's journal, trying to understand his mysterious death in Malta. There, in the pages of the journal, Stencil has discovered V., or rather, he has discovered the enigma called V. "*Who then is V.?*," Stencil asks Eigenvalue. "She's yielded him only the poor skeleton of a dossier. Most of what he has is inference. He doesn't know who she is, nor what she is. He's trying to find out" (164). Stencil's quest as a reader shapes the reader's own desires, prompting, for instance, each appearance of a woman or place whose name begins a *V* to feel like a clue. The sheer number of V.s in the novel is staggering: in 1898, there is Victoria Wren, the girlfriend of a British spy embroiled in the Fashoda crisis; in 1899 in Florence, Victoria Wren reappears, this time involved in a plot to steal Botticelli's *The Birth of Venus;* in 1913 Paris, a woman named V. falls in love with a young ballerina; Vera Meroving, a woman with a glass eye whose iris is painted with a tiny clockface, appears in South Africa in 1922; and, during World War II in Malta, a woman named V. appears in the guise of a figure called The Bad Priest. Several times characters also mention a mythical place named Vheisseu. As an object of readerly desire then, V. is also an amalgam of half-truths, cryptic mentions, and ephemeral traces in references spread across hundreds of pages that may or may not add up to the woman of the title. The longer that Stencil and the narrative pursue her, the more she seems both ever present and irreparably vanished. More than halfway through the novel, for instance,

Stencil admits: "Truthfully he didn't know what sex V. might be, nor even what genus and species, . . . If she was a historical fact then she continued active today and at the moment, because the ultimate Plot Which Has No Name was as yet unrealized, though V. might be no more a she than a sailing vessel or a nation" (244).

The enigmatic V. generates many of the same questions as the disappearing objects that populate the novels I have discussed thus far: is V. past or present? Everywhere or nowhere? Can she be possessed or is she forever lost? The answer is, maddeningly, "yes," all of these. In every instance, V.'s body is an uncanny amalgamation of human and nonhuman. This becomes, as much as her initial, V.'s hallmark: a glass eye, a sapphire sewn into her navel, a prosthetic limb. Stencil notes her "obsession with bodily incorporating little bits of inert matter" (542). On the one hand, this echoes Rachel's intimacy with her car, a strategy developed in response to the inevitable fetishization of women. The V. in Paris even asks of the young dancer with whom she is enamored: "Do you know what a fetish is? Something of a woman which gives pleasure but is not a woman. A shoe, a locket . . . une jarretière. You are the same, not real but an object of pleasure" (449). It would be easy to read V. herself as this kind of fetish, "not real but an object of pleasure" for Stencil and for the reader, who can enjoy the challenge of following the many versions of V. and the links between them.

But one particular object that V. incorporates into her body undoes this notion of the fetish in the way I have suggested. The object commands a different reading that uses the logics of transience to bring history, human, and artifact together in a single image. In the scene involving the art heist in Florence, V. is "Miss Victoria Wren, late of Lardwick-in-the-Fen, Yorks., recently self-proclaimed a citizen of the world" (176). Victoria is "unadorned save for an ivory comb, gleaming among all [her] plausibly English quantities of brown hair." The comb is five-toothed: "[The] shape was that of five crucified, all sharing at least one common arm. None of them was a religious figure: they were soldiers of the British Army. She had found the comb in one of the Cairo bazaars. It had apparently been hand-carved by a Fuzzy-Wuzzy, an artisan among the Mahdists, in commemoration of the crucifixions of '83, in the country east of invested Khartoum" (177). The comb is a relic of the conquest of Egyptian-held Khartoum by Mahdist forces, which were led by Muhammad Ahmad, a nineteenth-century religious and theocratic leader in Sudan. When the siege brought Sudan to

Great Britain's attention, the British government appointed General Charles George Gordon to evacuate the Egyptian government's garrisons in Sudan. But rebelling Mahdists surrounded Gordon's forces, and by the time relief forces arrived, Gordon was dead, his body discovered beheaded.

What are we to make of this comb and the grim history it embeds? Pynchon stresses the comb's significance by returning to it at the very end of the novel. In the epilogue, Stencil Sr. meets another V. in Malta, this time Veronica Manganese. The veiled woman turns her head to Stencil and "in the hair visible below the hat was a carved ivory comb, and five crucified faces, long-suffering beneath their helmets." "I wore the comb today," this V. says, "Knowing you would be here" (541). The comb is a marker of the sort of colonial violence that transpires throughout the novel. That history is one of white men seeking material wealth, treating both land and people as an object to be exploited for material gain. The comb symbolizes this exploitation and also suggests that the violence of colonialism is total: the "long-suffering" Englishmen are undone by the system that purports to give them power. Because it is made of bone, the comb is a reminder and a remainder of something alive. It is transient in the sense that it evokes a history never completely lost; as its teeth sink into Veronica's hair, it remains an object that is perpetually dying. The comb marks the uncanny persistence of the human body and the way that, while the human may be ephemeral, its physical form can reside in ephemera.

Since the comb is first and foremost an emblem of V. herself, it remains to be asked what the comb tells us about the woman. On this point, the narrator has only this to say: "Her motives in buying it may have been as instinctive and uncomplex as those by which any young girl chooses a dress or gewgaw of a particular hue and shape" (177). Readers looking for evidence that history is unknowable, that Pynchon's aim in *V.* is to insist that "everything" is random, might cite this explanation of the comb as evidence of that point. Why bother tracing the reference to Khartoum if Veronica chose the comb at random? One answer is that Pynchon insists on a history that remains present whether or not it is recognized. Likewise, the comb raises the question of whether it is possible to identify with an unrecognizable, unknowable subject. Can we feel with, or for, any human when we accept that they are only ever partially present to us? On this point, Pynchon is clear: even if the comb means "nothing" to Veronica, it comes to mean something for Stencil, who sees suffering in the carved faces. It makes meaning for the reader who recognizes that this V. is the same woman from many chapters ago. The comb is a narrative device, allowing the reader to reckon with the novel's own past through attention to matter and form. It is therefore not a conventional fetish object; it does not stand in for V., but rather embeds her in the history that she inevitably shapes. It links her actions in Florence and in Malta to the violence whose story the comb tells. "Because we are less human," another character tells another V. earlier in the novel, "we foist off the humanity we have lost on inanimate objects and abstract theories" (450). But the inanimate object returns to the human, into the human—the hair, the skin, the bones—and once there, it becomes not so much a sign of alienation, but a beacon that points back to the very thing assumed lost. Just like the objects that neither entirely vanish nor remain unchanged, the traces of the humanity and the humanness sloughed off upon them also persist, albeit compromised *because* they are held within the coarse matter of the postwar world.

In an oft-quoted passage, Eigenvalue reflects on the relationship between history, objects, and desire that lies at the heart of *V.*

> Perhaps history this century, thought Eigenvalue, is rippled with gathers in its fabric such that if we are situated, as Stencil seemed to be, at the bottom of a fold, it's impossible to determine warp, woof, or pattern anywhere else. By virtue, however, of existing in one gather it is assumed there are others, compartmented off into sinuous cycles each of which comes to assume greater importance than the weave itself and destroys any continuity. Thus it is that we are charmed by the funny-looking automobiles of the '30s, the curious fashions of the '20s, the peculiar moral habits of our grandparents. We produce and attend musical comedies about them and are conned into a false memory, a phony nostalgia about what they were. We were accordingly lost to any sense of continuous tradition. Perhaps if we lived on a crest, things would be different. We could at least see. (164–65)

Eigenvalue converts history itself into an object. The image of the fold suggests that history is both palimpsest and teleology, that there is a definite past, one that remains proximate to our present. Blindness to this past, however, generates "phony nostalgia": we are seduced by an effect of the past instead of attuned to past realities that give the present moment its texture. The musical comedies, like the "radio jokes" and "new songs" that Pynchon references in his essay on Watts, and like the artifacts sold in Childan's store in *The Man in the High Castle,* are symptoms of the epistemological crisis that arises from a lost sense of history. Through Eigenvalue, Pynchon names the critical nostrum of nostalgia but does not suggest that "any sense of continuous tradition" is entirely or irreparably lost. Pynchon's tactic of tethering his characters to a wide array of objects, from sports cars to dentures, is one way that he exposes the "warp, woof, [and] pattern" of the twentieth century. The persistence of past materials in the present literalizes Eigenvalue's historical metaphor. Those objects remind us of the continuity that a collective, cultural amnesia would seek to forget. But it must be noted that the objects Pynchon embeds in his novel (and his characters' bodies) are not the sentimental artifacts of a prewar past. Instead, Pynchon mines materials from the present: technological devices, synthetic materials, and pop-culture debris congeal in a contemporary archive. Like the futuristic objects of the world's fair, though, these artifacts perform a double operation: while speaking of the present moment and its promises for the future, they also flag their participation in a consumer culture predicated on excess and obsolescence.

The "thousands of newspaper pages" that blow through Sheridan Square (322), the automobile junkyard with cars "piled up high in rusting tiers" off of Route 14 in Elmira, New York (321), and even the "cellulose acetate butyrate" that scientists have used to construct a lifelike automaton (311) bespeak the logics of the capitalist war machine whose tentacles spread throughout *V.* The history that Pynchon makes present is one of rapid turnover: materials flit briefly across the contemporary horizon before decaying in junkyards and abandoned laboratories. Evoking the rapidity of these dynamics and the transience of the promises encoded in objects, Pynchon's material inventory refuses the kind of nostalgic desire Eigenvalue is so eager to avoid. Seen in this light, *V.* narrates the intimacy of the human and the nonhuman in order to account for the past without romanticizing it. The characters present themselves as curious object lessons, inviting readers to consider the specific histories that have produced their unusual forms. Readers learn that a precise history of the twentieth century requires attention to the subjects who coexist with the remains of the past, including those remains that can only point to what has vanished. The notion of Pynchon as a precisionist, searching for an accurate historiographical method, runs counter to a common view of him as a postmodern trickster. Despite Linda Hutcheon's insistence that writers of historiographic metafiction, like Pynchon, are committed to a rigorous "rethinking and reworking of the forms and contents of the past," the coarsest view of Pynchon as postmodernist suggests he wants to dispose of the past, or at least place the whole of history in a grinder set to blend.[25] Luc Herman, in his study of the first draft of *V.*, discusses Pynchon's explicit interest in historiography. He explains: "[In the novel's introduction,] historians such as James Frazer, Robert Graves and Henry Adams are antiquated because they only indulge in continuity and simple pattern. However, the poetic resilience of Stencil's historical imagination (also displayed by the narrator in the Epilogue) seems to compensate in part for the impossibility of coming to grips with the intimidating chaos of history in the first half of the twentieth century."[26] It is this stress on "impossibility," the legacy of poststructuralism with its unknowable lacunae and unspeakable gaps, that an emphasis on transience chafes against. Though Pynchon's novels certainly insist that history may well be chaotic, they search relentlessly for a form to document the mess.

HUMANS IN OBJECTS: *THE CRYING OF LOT 49*

Early on in *The Crying of Lot 49,* the protagonist, Oedipa Maas, sees an artwork that, like Eigenvalue's meditation on history, uses an image of fabric to reflect on the perspective that certain objects might make available. After learning that she has been named executor of her former lover's estate, Oedipa recalls a trip to Mexico City with the recently deceased real-estate mogul. She remembers wandering into an exhibition featuring paintings by the Spanish surrealist Remedios Varo. She focuses on one image in detail:

> In the central painting of a triptych, titled "Bordando el Manto Terrestre," were a number of frail girls with heart-shaped faces, huge eyes, spun-gold hair, prisoners in the top room of a circular tower, embroidering a kind of tapestry which spilled out the slit windows and into a void, seeking hopelessly to fill the void: for all the other buildings and creatures, all the waves, ships and forests

> of the earth were contained in this tapestry, and the tapestry was the world.[27]

Though critics commonly explain Oedipa's strong reaction to the painting as her recognition that she too is trapped by a destiny she cannot understand and from which there is no escape, the passage assumes other meanings when seen alongside Eigenvalue's history lesson.[28] The women respond to their captivity in the tower by creating a world of which they can never be a part. And yet they *are* of that world, their hair "spun-gold," as if the tapestry might be the thing giving the women their shape. This is a fitting metaphor for Oedipa to consider at the beginning of the novel, which details her reluctant quest to escape the confines of her sheltered life in Kinneret-Among-The-Pines. The world she encounters outside her suburb is one that may well be entirely of her making, but it is one in which those made objects seem at times to overtake their creator.

It's tempting to read the objects in Pynchon's fiction, and especially in *Lot 49,* as animate, assuming equal or even greater agency than his human characters. As one compelling example, take the rogue hairspray can that menaces Oedipa at the beginning of her quest to solve the mystery of Inverarity's estate. In the bathroom of a hotel room where she has met Inverarity's attorney, Oedipa knocks over a can of hairspray:

> The can hit the floor, something broke, and with a great outsurge of pressure the stuff commenced atomizing, propelling the can swiftly around the bathroom. . . . The can, hissing malignantly, bounced off the toilet. . . . The can knew where it was going, she sensed, or something fast enough, God or a digital machine, might have computed in advance the complex web of its travel. . . . The can collided with a mirror and bounced away, leaving a silvery reticulated bloom of glass to hang a second before it all fell jingling into the sink; zoomed over to the enclosed shower, where it crashed into and totally destroyed a panel of frosted glass; thence around the three tile walls, up to the ceiling, past the light, over the two prostrate bodies, amid its own whoosh and the buzzing, distorted uproar from the TV set. She could imagine no end to it; yet presently the can did give up in mid-flight and fall to the floor, about a foot from Oedipa's nose. (24)

If ever there was a prize for most agentic object in literature, surely this demonic can, animated to such a degree that only "God or a digital machine" could chart it, would be a winner. But what is the point of the hairspray's frenzied flight? The can symbolizes a consumer culture out of control: the hairspray's malignant hiss shows how, left unchecked, mass production alienates and weaponizes labor. The can also offers a comment on evolving media technologies, linked as it is to the "distorted uproar" from the TV set in the next room. But, in this mingling of reality and simulation, of real space and televised space, Pynchon's real interest lies in the woman who watches. For all the comedy of the scene, it contains real emotion. The can's flight is both terrifying and beautiful. Most of all, it feels interminable. Oedipa cannot imagine an end to the can's flight, "yet presently" it drops to the floor. This contradiction stresses the way that objects chart courses we cannot easily track; the processes that interest Pynchon are neither fully dynamic nor fully static. The can is transient insofar as it is both obstinately present and perpetually out of reach. The conclusion of the passage encapsulates a central tenet of the book: objects run amok and, therefore, make the world increasingly unknowable to Oedipa. Her suffering in the face of this uncertainty is real; it is made real to readers who follow Oedipa as their guide through a sprawling maze of conspiracy and chaos.

At first glance, it would seem that *Lot 49* features two distinct classes of objects: collections and assemblages of enduring materials and ephemera, largely paper, such as letters and stamps that degrade and disappear. But this distinction fails when we consider the way Pynchon describes them and their role in Oedipa's quest. If objects endured in any straightforward sense, there would be no need for Oedipa to become an amateur detective, no motivation to track the elusive traces of Inverarity and his convoluted networks. Like Himes's detectives, Oedipa must engage with the material world as it fluctuates: the narrative depends on her recognition of the fact that things rarely disappear, but are instead perpetually disappear*ing*. As they did in *V.*, recycled, repurposed bones in *Lot 49* make this contradiction legible. Once again, the bones invoke the war dead, this time not in a comb, but in the filters of cigarettes. At Fangoso Lagoons, a new housing development owned by Inverarity, prospective residents are enticed by "private landings for power boats, a floating social hall in the middle of an artificial lake, at the bottom of which lay restored galleons, imported from the Bahamas; Atlantean fragments of columns and friezes from the Canaries; real human skeletons from Italy; giant clamshells from Indonesia—all for the entertainment of Scuba enthusiasts" (19). As if the use of human skeletons for decorative garnish isn't sufficiently disturbing, during her visit to Fangoso Lagoons, Oedipa finds out about the cigarette scheme.

A former colleague of Inverarity explains that he is still owed money for human bones he procured:

> "These bones came from Italy. A straight sale. Some of them," waving out at the lake, "are down there, to decorate the bottom for the Scuba nuts. That's what I've been doing today, examining the goods in dispute. . . . The rest of the bones were used in the R&D phase of the filter program, back around the early fifties, way before cancer. Tony Jaguar says he harvested them all from the bottom of Lago di Pietà." (43)

Oedipa learns the story of Lago di Pietà, another bit of history like the story of Khartoum attached to V.'s comb, where American soldiers huddled in isolation, trapped by Germans who waited until they "died, every one, dumbly, without a trace or a word" (43). The Germans "put all the bodies into the lake," where they sank and stayed "till the early fifties" (44). The dredged bones have been ground into charcoal cigarette filters, consumed by unknowing smokers who inhale the imported remains of their country's military heroes. This revelation undermines the narrator's claim that the soldiers died "without a trace or a word." The problem here is *not* that the bodies or history have vanished, but rather that they have been repurposed by an unsparing consumerist demand, an insatiably hungry machine. Instead of ashes to ashes, Pynchon gives his readers dust to activated carbon, the remains of the dead incorporated into living bodies. This anecdote offers a cautionary tale about capitalism's blindness to history. When profit is the only goal, a moral attachment to the past or even an awareness of it becomes a hindrance. The human body becomes a vexed kind of ephemera: it is mortal, it dies and decays, it is easily effaced by the passage of time. And yet, here in *Lot 49,* those forgotten bodies undergo a vulgar reincarnation. This kind of capitalist recycling neither creates entirely new objects nor fully destroys the old ones. The charcoal filters demonstrate that when things *are* lost—even human bodies—they persist in new forms, waiting simply to be "activated" by an inquiring mind. The reader of Pynchon's novels sees, like Oedipa in this moment, that the consumerist landscape of postwar America is structured by transience, both our objects' and our own.

The first half of the novel is preoccupied with objects that are only half-vanished and foisted upon complicit but unknowing subjects. Along with the macabre cigarettes and the demonic hairspray can, *Lot 49* contains several objects that threaten humans with their staying power. The very first sentence of the novel references a Tupperware party that Oedipa has attended, poking fun at the conventions of 1950s housewives but also at the American mania for storage and infinite preservation. Early on, readers are also introduced to Oedipa's husband Mucho Maas, a disc jockey and used-car salesman who "believed in the cars" (4). The narrator goes on at length about the cars that people want to trade, cars that are heart-rending because they have been around too long, accumulated too many miles, collected too much residue of the lives lived inside them. Mucho is horrified and moved by the passengers who bring in "motorized, metal extensions of themselves, of their families and what their whole lives must be like, out there so naked for anybody, a stranger like himself, to look at, frame cockeyed, rusty underneath, fender repainted in a shade just off enough to depress the value, if not Mucho himself, inside smelling hopelessly of children, supermarket booze, two, sometimes three generations of cigarette smokers, or only of dust" (4). Like the Provos' belongings that Ellison's invisible man encounters on the streets of Harlem, the cars expose the private lives of their owners. Cigarettes, dust, motors, and metal comingle with the bodies that the cars are meant to shuttle across the gleaming freeways of southern California.

The cars are described as "extensions" of their owners, prostheses now worn and rusty. But it's what's inside the car that's most meaningful, the contents that disclose the everyday struggles of Mucho's customers:

> When the cars were swept out you had to look at the actual residue of these lives, and there was no way of telling what things had been truly refused (when so little he supposed came by that out of fear most of it had to be taken and kept) and what had simply (perhaps tragically) been lost: clipped coupons promising savings of 5 or 10c, trading stamps, pink flyers advertising specials at the

> markets, butts, tooth-shy combs, help-wanted ads, Yellow Pages torn from the phone book, rags of old underwear or dresses that already were period costumes, for wiping your own breath off the inside of a windshield with so you could see whoever it was, a movie, a woman or a car you coveted, a cop who might pull you over just for a drill, all the bits and pieces coated uniformly, like a salad of despair, in a grey dressing of ash, condensed exhaust, dust, body wastes—it made him sick to look but he had to look. (5)

The debris tells stories of unemployment, barely making ends meet, the labor of just getting by. And yet it remains unclear what is garbage and what is lost. In the same moment that the ephemera here seem to reveal intimacies and secrets, readers are reminded that these objects have been cast off. Is this the "residue of these lives" or rather something more like the surplus, the stuff on the margins that has been deemed meaning*less*? The cars and their piteous interiors seem like repositories for the humanity that has been threatened by the larger forces of war and capitalism. But Pynchon complicates the familiar literary strategy that intimates that humanity is secreted and stored in objects. Roger Bellin argues that Pynchon's "collection of details served as a way to prevent a false, too easy sense of totality, without the possibility of historical explanation entirely; that is, the collection serves as a ward against bad models of collectivity, as well as an always incipient model of good collectivity."[29] Certainly the "salad of despair" that Mucho sees day in and day out conjures collectives of exhausted strivers who populate L.A. But Pynchon probes the limits of this vision by emphasizing the cars' exchangeability, their reduction to identical units of (little) value.

Mucho's horror comes from the fact that these objects are offered up for trade: "He could still never accept the way that each owner, each shadow, filed in only to exchange a dented, malfunctioning version of himself for another, just as futureless, automotive projection of somebody else's life. As if it were the most natural thing. To Mucho it was horrible" (5). The callous logic of mass production and obsolescence, wherein a life is discarded and replaced by another, equally hopeless life, undoes the romantic idea that help wanted ads and the rags of old underwear give Mucho some kind of radical insight into his fellow humans. If these objects give rise to a collective, it is one that obliterates individuality, instead yoking people, cars, and trash together in an impotent assemblage. The cars, like the bones, are markers of persistent loss encroaching on the present. These fragments cannot be shored against the ruin that *Lot 49* goes on to chronicle; they can only make that ruin legible. The objects focalize empathy on everyday human suffering, on the death and the trash that Oedipa's suburban idyll is meant to block out.

The narrative stress on these objects, the space Pynchon devotes to their elaborate description, is therefore a ruse of sorts: it resurrects the debris in carefully curated prose while also suggesting that it may really be waste. These lasting objects, brought into threatening intimacy with the human body, preserve a dearth of meaning, a sense that the "sacred" dead and the discards of our daily lives are repurposed with equal ease. Greif describes the effect of this recycling as a disruptive flattening: "As communications technologies grow in significance, alongside material leftovers and remnants, something unnerving happens—the immaterial circulation of signs crosses over with material circulation, until one witnesses a further denudation of values. Stories and personal relations mix with leftover or forgotten objects, and are leveled down to the same neutral status, out of human control."[30] Though the persistence of transient objects in *Lot 49* is certainly unnerving, these objects are decidedly different from the "communications technologies" that are the focus of the novel's second half. The bones and the cars reappear in perverted forms, their endurance an affront to Oedipa and Mucho. But the communication artifacts that Oedipa tracks in the rest of the novel seem to have left behind only the occasional clue to advance her efforts. In short, the novel opens with objects that endure when they are thought to have vanished and then moves on to objects that are vanishing while we expect them to endure. This reversal might seem merely semantic, but I want to suggest that it is crucial to a new and nuanced understanding of *Lot 49* as a novel concerned with the affective and historical relays between humans that transience makes possible.

The vanished objects whose traces Oedipa must track to unravel the mystery of Inverarity's inheritance are media objects designed to relay messages and meaning between individuals. Many critics have noted that Oedipa's journey is an awakening, a rejection of her self-contained suburban lifestyle in favor of a more porous, communal existence within the alternative America she discovers along the California coast.[31] That awakening happens through contact and confrontation, by talking to the curious (and sometimes menacing) characters she meets along the way. This happens because Oedipa is chasing down an eight-hundred-year-old postal conspiracy, a story about (thwarted) communication. Letter-writing, postal delivery, and postage stamps become the mystery's emblems. Although Bernhard Siegert has memorably declared that "the empire is a postal system, and the postal system is war," these objects are not high technological weapons or grisly remnants of human bodies.[32] They are, however, the media that allow "users" to transmit messages of opposition. Kate Marshall points out that Pynchon's portrait of "reflexively produced communications systems" in *Lot 49* comprises a comment on the novel's "own operations as media," and her analysis helps us understand that the dead letters and elusive stamps reach out to unknown readers in much the same way as the novel itself.[33] Like the writers examined in earlier chapters, Pynchon uses the novel as a medium that reflects on the role of infrastructure through depictions of discrete objects. Systems and our ability to resist or revise them become visible in Pynchon's novels through the proxy objects that force his characters to look beyond the boundaries of their individual lives.

After Oedipa learns about the cigarettes, she begins to uncover a plot of postal intrigue: the Thurn and Taxis mail courier, which had a monopoly on mail in Europe from 1300 to 1867, gave rise to an underground rival mail organization, the Tristero. Oedipa begins to encounter "evidence" that suggests Tristero may still be in operation: the symbol of a muted postal horn etched onto bathroom walls and doodled on napkins; special trash bins that are (perhaps) mailboxes, emblazoned with "W.A.S.T.E," which (perhaps) stands for "We await silent Tristero's Empire." Oedipa marvels at her realization that there "were God knew how many citizens, deliberately choosing not to communicate by US Mail" (94). The muted horn and the traces of W.A.S.T.E. become the connective tissue that finally links Oedipa to these citizens. The narrator offers another long list, this time of the people Oedipa meets:

> Among her other encounters were a facially-deformed welder, who cherished his ugliness; a child roaming the night who missed the death before birth as certain outcasts do the dear lulling blankness of the community; a Negro woman with an intricately-marbled scar along the baby-fat of one cheek who kept going

> through rituals of miscarriage each for a different reason, deliberately as others might the ritual of birth dedicated not to continuity but to some kind of interregnum; an ageing night-watchman, nibbling at a bar of Ivory Soap, who had trained his virtuoso stomach to accept also lotions, air-fresheners, fabrics, tobaccos and waxes in a hopeless attempt to assimilate it all, all the promise, productivity, betrayal, ulcers, before it was too late; and even another voyeur, who hung outside one of the city's still-lighted windows, searching for who knew what specific image. Decorating each alienation, each species of withdrawal, a cuff-link, decal, aimless doodling, there was somehow always the post horn (94).

These are people harmed by the environment they inhabit. They are searching and waiting like Oedipa: for relief, for redemption, for something unknown. But they are also connected to one another and to Oedipa by the enigmatic post horn. These people, "deliberately choosing not to communicate," in fact use their cuff links and doodles to signal their belonging to a resistant collective. Not only does the post horn transform their alienation into communication; it also embeds these characters in the long history of Tristero. As in *V.*, the postwar period, with its late capitalist distortions, is linked to a much longer arc of corporate control and violence. This is one reason why Oedipa first learns about the Tristero from a Jacobean revenge play. Neither the fact of subterranean resistance nor the fact of corporate control, *Lot 49* suggests, is unique to the twentieth century. Moreover, as John Durham Peters observes: "Mediated communication blurs 'live' and recorded contact. . . . It is utterly routine to read words from people who are dead; much of the uncanniness of that act has rubbed off, though the voice calling from the beyond can still take us by surprise."[34] This fact of mediated communication is central to *Lot 49*, whose entire plot is motivated by a phone call concerning Inverarity, a dead man. The past quite literally communicates to Oedipa through the post horn, relaying a history of human communication (and its failure).

Despite the novel's attention to the newer technologies of radio and television, it is the medium of the letter that most poignantly exposes how the excesses of postwar consumerism are a paltry screen for the deficits and voids of American culture. Pynchon conveys how aptly the written letter and postal infrastructure embody the logics of ephemera. Though both by now seem banal, largely obsolete, or even quaint thanks to digital communication, letters and the postal network popularized in the mid-nineteenth century "laid the cultural foundation," as David Henkin has argued, "for the experiences of interconnectedness that are the hallmarks of the brave new world of telecommunications."[35] Henkin's examination of how antebellum Americans experienced writing and receiving letters emphasizes the same tension between presence and absence that is central to Pynchon's treatment of the postal system. The presence of a letter implies the absence of its sender; this is one reason Henkin claims that, "despite its evident modernity and its association with mundane commercial transactions, observers could find something otherworldly about the postal system in the middle of the nineteenth century."[36] The ghosts that reach Oedipa from the past are both individual and infrastructural, dead letters retrieved belatedly by a twentieth-century woman trying to decode both levels of meaning.

The dual logic of ephemera (what is perceived as lost in fact remains, and what remains may also vanish) is twice instructive here. It illuminates the narrative axis along which Oedipa proceeds, at first pursuing meager evidence of a Tristero that seems all but vanished, and then ultimately overwhelmed by the sense that Tristero is everywhere, its emblem scratched on the backs of bus seats and chalked on sidewalks. But Pynchon's choice of infrastructure—a postal scheme—to place at the center of his novel also calls attention to the materiality of letters and of postage stamps. Lisa Gitelman points out that paper is "familiarly the arena of clarity and literalism—of things in black and white—at the same time that it is the essential enabler of abstraction and theory, as in mathematics and theoretical physics."[37] The paper objects in *Lot 49* evoke the duality that Gitelman notes: they are the traces of a vanished past and definite but inscrutable evidence that the past exists. The postage stamps in Inverarity's collection are physical markers of letters sent and value accrued, but they also circulate in a mysterious network of forgery that leads to maddening abstractions and competing theories. Like Philip's collection in *The Plot Against America,* Inverarity's stamps also act as a commentary on the novel, a printed object that transmits sometimes cryptic messages to its readers. And like Himes's layered signs, the stamps reveal the different historical moments and registers that the novel seeks to conjoin.

The stamps link Oedipa's personal history with a broader, political one. Like the stamps in *Plot Against America,* Inverarity's stamps remind the reader that the personal dramas always unfold against a historical horizon. In the case of the *Lot 49,* this history is even broader than the national story that Roth tells, since Pynchon imagines the Tristero's transnational tentacles spreading around the globe. As Oedipa learns to read the stamps, she begins to see that an awareness of history facilitates an awareness of the people with whom she inhabits that history. The narrator describes, in retrospect, her perception of the stamps before she has begun her investigation of the Tristero:

> Much of the revelation was to come through the stamp collection Pierce had left, his substitute often for her—thousands of little colored windows into deep vistas of space and time: savannahs teeming with elands and gazelles, galleons sailing west into the void, Hitler heads, sunsets, cedars of Lebanon, allegorical faces that never were, he could spend hours peering into each one ignoring her. She had never seen the fascination. (29)

The stamps unfurl a romantic history of war and imperialism. At first, however, Oedipa cannot understand the collection. She is unable to see the stamps as "windows" into the history in which she is embedded, nor can she imagine that to collect these stamps might be an attempt at mastery, at bringing the "deep vistas of space and time" into a single narrative kept at close proximity. She instead feels something like rivalry toward the stamps, resentment that Pierce chose to look at the stamps instead of her. From the present moment still looking back, the narrative implies that Oedipa eventually learns to see the stamps differently:

> The thought now it would all have to be inventoried and appraised was only another headache. No suspicion that it might have something to tell her. Yet if she hadn't been set up or sensitized first by her peculiar seduction, then by the other, almost offhand things, what after all could the mute stamps have told her, remaining then as they would've only ex-rivals, cheated as she by death, about to be broken up into lots, on route to any number of new masters? (29–30)

The curious temporality of this passage is no coincidence. The past conditional that names what will or would have been, a tense we have come upon repeatedly in representations of ephemera, allows readers to see the stamps simultaneously in Oedipa's naïve perspective and as they appear once she has been "sensitized" to the story of the Tristero. This narrative duality evokes the type of projection that is unique to the letter. Stamps like the ones in Inverarity's collection draw upon imagery of the past and are sent to a recipient somewhere in the future. In the recipient's hands, the stamp and the letter become artifacts of the past, the markings and words of a time prior to the one in which they hold the document. These stamps recall the layered signs in Himes's Harlem that testify to the past as a process of accrual and erasure. The stamps, even as they are embedded in a conspiracy that may not be real, help Oedipa encounter history. As in Himes's novels, history is not a static artifact. Like Pynchon's stamps that contain it, history is a fluctuating, paradoxical affair that cannot be pinned down, only seen more clearly. *Lot 49* is, as Paul Saint-Amour says of *Gravity's Rainbow,* "aswarm with untimely counterforces," such that no sense of linear time and no historical narrative can be gleaned from its pages.[38]

Much later in the novel, Oedipa discusses Inverarity's stamps with Genghis Cohen, a stamp expert hired to appraise the collection. Cohen has found forged and altered stamps used by the Tristero: "stamps that were almost kosher-looking, but not quite" (134). While Oedipa found the stamps irksome before, she has by now become something of a philatelist herself. A long passage describes the Tristero forgeries in Inverarity's collection:

> Oedipa knew them by heart. In the 15c dark green from the 1839 Columbian Exposition Issue ("Columbus Announcing His Discovery"), the faces of three courtiers, receiving the news at the right hand side of the stamp, had been subtly altered to express uncontrollable fright. In the 3c Mothers of America Issue, put out on Mother's Day, 1934, the flowers to the lower left of Whistler's Mother had been replaced by Venus's-flytrap, belladonna, poison sumac and a few others Oedipa had never seen. In the 1947 Postage Stamp Centenary Issue, commemorating the great postal reform that had meant the beginning of the end for private carriers, the head of a Pony Express rider at the lower left was set at a disturbing angle unknown among the living. The deep violet

> 3c regular issue of 1954 had a faint, menacing smile on the face of the Statue of Liberty. The Brussels Exhibition Issue of 1958 included in its aerial view of the US pavilion at Brussels, and set slightly off from the other tiny fairgoers, the unmistakable silhouette of a horse and rider. There were also the Pony Express stamp Cohen had showed her on her first visit, the Lincoln 4c with "US Potsage," the sinister 8c airmail she'd seen on the tattooed sailor's letter in San Francisco. (134)

Like Roth in *Plot Against America,* Pynchon refers here to real stamps, embellishing historical artifacts with the details that have been changed by the Tristero. And like Roth, Pynchon chooses stamps that celebrate America's march forward into and across the twentieth century. The Columbian Exposition stamp commemorates the world's fair in Chicago that commemorated Columbus's "discovery" (Figure 19); the 1947 Stamp Centenary features the heads of George Washington and Benjamin Franklin above a pictorial time line of transportation history (Figure 20); the 1954 four-cent Lincoln depicts the beloved president in rose-tones, looking very much like a friendly father from a Norman Rockwell painting (Figure 21). The stamps are tokens of a subversive, alternative infrastructure, and thus perform the historiographical critique that lies at the core of *Lot 49.* Or rather, the Tristero perform that critique with their slight, mocking alterations to the iconic images on the stamps. The changes, invisible to an inattentive eye, poke fun at America's narrative of itself, its bombast and self-veneration. They also show that "progress" happens at the expense of someone or something, causing the deformities and excesses that are everywhere in the novel. Conventional readings of Pynchon's postmodern sublime tend to reinforce a hypermodern America, rather than an America degraded by its immoral entanglement in transnational capital and its war machine. The latter vision of America is the one that emerges through a reading of these doctored stamps. Recognizing the transience of Pynchon's objects allows us, like Oedipa, to better see that, both as construct and as narrative, America is dying even as it appears to be hurtling into a gleaming technofuture.

The objects of the novel—the Tupperware and the used cars, the stamps and the W.A.S.T.E. bins—must be repurposed to work against the cultural and economic forces out of which they are made. Pynchon works within the constraints of the novel in order to find

FIGURE 19. Columbian Exposition Commemorative Stamp, based on John Vanderlyn's painting *Landing of Columbus.* Issued by the U.S. Postal Service in 1893.

FIGURE 20. Three-cent U.S. Stamp Centenary commemorating America's first postal stamps. Issued by the U.S. Postal Service on May 17, 1947. Author's photograph.

FIGURE 21. Four-cent Abraham Lincoln Liberty Series stamp, based on a portrait by Douglas Volk. Issued by the U.S. Postal Service on November 19, 1954.

a new form for historiography, for narrative, for the novel itself. The notion of "resistance from within" is not limited to the plot of *Lot 49,* but describes Pynchon's relation to the fictional form that he simultaneously explodes and preserves. Here the logic of ephemeralization *eclipses* the logic of obsolescence. It is not simply that things fall out of fashion and become obsolete, but that they persist and leave traces even as they cease to exist in their original form. A great deal has been said about the obsolescence of the things Pynchon's fiction depicts: communication technologies, car culture, the suburbs and the city. So much has also been said about the many things Pynchon's fiction apparently *makes* obsolete: readerly identification, a familiar version of humanism, the novel. But critics have too easily collapsed Pynchon's critique of outdated forms with his interest in them *as* the raw material out of which he might construct a new type of fiction or a new mode of historiography. His novels insist that there remains real value in the traces and remnants of the things we have apparently left behind. This point is literalized by the final scene of *Lot 49,* in which value becomes an explicitly material *and* literary term.

Cohen informs Oedipa that Inverarity's stamp collection will be sold at auction, the Tristero stamps parceled separately as lot 49. A mysterious stranger has registered to bid anonymously by mail on the stamps. But the "conservative" auction house has refused the request and insisted that the bidder appear in person. Cohen and Oedipa speculate that the bidder may be from Tristero who "saw the description of the lot in the auction catalogue," and wants "to keep evidence that Tristero exists out of unauthorized hands" (136). Oedipa decides to go to the auction, desperate to meet the bidder and finally learn whether she has been "in the orbiting ecstasy of a true paranoia, or a real Tristero" (140). The "crying" of the novel's title, it becomes apparent, refers to the auctioneer who "cries" a sale. Oedipa takes a seat in the back of the room and tries to guess who could be the mysterious bidder. The novel's last lines leave Oedipa, and readers, in a state of ominous suspense: "An assistant closed the heavy door on the lobby windows and the sun. She heard a lock snap shut; the sound echoed a moment. Passerine [the auctioneer] spread his arms in a gesture that seemed to belong to the priesthood of some remote culture; perhaps to a descending angel. The auctioneer cleared his throat. Oedipa settled back, to await the crying of lot 49" (141–42). Rather than focus on the way that this conclusion seems to slot neatly into a postmodern ambiguity in which conspiracy and reality cannot be distinguished from one another, as have many critics, I want to stress instead the plea for empathy that this ending makes.

The scene returns us to Oedipa's earlier reflection about the stamps, the pathos she feels about the collection that is "about to be broken up into lots" and set "on route to any number of new masters" (30). The "crying" at the auction evokes the pathos of destruction, the sadness and sickness that Oedipa has uncovered in her explorations of America. The stamps and their crying serve as the novel's final variation on Pynchon's theme that writers can make visible the human suffering inherent in objects. But what about the way that, here at the novel's end, its title is finally explained? The ludic reveal gives readers a fraught moment of pleasure. "Aha!" we think, "so *that's* the crying of lot 49!" But this revelation is compromised: like Oedipa, we are left awaiting the crying, unaware of the bidder's identity, still unsure whether the Tristero is anything more than an imagined conspiracy. We wait like Oedipa and with her; by traveling with her, we have also become "sensitive," attuned to the stories in things.

POSTAL, POSTMODERN, POSTHUMAN

Pynchon does not dispose of empathy any more than his characters manage to dispose fully of the objects of the past haunting their present. This is yet another way that *V.* and *The Crying of Lot 49* are usefully read through the dual logic of ephemera, through an awareness that disappearance might be constitutive of more than just loss. By feeling the material textures of the world, by reading them with sensitivity, Pynchon suggests, we might find ourselves more connected to fellow travelers. So, while his characters fetishize an ivory comb, a used car, or a postage stamp, Pynchon does not lavish attention on those objects so that readers will similarly fetishize them. The objects instead narrate contorted and unseen histories to show readers the human suffering that has been wrought by an unchecked fetishism of the material. Pynchon's object world invites us to look at things and see what might be crying out from within them. This emphasis on *human* suffering is particularly important in the current moment, when it has become harder than ever to resist the temptation to read Pynchon as an early or prophetic posthumanist. Given Pynchon's profound interest in the ways that objects infect and inflect human bodies, his work has become a likely source for scholars looking for representations of agentic objects and the humans displaced by them.[39] Bill Brown writes that Philip K. Dick's "animate object world seems to prefigure Bruno Latour's conceptualization of a sociality that includes both persons and things"; the same could be said of Pynchon's hybrids and quasi objects.[40] But, even if Pynchon's early works offer a glimpse of Latour's "symmetry" in which nonhuman and human entities have the same agency, the real work of the cars and the stamps and the bones and the letters is to remind readers that we can't escape our humanness or our history. Another way of phrasing this is that Pynchon's politics cannot rightly be called posthuman because his works do not decenter the human so much as they investigate the outcome of human industry and warfare. *V.* and *Lot 49* protest against the reification and instrumentalization of human beings. When Pynchon's characters are enthralled or held captive by the objects around them, the author never lets his readers forget that these objects are of human making. Rachel's car and Oedipa's hairspray, like the sardine tin bobbing on the sea that refuses to look back at Lacan, are more banal than sublime: the metallic rem(a)inders of late capitalist life.

The historical horizon against which these objects appear challenges a posthumanist Pynchon. With some notable exceptions, posthumanist work eschews historical specificity as it reaches for an imagined world beyond or without the human.[41] Though posthumanism is used to describe a historical condition that can be pegged to various timelines—the state humans increasingly find themselves in vis-à-vis technology, other species, and their own bodies—it destabilizes the conventional ways we narrate history. Decentering human actors means that timescales expand and history becomes a fact of geologic shifts, genetic mutation, machinic evolution, and so on. When Timothy Morton, for instance, creates a thought experiment involving a microwave parked on the middle of a frozen lake to insist that objects act independently of humans, his point is that *how* and *why* the microwave arrived there is irrelevant to how molecules of frozen water interact with the mass and weight of the ceramic and glass oven.[42] Reading Pynchon's depiction of objects along similar lines would make little sense. Pynchon is interested in how and why the material world has assumed its present contours, but he is also committed to the idea that understanding these dizzying historical currents is crucial to inhabiting them more empathetically and even more ethically. No matter how object-oriented Pynchon's fictions are, they ultimately tell human-oriented stories, stories about the subjects we have been and can become amidst so many objects. As posthumanist work has grown increasingly popular, this kind of humanist and historicist work can seem old-fashioned. But certainly the links between our history and the materials we consume, produce, and desire to possess can remain dangerously opaque. These are the links that Pynchon's early novels investigate by representing ephemera and their strange temporal vectors. History and humanity, like transient objects, are neither wholly vanished nor fully present. Although it seems that such an ambivalent, liminal state should be one made legible by posthumanism, Pynchon's perpetual and material in-betweenness irritates its conceptual frames. Because transience always raises the specter of loss, of time passing, and of mortality, Pynchon's portraits of ephemera ask readers to reckon with these concerns as his characters do. In this reading, we do not allow ourselves to be blinded by Pynchon's dazzling narrative acrobatics, but rather we see them as a means for illuminating the vulnerable subject who wanders the ruins and the chaos of postwar America. The allure of surface, the uncanny seduction of hybrid bodies, the mesmerizing parade of objects: these aren't the marks of a posthumanist writer, but instead a reaching, a feeling for the compromised but remaining humanity that we seem to have forgotten, that we wish to have left behind, traded in, or made to vanish altogether.

5

The Disorder of Things

MARILYNNE ROBINSON'S TRANSIENT WOMEN

SYLVIE AND THE STAMPS

Oedipa Maas's dizzying quest in Pynchon's *The Crying of Lot 49* begins because a stamp collector has died. Marilynne Robinson's first novel, *Housekeeping* (1980), also begins with the death of a stamp collector. Although this observation might seem to point to a mere plot coincidence between a novel generally taken as the very avatar of heroic male postmodernism and one that surely stands for many as an icon of stalwart domestic realism, Robinson, like Pynchon, presides over a westward adventure in which a previously "domesticated" female protagonist finds her way forward through a collection of uncanny, undead objects. Robinson's novel tells the story of two young girls growing up in Fingerbone, a small town in the state of Washington. After their mother, Helen, commits suicide by driving off a cliff into a lake, the girls are cared for by their grandmother until her death, then briefly by their two great aunts, and finally by their Aunt Sylvie. Upon Sylvie's arrival, the two girls are desperate to hear about their mother. "But what was she *like?*" they ask Sylvie, who has little to offer:

> "It's hard to describe someone you know so well. She was very quiet. She played the piano. She collected stamps." Sylvie seemed to be reflecting. "I've never known anyone so fond of cats. She was always bringing them home."[1]

Sylvie can answer the question only through indirection: not what Helen *was* like, but what she liked. Though Sylvie's laconic answers disappoint the girls because they seem to reveal so little, this detail about Helen's collecting is not insignificant. The stamps' appearance in a novel centrally concerned with what kind of things might resist the ravages of time and the pull of transience draws an unlikely line between Roth, Pynchon, Robinson. If, as we have seen, stamp collections can evoke the possibility of communication, the melancholy of dead letters, and the desire to bring order to a chaotic world, what do they mean here at the outset of *Housekeeping*? Neither Helen nor her stamps have survived, and even Sylvie's memory of them seems incomplete, inadequate. But their mention links the absent Helen to the object world of the novel, which is overflowing with stuff: newspaper clippings, magazines, dress patterns, tin cans, pressed flowers, brass buttons, and odd socks, as well as an elaborate catalog of nature's leaves and vines and raindrops and riverbeds. The stamp collection is named but never known or seen; it is only a gesture to what might be a material tether between the two girls and their mother. Helen's collection is not a privileged object with imagined explanatory power like Pynchon's titular *Lot 49,* but an emblem of the transience that structures Robinson's novel about women seeking to renegotiate and escape the object relations to which they are traditionally assigned.

Characters in the novels I have discussed thus far often respond to the surprising reality of transience by attempting to create or shape the material world: Edgar's time capsule in Doctorow's *World's Fair,* Philip's stamp collection in Roth's *The Plot Against America,* and the invisible man's profusion of light bulbs in Ellison's *Invisible Man* are just a few such instances. In *Housekeeping,* Robinson seems to be asking readers to consider what happens when the object world is gendered to the extent that such material strategies are unavailable to women or might reproduce the very conditions they wish to escape. As a property of objects and a state of being, Robinson's transience makes a particular appeal to women wrestling with the gender norms of small-town life in postwar America. Like the male-authored and male-centered texts I investigate in the other chapters, *Housekeeping* features catalogs of stuff, artifacts that circulate between people and over time, prose that captures objects *and* their disappearance. But unlike those other texts, Robinson's novel insists that the death of things holds special meaning for the women expected to maintain them, to keep them.

Housekeeping, set just after World War II, is narrated in the first person by Ruth, who endures the loss of her mother with her sister Lucille and describes the series of caretakers who pass through their lives, including Sylvie. Before returning to Fingerbone to look after her nieces, Sylvie has led the life of a transient, and she refuses (or is unable) to fully surrender her itinerant ways and embrace the domestic role into which she has been thrown. Sylvie's habits pit her against "the stiff social fabric of Fingerbone, with its church ladies, sheriff and school."[2] The governing opposition between domestic settlement and radical transience seems to organize the whole plot of the novel, eventually causing one sister, Lucille, to literalize the conditions of domestic realism by moving in with a home economics teacher while the other, Ruth, faces the threat of banishment from home and town. In response to the threat of removal and the dissolution of their ward–guardian bond, Ruth and Sylvie set fire to their house and strike out for a life on the road. Ruth concludes of their transient lifestyle: "Now we were truly cast out to wander, and there was an end to housekeeping" (179). In this resonant but plainspoken retelling of the exodus plot, Robinson neatly opposes home economics to domestic conflagration and provides readers with what seems like a basic feminist roadmap for interpreting the core motif of transience in the novel. Paula Geyh, for example, identifies the text's investment in "transient subjectivity," which, she writes, "is located in a place outside all patriarchal structures" (104).[3] Certainly the novel charts a feminine subjectivity through fluidity, disappearance, decay, and transience; but can such a subjectivity in fact exist outside patriarchal structure altogether, outside the history of gender and power? For Robinson, and for this chapter, it cannot.

Indeed, despite her warm reception as feminism's answer to the "great American (male) novel," Robinson has been somewhat persistently misrecognized by her admirers as well as her critics. This chapter attempts to redress that misrecognition by mapping new intersections between ephemera and gender, arguing that a better understanding of the death of things in Robinson clarifies not just the contours of her feminist politics but also the aesthetic force of her prose style. In Robinson's critically acclaimed, best-selling novel, minor and fleeting objects speak to the historical conditions of womanhood, to the problem of gender in time, to gendered subjects viewed through the logic of uncanny objects that are vanishing but never quite gone. Robinson's perspective thus reminds us that, were Freud's story of the countryside to be told by Lou Andreas-Salomé, its position on loss and its formula of "transience value" might look very different. Telling that story invites a turn to recent feminist and queer theories of feeling and objecthood, theories that, when overlaid onto Freud's treatment of transience, illuminate how both holding on and letting go have distinct consequences for women. Robinson's novel helps make visible a longer lineage of women's writing on ephemera, and points to the vexing status that women's writing has long had *as* ephemeral. In what follows, I trace Robinson's leads into the past, considering her discussions of Emily Dickinson and American transcendentalism as fundamental to her treatment of transience. After tracing these lines of influence, I discuss the figure of the house as an infrastructural space that Robinson transforms to upend conventions of gender and of genre. At this point, the stakes and necessity of a new reading of *Housekeeping* should be clear, and thus I offer a new analytic of transience to make sense of the novel's conclusion, one shaped by feminist and queer theories. Before exploring these broader historical contours and contemporary claims, however, I want to briefly consider the existing scholarship on *Housekeeping* to clarify the need for a new reading of the novel centered on the death of things.

POOR HOUSEKEEPING

Most critics have read *Housekeeping* as a novel that details two poles of existence: one of social conformity, order, and stability, and the other of independence, disorder, and transience. The primary site of struggle between these two positions is the house that the narrator Ruth and her sister, Lucille, occupy. Given the novel's focus on the house "at the edge of a town on a little hill," and on the women and girls who occupy it, scholars have mostly treated the novel as domestic fiction. As Elizabeth Meese points out, Robinson's novel subverts expectations by offering a narrative of small-town American life in which men appear only marginally.[4] And across the board, criticism on *Housekeeping* explores the relationships among the space of the home, the traditionally feminized forms of labor required to maintain it according to social conventions, and the gender of the inhabitants who follow or buck those conventions. Geyh argues that "feminine subjectivity both constitutes and is constituted either through or in opposition to the space of the 'house' or the 'home' in *Housekeeping*."[5] The critical consensus sees *Housekeeping* as a transgressive text that invites feminist readings, a kind of early poster child for the prosaics of the Bechdel Test, and such readings affirm the novel's woman-centric narrative and the challenge it poses to normative gender roles. Reading through this criticism today can have the curious effect of flattening the novel, reducing it to an oppositional text whose only goal is to trouble conservative notions of women's roles and women's fiction. However valuable such interpretations have been in the first phase of Robinson reception, they come to feel reductive and redundant because, as Christine Caver puts it, "*Housekeeping*'s feminist markers . . . are almost over abundant."[6] That this is a novel about mothers, daughters, femininity, domestic labor, and the restrictions placed on women's bodies is not to be contested. But what story do the novel's ephemera tell that might complicate or exceed such oppositional readings, and how might they help us place Robinson's objects in a longer, more complicated literary history of American ephemera?

Existing readings often overlook Robinson's deliberate portrayal of ephemeral objects to focus instead on Sylvie's nonconformist behavior. When critics discuss the way that Sylvie defies or ignores the patriarchal expectations of femininity, they emphasize her refusal to maintain order in the family home. Ranging from statements about her "eccentric housekeeping" (Sinead McDermott) and her "failure of good housekeeping" (Geyh) to her "extreme un-housekeeping" (Sarah Hartshorne), critics seem to unintentionally replicate the same value judgments of the society that labels Sylvie a "primarily disruptive" (Kristin King) "hoarder of trash" (Elizabeth Klaver).[7] Since this novel's time of publication, the problem of hoarding (and more recently, the solution of KonMari tidiness) has occupied center stage in American culture, defining good subjects by the objects they (don't) keep. Rebecca Falkoff, Stephanie Foote, Priyanka Jacob, and Patrick Moran, among others, have addressed the importance of hoarding in twentieth-century literature, especially the way that the figure of the hoarder focuses attention on the pathology of the individual who fails in his or her feminized, domestic stewardship, rather than on the cultures of accumulation, pathology, and voyeurism that underwrite the behavior.[8]

Beyond this changing motif of good housekeeping as a marker of middle-class fitness for American women, Robinson's prescient and subtle approach to domestic order is already a bit more complicated than it might seem. Even a quick look at the materiality of a passage frequently used to support classic feminist readings suggests that something more is afoot than a simple binary between sanctioned order and emancipatory neglect. Ruth describes a scene from the house on an autumn day:

> I remember Sylvie walking through the house with a scarf tied around her hair, carrying a broom. Yet this was the time that leaves began to gather in the corners. They were leaves that had been through the winter, some of them worn to a net of veins. There were scraps of paper among them, crisp and strained from their mingling in the cold brown liquors of decay and regeneration, and on these scraps were sometimes words. One read *Powers Meet,* and another, which had been the flap of an envelope, had a penciled message in anonymous hand: *I think of you.* Perhaps Sylvie when she swept took care not to molest them. Perhaps she sensed a Delphic niceness in the scattering of these leaves and paper, here and not elsewhere, thus and not otherwise. . . . Thus finely did our house become attuned to the orchard and to the particularities of weather, even in the first days of Sylvie's housekeeping. (85)

The majority of critics read such a scene as evidence that, by exposing the inside of the home to the elements outside, Sylvie dissolves boundaries and eschews order. For instance, it is taken as evidence of the latter of the "two models of feminine subjectivity" that Geyh sees the novel offering: "the *settled* and the *transient*" (105). But look more closely: the narrator does not call Sylvie's habits "extreme unhousekeeping" or denigrate her efforts as failure; rather, Ruth's narration suggests Sylvie is anything but careless. Her care assumes an unusual form, but it is deliberate. As Ruth notes, "Sylvie believed in stern solvents, and most of all in air" (85). Scholars' emphasis on Sylvie's rebellious nature and her refusal to adhere to feminine, domestic norms obscures what passages like this one stress time and again in the novel: that transience is not the site of neglect and inaction, but something that can be cultivated. Sylvie's unconventional behavior seems to grant her a measure of freedom; it also brings Ruth and the novel's readers a host of pleasant affects. Ruth's lyrical description of the eddied pools of leaves and papers makes beauty of transience, so that air—the agent of material change in this vignette—is itself a kind of strong solvent that dissolves dying things into poetic forms.

Robinson establishes a framework in which preservation and dissolution are not opposed simply, but are rather deeply interfused. Moreover, each involves a craft and a commitment. An older feminist take on this novel tends to stabilize for readers the notion that housekeeping is a standard of good womanhood, a standard that characters in the text can choose, like so many first-wave feminist subjects, to heed or to flout. But the texture and tone of the novel demand that we see the process of dwelling, whether in houses or in time, as subject to a logic of ephemeralization in which objects are always vanishing. And yet, Robinson insists, the decay and dissolution of household things does not mean that women (or men) can suddenly, voluntarily liberate themselves from the uncanny persistence of domestic forms. Robinson's treatment of the house as a palimpsestic space of different temporal registers, like Ellison's and Chester Himes's treatment of the neighborhood as a palimpsest of black life in Harlem, emphasizes the continuous vanishing, but also uncanny legacies, of historical content underneath the surface, lodged in the infrastructure of both exurban and urban America. The house is not opposed to the many other objects in the text, but *like* them; it is infrastructural in the sense that Kate Marshall names when she writes of William Faulkner's novelistic houses: "These built structures, in their explicit communicativeness, are like looms, letters, and other writing and print technologies."[9] For Robinson, the space of the home is no magic, feminine bulwark against time, but an index of its omnipresent, corrosive effect on subjects and ideologies.

The leaves and the paper in Sylvie's and Ruth's home are fragmented, fading ephemera that record the passing of time. This time is not purely a melancholic one, proceeding toward absence of death. The piles contain evidence of "decay and regeneration," but Sylvie's housekeeping preserves the messages, even as they remain inscrutable and anonymous. She is a deliberate housekeeper; she does not hoard or tidy, but rather curates the evanescent and dissolving material culture in which she dwells. Her care allows exterior *Powers* to *Meet* interior ones, and Ruth's description suggests this may be more "natural" than their segregation. Ruth does not lament what is happening to her house, but sees it as increasingly meshed with the outside world, a more sensitive measure of light, weather, and seasons. Sylvie's housekeeping remakes the home as a transient space whose vanishing objects call forth some of the most distinctive affordances of Robinson's poetic prose. Moreover, by allowing the leaves and scraps of paper to comingle in the house, Sylvie equates the natural world and the printed word.

That Sylvie even holds onto copies of *Good Housekeeping* magazine, allowing them to grow into dusty, moldering stacks, is a wry comment on the subversive nature of Sylvie's behavior. But that magazine's actual history, worthy of a brief detour here, illustrates how even this detail does not entail a straightforward critique of domesticity or its rejection. Although the magazine *Good Housekeeping* is ephemeral insofar as it is not meant to be saved, Sylvie's collecting practices overturn that, as does the magazine's own story of endurance. Founded in 1885 as a fortnightly magazine with the stated mission "to produce and perpetuate perfection—or as near unto perfection as may be attained in the household," it is still produced today by the Hearst Corporation as a monthly. *Good Housekeeping* has proven a remarkably resilient publication. Its circulation topped one million in the mid-1920s and continued to rise even during the Great Depression. In 1938, a year in which magazine advertising plummeted, *Good Housekeeping* posted an operating profit of more than three times that of Hearst's other eight magazines combined. And while the magazine has been, for over 130 years, devoted to women and their conventional role in the home as wives and mothers who cook, clean, and rear children, it has also been a surprising forum for feminist authorship. In addition to publishing work by female writers like Virginia Woolf and Edna St. Vincent Millay, the magazine printed Betty Freidan's 1960 article "Women Are People Too," which was the precursor to her book that sparked second-wave feminism, *The Feminine Mystique.*[10] What even this short excursus into the magazine's history reveals is that women's roles, like the objects that document or prescribe them, are riddled with contradiction. So too, is Sylvie's supposed refusal to keep house.

A DETOUR THROUGH DICKINSON

Sylvie's housekeeping, Ruth's voice, Robinson's style: these are the embedded layers of the novel's poetry of the everyday—not monuments but scraps, not landscapes but leaves. Or to be more precise, Robinson takes a domestic scene, a detail from a woman's quotidian routine, and reveals its weight by extracting and unfurling it. Ephemera here congeal the passage of time with the precarity of prose. They remind readers that women's labor, especially women's writing, is itself often ephemeral. Diaries, letters, shopping lists, household ledgers, housekeeping guides, and pamphlets about ethical and social issues name just a few of the forms frequently authored by women and deemed unworthy of archiving. Robinson thematizes this fact, turning the novel into a catalog of fleeting objects and insisting on their aesthetic value. The link between transient objects and women's writing is made explicit early in the novel, when Ruth recounts an assignment in school: "Once I was required to stand by my desk and recite 'I Heard a Fly Buzz When I Died'" (77). The reference to Emily Dickinson is another marker of Robinson's intent to craft a poetics out of the everyday not by sacralizing the act of "keeping," but by preserving the process of loss. Robinson brings Dickinson's verse into the house of her prose in order to press this point that a feminist poetics depends not on separating the sphere of the home from the sphere of the public, and still less on conserving objects and subjects in the amber of domestic care or literary faith, but precisely on capturing the paradoxical logic of keeping as losing.

Though it has by now been productively nuanced, the image of Dickinson as a reclusive, solitary woman devoted to her poetry has much in common with the image of Sylvie, or at least with the way the residents of Fingerbone see her. Clearly Robinson's allusion to "I Heard a Fly Buzz" is meant to signal this biographical resonance, but it cuts deeper to the core of Robinson's purpose in establishing a feminism based neither in good keeping nor in the pure rejection of that logic of women's conservatorship. It is a feminism made of the coincident, overlapping life and death of things, viewed through the distinctively gendered lens of those who have been made most responsible for the domestic war on time: the housekeepers, the home economists, the interred subjects of female interiority. Dickinson compacts all of this into sixteen lines that inscribe the problematic of an outside that is already inside the space of the home: the mortal subject and the punctual text commingling with what they are not, an eternity just outside the glass:

> I heard a Fly buzz—when I died -
> The Stillness in the Room
> Was like the Stillness in the Air -
> Between the Heaves of Storm -
> The Eyes around—had wrung them dry -
> And Breaths were gathering firm
> For that last Onset—when the King
> Be witnessed—in the Room -
> I willed my Keepsakes—Signed away

What portion of me be
Assignable—and then it was
There interposed a Fly -
With Blue—uncertain—stumbling Buzz -
Between the light—and me -
And then the Windows failed—and then
I could not see to see -

By collapsing time and space, the poem narrates the moment of death, the cusp of human transience. Like the home in Robinson's novel, the room in the poem is the screen onto which death is projected and becomes legible. In the poem, the speaker famously narrates the moment of her death not with grand gestures, but through attention to a fly that she says "interposed . . . Between the light—and me -."[11] The poem focuses on the fly but also on the space where the speaker lies: "The Stillness in the Room," she says, "Was like the Stillness in the Air - / Between the Heaves of Storm -." The time of (near) death becomes the stillness in the room, which in turn becomes the pause in a storm. Time's passing, as well as life's, is palpable because Dickinson translates moments into images: the fly's "Blue—uncertain—stumbling Buzz -" and the windows that "failed" allow the poem's readers to inhabit the moment of death *as* a space. This is the space of the room, but also of the poem itself. "I Heard a Fly Buzz," with its dashes and line breaks that mark time in Dickinson's signature way, takes up space; it becomes a kind of room that the reader inhabits in the time it takes her to read the poem. Like the leaves that Robinson describes as "worn to a net of veins," Dickinson's poem makes time and its passing material.

This dimension of Dickinson's poetry that makes it a touchstone for Robinson is also of current critical interest. There has been considerable excitement over discovering in Dickinson some of our own recent enthusiasm for the materiality of language, for the text's literal surface, and for the scene of writing as it is self-reflexively described in her poems. Susan Howe was among the first critics to insist on the material specificity of Dickinson's poems. Howe argued early on that Dickinson's writing practice needed to be reevaluated as a radical artistic act, that her "manuscripts—some sewn into fascicles, some gathered into sets—may have been demonstrating her conscious and unconscious separation from a mainstream literary orthodoxy."[12] Especially since the publication of *The Gorgeous Nothings* in 2013, the first full-color facsimile edition of Dickinson's manuscripts that presents her late work as she wrote it (on scraps of envelopes), the long-standing sense of Dickinson's poems as objects has been reinforced by the materiality of her writing practice. In the midst of this critical ferment, it is important not to lose sight of the fact that Dickinson seems to have been aware of this drift toward the material, and insisted on complicating it. Her poems, and poems more generally, are often described as objects: language compressed and crystallized until it takes on a heft, a density.

But read in the context of Robinson's novel, Dickinson's poem also stages itself as ephemeral: short, intended to be read aloud, conveying a kind of artlessness that makes it seem as if it was perhaps written on the fly. Writing about Dickinson's textual practices, Bill Brown suggests that one reason her poems are so provocative is that they make visible the way literary language shuttles between registers: "You might thus say that language is the material means by which to virtualize the literal object, with material here effectively signifying the textual materialization of language."[13] Dickinson's poetry addresses this virtualization by thematizing the tension between the durability and transience of the poem, and of objects more generally. In doing so, her poems suggest that all our object relations have the potential to be poetic insofar as they require us to negotiate between loss and gain, between distance and intimacy.

That negotiation is staged most explicitly as one between the writer and object in a lesser-known poem by Dickinson. Written around 1866, "Perception of an object costs" (poem 1071) describes the fundamentally negative relationship we have to all things, insofar as we can never grasp them in their entirety.[14]

Perception of an object costs
Precise the Object's loss—
Perception in itself a Gain
Replying to its Price—
The Object Absolute—is nought—
Perception sets it fair
And then upbraids a Perfectness
That situates so far—

The poem tells us that the absolute being of any Object is lost the moment when it is perceived. This is, in fact, what turns it into an object. Any attempt we make to approach it, to capture it in our gaze or on the page, only pushes the truth of the object further away. To be a perceiving subject then, is to constantly confront the endless receding of things, the self-defeating nature of our senses. But this is not to say that the world is impoverished; Dickinson's negative theology allows for intensity, pathos, and beauty. The poem is an act of perception, "itself a Gain," such that its eight short lines convey not a nihilistic realization that we can never access "The Object Absolute," but a meaningful examination of our limits and the longing they generate.[15] Such an examination seems to me the main project of *Housekeeping,* and the reason that it is filled with objects that are an imperfect record of a world just beyond reach: pressed flowers that fall out of a dictionary's pages, *Good Housekeeping* magazines stacked in untidy piles, the scraps of paper blown into the house among dead leaves. These are objects that attest to time's effect on the supposedly enduring ideals of domesticity, objects that Robinson "sets fair," to use Dickinson's phrase, so that we can better see their transience.

With transient things set fair as the symbolic site neither of absolute loss nor of sudden liberation, Robinson recovers the historical force of Dickinson's poems, which themselves offer a counterpoint to the industrious, male autonomy lauded by Thoreau and Emerson. Robinson's novel, like Dickinson's poems, does not depict a human subject who tames nature or stores symbolic capital against the depredations of time, but rather one who recognizes a kinship between the transience of the self and the transient objects around her. Though Sylvie, like Thoreau, "talked a great deal about housekeeping," her habits hardly resemble those narrated in the prose and charts of *Walden,* where to court dispossession means also to initiate a masculine romance of recuperative value. In an essay for *The New York Times Book Review* in 1985, Robinson addresses her desire to revive, but also to revise, American Romanticism. "Emerson and Whitman," she notes, "solved the problem of developing a democratic esthetic by finding the origins of poetry in the workings of consciousness, perception and language." Though she claims that her goal is to dispense with the prevailing notion that history entails "a before and an after with some Catastrophe in between to account for a grand-scale qualitative decline,"[16] Robinson's resurrection of the literary past in *Housekeeping* proceeds under the sign of Dickinson, not Emerson, Whitman, or Melville (whom she also names in the 1985 piece). Dickinson's appearance underscores a gendered legacy in which men are celebrated for transcending their material belongings and women asked merely to act as stewards of domestic goods. It makes sense, then, that Robinson turns in her most important fiction to the nineteenth-century poet with a similarly patronymic surname in order to rework and regender the romantic tradition.

REGENDERING LOSS

This regendering runs the course of the novel, shaping its plot and setting, driving its story arc of a woman disappearing from a disappearing home. *Housekeeping* opens with Ruth's account of an apparently stable house in which generations of women have lived:

> I grew up with my younger sister, Lucille, under the care of my grandmother, Mrs. Sylvia Foster, and when she died, of her sisters-in-law, Misses Lily and Nona Foster, and when they fled, of her daughter, Mrs. Sylvia Fisher. Through all these generations of elders we lived in one house, my grandmother's house, built for her by her husband, Edmund Foster, an employee of the railroad, who escaped this world years before I entered it. It was he who put us down in this unlikely place. (3)

"One house," Ruth notes, has held "all these generations." But the list of women who have passed through it stresses the transience of the house's inhabitants, as if it has always been a temporary way-station. Died, fled, and escaped: the house stands as a witness to a stream of departures.

The house itself stands poised on the verge of dissolution from the outset. Ruth explains that "the terrain on which the town itself if built is relatively level, having once belonged to the lake" and that "sometimes in the spring the old lake will return." At such times, water creeps into cellars, such that Ruth finds "a black pool in our cellar, with a few skeletal insects skidding around on it" (4–5). Given that the house is defined immediately by its porousness to the natural world beyond its walls, Sylvie's supposed transgressions against domestic order might be read instead as a way of preserving its character, allowing the house to bend toward its destiny. Sylvie exposes a truth of infrastructure that we have seen in the work of other writers. The stray paper and magazine scraps are objects vanishing in a built environment that is not much more durable than its frail and random contents: larger objects, like houses and even towns, also shift, settle, and decay. Infrastructure here is no longer what interposes between people and their environment, but another object that reveals the ways both are subject to the passage of time. Robinson's use of the term "infrastructure" slightly later in the novel, undoes its conventional meaning as a stable component of the built world. Exploring Fingerbone in winter, Ruth describes how: "If one pried up earth with a stick on those days, one found massive shafts of ice, slender as needles and pure as spring water. This delicate infrastructure bore us up so long as we avoided roads and puddles, until the decay of winter became general" (93). The paradox here of the phrase "delicate infrastructure" recalls Ellison's and Himes's notion that infrastructure remains always *in between,* never the bulwark that we imagine it to be, but something more fleeting and reflective of the vulnerability of human making and of the human subject itself.

Like the midcentury black writers who made urban infrastructures visible by attending to the dense object worlds surrounding them, Robinson is a virtuoso of scale-shifting transience from the hand-held to the dwelling-sized. We who would think little of discarding an oyster shell, crumpling up a ticket stub, or donating used clothes may balk at the destruction of a house or the transformation of a neighborhood. Yet all of these human-made objects are in a state of permanent transience: no art of preservation saves mega-objects simply because we want to live inside them and call them home. Little wonder, then, that Ellison's invisible man sets alight the objects and space from which he once made a dwelling; he anticipates the actions of Robinson's protagonists who decide to confront the unkeepability of their porous, decaying, mortal home by literalizing its transience into flame. Here Ruth reflects on that decision:

> Sylvie and I could not leave that house, which was stashed like a brain, a reliquary, its relics to be pawed and sorted and parceled out among the needy and the parsimonious of Fingerbone. . . . For even things lost in a house abide, like forgotten sorrows and incipient dreams, and many household things are of purely sentimental value, like the dim coil of thick hair, saved from my

> grandmother's girlhood, which was kept in a hatbox on top of the wardrobe, along with my mother's gray purse. In the equal light of disinterested scrutiny such things are not themselves. They are transformed into pure object, and are horrible, and must be burned. (209)

Once again, if the inner nature of a house is its transience and not its permanence, then an act of housekeeping is also an act of destruction: these are not the two choices of a voluntarist, first-wave feminist protagonist, but the revelation—in the material culture of wood and ash—of an ambiguous condition underlying the social and ideological action on the surface of the text.

Just as Ellison and Himes found a route to and through their inherited literary genres by attending to the fragility of proxy objects set in urban infrastructures, so does Robinson revise the domestic novel by attending to the fragility of kept objects in exurban space. Ruth reflects on the nature of her own memory: "At Sylvie's house, my grandmother's house, so much of what I remembered I could hold in my hand—like a china cup, or a windfall apple, sour and cold from its affinity with deep earth, with only a trace of the perfume of its blossoming" (124). The cup that is both sturdy heirloom and delicate china and the apple that conjures scents of both fertility and morbidity stand in for the house that is the genesis of Ruth's story and its undoing. In a discussion of the embodied contours of mourning, Laura Tanner writes that "Ruth continually refigures the consolation of memory not as a form of material transcendence but as a kind of haunting entrapment within the image" (97).[17] Although Ruth's recollections here may not be readily called transcendent, they are resolutely material, taking into account that material's transience. This is why, after remembering the cup and the apple, Ruth can comment on her aunt's relation to the tension inherent in objects: "Sylvie, I knew, felt the life of perished things" (97). The cup, the apple, and the house they evoke may be dying, but they stay alive in their perishing, a paradox of preserved loss that determines the meaning of this novel for its readers as much as for its characters.

Since Robinson's aesthetic holds so firmly to a dialectical logic of creation and destruction, of keeping and losing, of keeping *as* losing, it is important that the objects and environments defining the material world of the text can be refashioned and remade, not just abandoned, dissolved, or destroyed. Ruth narrates the act of remaking over and over again, especially in relation to Sylvie's treatment of the house:

> Sylvie in a house was more or less like a mermaid in a ship's cabin. She preferred it sunk in the very element it was meant to exclude. We had crickets in the pantry, squirrels in the eaves, sparrows in the attic. Lucille and I stepped through the door from sheer night to sheer night. (99)

Though Lucille comes to disdain what she sees as Sylvie's failure to properly maintain the house, Ruth's empathy and, most of all, Robinson's prose lend a sense of wonder to the scene. The image of the mermaid, the whimsical series of creatures who inhabit spaces in the house, and the epiphora of the night that enrobes it make the scene more magical than repellent. Since the dissolution of boundaries and the slow vanishing of things create beauty and these processes are underway from the beginning of the novel, we need a new way to read *Housekeeping* that does not reproduce the distinction between order and disorder and between presence and absence that the narrative itself undoes. If we forgo a reading in which Sylvie is an entropic force that leads to disrepair in the home, we shift attention away from a somewhat hackneyed or entrenched battle pitting women against the sexist order of things, and we shift attention toward the essential transience of what may otherwise seem fixed and toward the vivid afterlife of what may otherwise seem absent. No less than for Freud, or Pynchon, or Roth, this core act of perception of the death of things defines the novel's story arc and stylistic achievement.

The Freudian ambivalence I have relied on to help explain the social and affective work of ephemera in postwar American novels takes on new forms and yields new implications in *Housekeeping.* Because Robinson is explicitly interested in what transient objects and transience as a state of being make possible for women, it is necessary to place Freud's notions of loss and preservation within a more deliberately gendered framework. In an article from 1988, Thomas Foster turns to Julia Kristeva's essay "Women's Time" to argue that *Housekeeping* organizes a "narrative of women's resistance to the historical limitations imposed on them." Foster suggests that *Housekeeping* "offers some support for the conclusion that women have in practice already begun" to do what Kristeva describes as "operat[ing] from displacement as such."[18] The novel indeed portrays Sylvie, Ruth, and her sister as subjects who are literally and figuratively displaced. But what form does this operation take? In "Women's Time," Kristeva uses the term "future perfect" (in quotes) to name the cyclic temporality associated with women's subjectivity.[19] Certainly *Housekeeping* outlines a nonlinear temporality that its women might inhabit: one of generations, seasons, even weather patterns and train schedules. It is tempting, perhaps, to think of the novel as positing a cyclical, women's time in opposition to a conventional, and conventionally male, linear time. But the novel's preoccupation with transience complicates such a reading and moves us beyond some of the coordinates of classic feminist analysis.[20] As a material property and as a temporal one, transience seems both cyclical and linear. It moves toward a vanishing point, neither in a straight line nor in a sequence of repetition and return. Robinson's novel feels neither wholly melancholy nor wholly redemptive, but instead lingers in a perpetual in between, in the past participle of the fading, the fleeting, the dying but not dead. For this reason, I find it helpful to read the novel's affinity for transience in light of recent feminist and queer scholarship that seeks to make sense of negative and minor affects. Several scholars in queer and cultural studies have written about feelings that usually go unnoted, either because they are too shameful (Eve Kosofsky Sedgwick, Michael Warner), too ugly (Sianne Ngai), or seemingly too apolitical (Anne Anlin Cheng, Heather Love). Their critical terms can help us unravel the affect and the unexpected import of minor objects populating a novel about marginalized subjects living on the edge and eventually outside the limits of a small town.

Heather Love has written about the representational strategies of modernist authors who were, as she puts it, "in various ways marked as backward." She describes texts that find literary strategies for turning away from normative constructions of progress, but she is careful to note that such rejection is not a form of solipsism. Rather, "backward feelings serve as an index to the ruined state of the social world; they indicate continuities between the bad gay past and the present; and they show us the inadequacy of queer narratives of progress."[21] Robinson's choice to set her novel some twenty to thirty years prior to the time of its writing and publication attests to her interest in the enduring effect of the social norms for women that were consolidated in the 1950s. Though not explicitly queer, *Housekeeping*'s focus on relations between women who evade heterosexual bonds clears a space for Robinson to critique the reproductive domesticity expected of her female characters. Sylvie's decision to live as a transient and Ruth's choice to accompany her at the novel's end comprise a survival strategy, a way to maintain a self amidst the "ruined state of the social world," if not a means of remaking that world. Precisely because this strategy entails the rejection of various bonds and results in both vulnerability and solitude, it casts a melancholy pall over the novel. But Love's work reminds us that melancholy is not a futile mode, and in *Housekeeping* it represents the outcome of any attempt to escape the normative grid of sexual destiny and domestic space imposed on women.

Ruth and Sylvie's decision to burn the house and begin a life of transience by climbing aboard a westbound train and drowsing "among the poultry crates all the way to Seattle" (216) thus marks a refusal of what Lauren Berlant has called "cruel optimism." Berlant argues that "one of optimism's ordinary pleasures is to induce conventionality, the place where appetites find a shape in the predictable comforts of good-life genres that a person or world has seen fit to formulate."[22] Ruth's life of constant motion—"we had no particular reason to go to one town rather than another, and no particular reason to stay anywhere, or to leave"—foregoes the conventions and comforts of the "good life," the life pictured in women's magazines and outlined by her school teachers. The novel ends with Ruth narrating her transient lifestyle in a minor key, as if it is a melancholy inversion of the life that has come before. In fact, what Ruth narrates is a fantasy of the life of her sister who has not abandoned convention. Imagining Lucille in Boston, Ruth concludes the novel with the following lines:

> We are nowhere in Boston. However Lucille may look, she will never find us there, or any trace or sign. We pause nowhere in Boston, even to admire a store window, and the perimeters of our wandering are nowhere. No one watching this woman smear her initials in the steam on her water glass with her first finger, or slip cellophane packets of oyster crackers into her handbag for the sea gulls, could know how her thoughts are thronged by our absence, or know how she does not watch, does not listen, does not wait, does not hope, and always for me and Sylvie. (218–19)

A cascade of nowheres, no ones, and nots, the passage effectively negates its own utterances until it becomes difficult to discern who is not doing what. In Ruth's imagination, Lucille's thoughts are "thronged by" absence but she does not wait or hope for her sister and aunt's return. And yet, the final clause, "and always for me and Sylvie," contains no negative, such that the novel ends with a statement of enduring love wrapped in its own impossibility: the return of Ruth and Sylvie is an enduring but refuted fantasy that acknowledges the incommensurability of Lucille's choices with Ruth's rebellion.

Housekeeping ends, then, not with a nostalgic glance to the home Ruth has left, nor with an exuberant view of the future she might have. Instead, Robinson leaves readers with the image of a solitary woman and her cellophane packets of oyster crackers, a literary and fully feminized version of Edward Hopper's famous painting *Nighthawks*. Certainly, the emotions evoked here might rightly be called "feeling backward" or the aftermath of "cruel optimism." But the fleeting inscription of initials in steam and even the cellophane packets remind readers of the novel's relentless concern with ephemera, with the fleeting and fragile stuff of even the most "stable" domestic spaces. In these final lines, Robinson returns to such materials to emphasize that, although Lucille has not left with Ruth and Sylvie, her existence is also shaped by a mood of transience. This mood or orientation is one that looks to a future in which attachments have begun to vanish. Because these attachments are perniciously gendered and classed in Robinson's novel, their prospective dissolution is not necessarily something to be mourned. Instead, the nebulous negation at the novel's end depicts a gynosocial mood and double-stacked temporality not yet named by critics.[23] Seen in concert with the novel's treatment of transient objects, a disappearing subject is less a pure negation than a leaning into, or living with, the historical world as it really is, thronged by absences.

Robinson's portrait of a female subject uncoupling herself from future attachments aligns with its memorable inventory of fragile objects and gives aesthetic definition to her literary style. As we saw in the Dickinson intertexts, this is also, always, a metatextual sign of Robinson's ability to capture the transience of the text itself, and not just the object and subjects it describes. Writing and print media are framed in the novel as ephemeral. Thus, for Robinson, "the life of perished things" is not just a leitmotif, but the ground on which form and content meet. In a recent essay on what he calls Robinson's "panpsychism," Jonathan Kramnick writes that, in *Housekeeping*, "the way that an image can be animated by its object—their literal dwelling in the same stuff . . . —turns on the way that point of view may be realized at the level of the sentence."[24] Such formal operations also happen in the novel beyond the level of the sentence. Returning to Berlant's explication of cruel optimism, we can see that Robinson is herself attuned to the blandishments of what Berlant describes as "good-life genres." Berlant's use of "genre" is a provocative invitation to consider whether Robinson's novel, in depicting characters who reject the "good life," also refutes the generic categories into which it might be slotted. The recurring images of decaying print, such as the magazine and newspaper clippings that Sylvie saves and the dress pattern, board games, and lithograph that interest Lucille and Ruth, invite readers to reflect on the status of the printed object that is the book. But rather than read this compendium as one that betrays anxiety about the death of the book, we might treat it as the material proxy for the genre(s) that Robinson hopes to redefine in *Housekeeping*. This is another reason that the house is so central to the novel: it stands in for the domestic fiction that Robinson evokes in order to undo.

The way that Robinson aims to trouble the conventions of domestic fiction accounts for the novel's opening in which the house in Fingerbone is identified by the generations of women who have passed through it *and* by its ongoing dissolution. As the house first succumbs slowly to the lake that once covered the ground and eventually into the flames the cover Ruth and Sylvie's escape, the central figure of the genre is resurrected only to be erased. Given that the novel, in this sense, enacts a real-time dying of domestic fiction as a genre, it makes sense that it ends with Ruth's image of Lucille in a city diner. This movement from the pastoral terrain of a small Midwestern town to rumbling train cars and a lonely Boston diner also marks Robinson's desire to depart from the transcendentalist tradition that informs the novel. In her *New York Times Book Review* essay, Robinson voices her intention to dispense with the literary traditions she sees constraining contemporary writers. Turning to a series of vivid—and material—metaphors, Robinson avows: "For myself, I will write what I will, as I can, chucking out what I have inherited of Piltdown anthropology, Wedgwood classicism and mercantile metaphysics. Somebody has stuffed Minerva's owl. It's time to clean house." In a single sentence, Robinson condemns the pseudoscience, orientalism, and capitalism that forms her inheritance. Though her final remark also seems to repudiate *Housekeeping*, published five years prior to the essay, the enjambment of metaphors, another collection of objects waiting to be discarded, feels of a piece with the novel's materialist approach.

Housekeeping draws on tropes of the domestic novel and themes of transcendentalism in order to consider what might happen as they decay and vanish without ever quite leaving the scene of American literary history. Like the novel's treatment of ephemera, its reimagining of genre is not entirely melancholy. Rather than lament the mortality of humans, the fleeting nature of objects, and the passing of familiar literary conventions, *Housekeeping* suggests that, in the transience of things, we might locate a model for subjectivity, albeit one that is unmoored and itinerant. Such a relation to the world, Robinson stresses time and again, is not without its comforts: it is not only a flight from oppressive norms for the novel's female characters but also a way of seeing in transience both mutability and possibility, sobered and salted by an acute sense of history's capacity to leave indelible marks on subjects in flight. Such a perspective is, as I have shown, fundamental to Robinson's aesthetics, her sentences woven from the poignant effects of time on matter. In her discussion of Robinson, Amy Hungerford contends that "Robinson is a formalist in both religion and in fiction." Of *Housekeeping* in particular, Hungerford argues that "Millennial images, Biblical allusions, and scriptural cadence imbue" the novel with "specifically religious overtones." Moreover, Hungerford sees "reconciliation" as the project of *Housekeeping*. "The narrative," she writes, "is designed to knit up a broken world into a whole, through simile and analogy, or through the idea that absence produces the present thing through the intensity of longing."[25] Hungerford's assessment is compelling, and certainly Robinson's liberal Protestantism has informed all four of her novels to date. But the drive toward wholeness that Hungerford identifies, though it occurs perhaps in a discrete longing for ordered forms, is no match for the novel's underlying material and historical substrate, in which the brokenness of the world and its objects can be neither forgotten nor erased.

Another example helps illuminate this distinction between a partial drive toward wholeness and a deeper acceptance of transience, of the temporal disorder of things. When they are still together, Ruth sits at the edge of the bay with Lucille and looks out: "Set aside from the drifts and rides and lucifactions of the open water, the surface of the bay seemed almost viscous, membranous, and here things massed and accumulated, as they do in cobwebs or in eaves and unswept corners of a house. It was a place of distinctly domestic disorder, warm and still and replete." The passage is full of inversions: the water's surface holds secrets; disorder is domesticated; dirt and dust figure as plenitude. And stillness here, though it allows for the adhesion of "things massed and accumulated," is temporary, a tenuous beauty that Robinson writes into being with a series of "ands" joining items in a list that bobs gently like the bay's surface might. By reversing and blurring the usual order of things, as she does here, Robinson troubles any easy distinction between inside and outside, surface and depth, and ultimately center and margin. The novel asks whether a house can be like a bay, a train be like a house, and a small town that is "chastened . . . by an awareness that the whole of human history had occurred elsewhere" be the setting for a drama about humans attempting to escape and remake their history (62).

Published in 1980, when the urban postmodernism of writers like Pynchon and Don DeLillo reigned over much of the literary market, *Housekeeping* contemplates the big questions of those authors: What relationship can we have to the history that eludes us? How can we make sense of changing, accelerating material relations? What does it mean to live through the waning of the American century? But it does so in a markedly different setting. I have already discussed the importance of this setting with regard to the genre interventions the novel makes, but I want to end this chapter and look ahead to the one that follows by reflecting briefly on the way that *Housekeeping* reframes some of the foundational questions of postwar literature, as well as those of my own arguments about ephemera, through its setting in a small, far-west town. The hills and woods of Fingerbone are a far cry from the bustling streets of Doctorow's Bronx, the tumult of Ellison's Harlem, and the heady chaos of Pynchon's San Francisco. But like these other novels, *Housekeeping* shares an overarching concern with transience. It harbors no pastoral fantasy of the Western exurbs as our collective national time capsule that could stay proof somehow against the ebb tide of our postindustrial historical fate. Like these other novelists, Robinson depicts ephemera in order to disclose the material relays between postwar subjects and their environments. She suggests that the promises of American modernity and its attendant object relations (produce more, consume more, have more) are untenable, not only for the gendered and raced subjects who have been excluded from or disproportionately vulnerable to these false promises, but also for the white, middle-class subjects of the American "heartland." Robinson's novel, with its many portraits of decline and disappearance, shows that transience is as much a concern for the writer who sets her fiction in rural or small-town America as it is for the urban writer and his urbanely dystopic visions. Writing in this setting, and writing within (and against) the conventions of the domestic novel and the transcendentalist text, Robinson marks her novel as thoroughly American. At the story's end, Ruth lists the names of destinations on her rambling train route: Seattle, Portland, Crescent City on the West Coast, Butte, Billings, and Deer Lodge in Montana, and finally Boston. Sketching a map of the country that is littered with the "gum wrappers and ticket stubs" carried in "small damp heaps" in the transient women's pockets, *Housekeeping* insists that minor objects are constitutive of the national subject *and* the national novel (218). Ephemera are everywhere, Robinson tells us, and the paradox of their persistent, pervasive vanishing is the very stuff of American fiction.

6

Ephemeral Gods, Billboard Saints

DON DELILLO'S APPARITIONS

OBJECTS AND APPARITIONS

This book began in an unnamed countryside where Freud wandered with a melancholy poet and his companion. In "On Transience," Freud composes an anticipatory elegy for the twentieth century that is yet to unfold. After making my way through the decades that followed Freud's reflections on the First World War, I turn now to a writer whose most important works are widely understood to cast a reflective eye back on the twentieth century. Don DeLillo is often hailed as the preeminent elegist of the previous century, an author whose novels from the 1980s and 1990s mourn the passing of time and the fading of America's postwar promises for a brighter future. Summing up this view of DeLillo, Peter Boxall has recently described DeLillo's oeuvre as chronicling "the postwar history of western modernity—from the fifties to the millennium, from the rise of US imperialism in the wake of 1945 to the globalization of US power after the end of the cold war."[1] In novels like *Americana* (1971), *White Noise* (1985), *Mao II* (1991), and *Underworld* (1997), DeLillo attempts to make sense of the legacy that the twentieth century would leave behind as it drew to a close. DeLillo's proleptic perspective makes him a logical bookend for an investigation of the transience documented in twentieth-century fiction and encoded into the dying objects that are stockpiled in the postwar canon.

Most readers understand DeLillo as a writer with curatorial impulses, one whose novels preserve both relic and refuse as they march toward a millennial horizon. DeLillo's "repeated invitation to think historically" is issued via an expansive attention to objects.[2] His novels stage encounters with history as encounters with things: weapons, pollutants, consumer goods, art objects, souvenirs, and even food evoke both the sweep of collective history and the more local "practical archive of stories" that people create as they lead their individual lives.[3] Describing the "maximalist" impulse of *Underworld,* Stefano Ercolino notes that, in the novel's 827 pages, we find an encyclopedic array of objects, as well as media illusions and allusions, "half a century of American history, an ominous technological obsession with nuclear arms, a large spectrum of literary genres, . . . and pervasive references to painting and cinema."[4] The novel is packed with the stuff of the waning century, a tome that records American materialism run amok. This critical consensus, with its emphasis on DeLillo the preservationist, appears to contradict the work of DeLillo the elegist. Alongside this contradiction is another uncertainty about whether, on the one hand, DeLillo's attention to objects is a kind of realism, documenting the stockpiling stuff of the twentieth century, or on the other, his fiction in fact derealizes things, dissolving them in the solvent of elaborate prose. How is it that his novels can palpably evoke a sense of decay and diminishment while resurrecting and reanimating so many objects? What is it about his object worlds that convey the "cross rhythms of gathering and dispersal" instead of just fixing matter in place?[5] The central logics of transience help to answer these questions. Reading DeLillo as a writer of ephemera reconciles the conflict in his work between preservation and elegy, realism and de-realization. In this reading, DeLillo is an uncanny chronicler, not just of objects, but of the process by which these objects are always being lost.

Like the other authors I have considered, DeLillo presents his readers with extensive catalogs of objects; like those of these other authors, DeLillo's catalogs do not index postwar America in a straightforward, realist way. Mark McGurl labels DeLillo a "technomodernist" writer whose work, like Pynchon's, explores how "technicity, no less than ethnicity, might be imagined to be prosthetically lodged in the body."[6] James Wood has also linked DeLillo and Pynchon (as well as David Foster Wallace, Salman Rushdie, and Zadie Smith), calling them writers of "hysterical realism" because their novels are "evasive of reality while borrowing from realism itself." A central formal device linking these writers together is what Wood calls their "cabinets of wonders" and criticizes as poor substitutes for "the drama of vitality."[7] But the catalog of catalogs that I have been writing thus far suggests that both cabinets and wonder do important work in postwar fiction. With Pynchon, for example, we saw how objects concretize and resist conventional definitions of high-postmodernism by yielding historical knowledge. While Pynchon's turn to objects represents a search for the real amidst the proliferation of postmodern surfaces in the 1960s, DeLillo uses objects, paradoxically, to reach beyond the ruthlessly materialist tides of Cold War America. Where Pynchon's objects hold the residuum of historical meaning, DeLillo's stockpile of things contains the remnants of transcendence and belief. But this belief, what Amy Hungerford calls DeLillo's "general mystical sense," does not represent a turn away from the world toward something beyond; it seems instead to inflect his objects so that they give readers a glimpse of communal forms and practices that are yet to be fully captured by the history he narrates.[8] In this chapter, I track the lines of influence that run to DeLillo not only from Pynchon, but also from Ellison and Himes. Like these major black writers, DeLillo shows how objects reveal the historical forces structuring urban spaces and their racial hierarchies while also showing how those structures may be repurposed. His object world attests to the persistence of imperialism and injustice, but it also presents opportunities to resist and remake these forces.

The objects from DeLillo's work that I discuss make a fitting end for this book on vanishing things. Drawn from the final pages of DeLillo's final novel of the twentieth century, *Underworld*, these objects collapse the ephemeral and the eternal. In doing so, they ask readers to reflect on the challenges confronted by Freud in "On Transience," which opened the pages of the present book: What happens if we recognize that even our most enduring objects and values are liable to vanish—and continue vanishing without ever fully disappearing? What kind of political efficacy does such transience make possible? If even material forms are mutable, what is left to hold onto? DeLillo's objects also lead us from fictional streets in the pages of novels into real ones. As readers of *Underworld* will recall, DeLillo ends his novel with a scene in which a conservative nun is transformed by a vision of a murdered girl whose face appears on a billboard in the South Bronx. This fictional vision bears an uncanny resemblance to a concrete image said to resemble the Virgin Mary that materialized in Chicago in 2005. Reading these two images together, one from the final pages of a canonical postwar novel and the other from the walls of a highway underpass, might seem a bizarre endeavor. But situating the fictional apparition next to a "real-life" counterpart illustrates that literature dramatizes the social energies consolidated by ephemera both in their sudden appearances and in their perpetual disappearance.

Both examples explored here suggest that urban apparitions galvanize questions not just of individual faith, but of collective practice, and reveal the mutable, layered nature of modernizing cities that the novels in previous chapters have also exposed. DeLillo, for his part, has not always been recognized as a chronicler of gentrification and racial stratification, though he is often taken to tread a fine line between corrosive skepticism and residual belief. Indeed, plenty has been written about the religious dimensions of DeLillo's work. From John McClure's reading of the "earth-centered mysticism" in *White Noise* to Jeffrey Nealon's account of reading as belief in *Mao II,* several scholars have addressed the way that DeLillo's fiction often registers spiritual forces at work in the world.[9] Ample attention has also been paid to the apparition at the end of *Underworld*: among others, Boxall, Hungerford, John Duvall, Mark Osteen, and Timothy Parrish have incisively examined the novel's final tale of a holy vision amidst poverty, squalor, and violence. But the link between DeLillo's treatment of objects and his turn to religion remains opaque, in part because critics tend to posit spiritual thinking as one way the writer moves beyond the profane world and this way of thinking elides a central tenet of DeLillo's work: faith and religious practices call attention above all to the material conditions of urban life. In *Postmodern Belief,* Hungerford, for example, aptly suggests that *Underworld* establishes a mystical relation to the material world, insisting that religious practice attends to the physical details and textures of even the most unassuming objects.[10] We are left to wonder, though, why DeLillo turns to religion and its object relations? Is it the consequence of his own residual Catholicism? A reflection of his desire, through fiction, to re-enchant the world?

I will suggest that DeLillo depicts the religious dimensions of transience to offer not a flight from reality, but instead a more intense immersion in it. Indeed, as McClure writes, religious experience in DeLillo's fiction does not emanate "from some transcendental beyond but from the world itself and its inhabitants."[11] The "world itself" is cast into relief by the spiritual capacities of material objects. In particular, the apparition at the end of *Underworld* calls attention to the entrenched inequality of late-twentieth-century American life. For DeLillo, religion facilitates a startling encounter with loss. More to the point, it enables the public, collective expression of grief. To grasp the particular contribution of DeLillo's craft, it is helpful to recall the distinction that Anne Cheng has traced between grief and grievance.

Cheng notes the problems that arise when courts and other institutional bodies seek to redress racial injury by "transforming the marginalized, racialized person from being an object bearing grief to a subject speaking grievance."[12] The language of loss that DeLillo locates in his ephemeral objects represents his attempt to express private grief while simultaneously joining in a shared call for political visibility and agency.

The attention DeLillo pays to the power of transient objects, and indeed to the most transient of all materializations, the apparition, galvanizes the epic energies of *Underworld,* training readers' gazes on a community formed around objects that seem to absorb their collective memories. And it is in this sense that DeLillo helps us to draw out the wider social implications of a psychic model of loss that I have been tracing through postwar American fiction by combining the interpretive tools of material cultural studies with Freudian insights. Freud's notion of loss helps us make sense of the dead and dying things that appear throughout the second half of the twentieth century in American novels. But the apparitions at the end of *Underworld* and on the streets of Chicago are best understood by turning to Walter Benjamin's concept of the wish image (*das Wunschbild*). DeLillo's apparition, to begin in the fictional realm, seems precisely to braid together the materialism, spirituality, and political subjectivity that animate Benjamin's influential concept. The wish image articulates a collective fantasy by reaching back to the past. In *The Arcades Project,* Benjamin explains that the wish image "is that wherein what has been comes together in a flash with the now to form a constellation."[13] He understood this shared ability to recognize the past as a dialectic encounter in which political consciousness emerges from an almost spiritual attunement to the artifacts of the modern metropolis. The wish image is like the apparition, insofar as it is not "uncanny" in the Freudian sense, but rather names an object relation that illuminates the structural underpinnings of the environment in which it takes shape. As we turn to the final arc of *Underworld,* then, Benjamin can help us understand how DeLillo's religious thinking is not only material, but materialist in the political sense.

ESMERALDA OF THE OVERPASS

The final scene of *Underworld* is assembled from the grit and grime of the American city, the waste that DeLillo's sprawling novel catalogs.

The narrative winds its way from the New York Giants' Polo Grounds in 1951 to the Bronx in the late 1990s via a juvenile detention center in Minnesota, a desert dotted with artfully repurposed military planes in New Mexico, and the graffiti-covered, garbage-strewn streets of New York City in the 1970s. The novel is loosely structured around its protagonist Nick Shay, an Italian-American waste-management executive who was abandoned by his father as a child and charged as a teenager on a count of criminally negligent homicide in the death of a troubled drug addict. But it spends equal time pursuing the trail of the baseball hit into the stands to win the pennant for the Giants over decades, from the hands of a boy who left the stadium that day with it to Nick's. This baseball has perhaps received the most attention of any object in the novel, but it is just one among many in a text that chronicles the twentieth century by cataloging its things: pages of *Life* magazine, Lucky Strike cigarettes, Soviet weapons, and a Zapruder film are just a few of the many objects that DeLillo vivifies to narrate a "Virgilian underground history of Cold War America."[14] Although the baseball has received its fair share of scholarly attention, the novel is clearly focused on the link between waste and human identity, including national identity. When, late in the novel, Nick visits the former Soviet Union to observe nuclear waste disposal methods, his Russian counterpart says that "waste is the secret history, the underhistory, the way archaeologists dig out the history of early cultures, every sort of bone heap and broken tool, literally from under the ground." Nick replies that "in our case, in our age. What we excrete comes back to consume us."[15] DeLillo is deliberate in pointing out that the detritus that Nick attempts to keep at bay in his job is the unlikely source material for the novel's final, miraculous vision. The novel's focus on waste raises a question: in a culture of so much excess, how can faith survive? Nick offers a cryptic answer: "Waste is a religious thing" (88). In American life at the turn of the millennium, waste itself has become something sacred. Nick says this as he describes his job, the reverence and dread he sees reserved for trash as it is separated, packed, buried, shipped, and handled with great care.

Like Doctorow, Ellison, Himes, Pynchon, and a number of postwar artists, DeLillo reclaims trash from the hidden margins and puts it on display.[16] Assembling trash into a religious vision, DeLillo narrates an uncanny instance in which the ephemeral, by evoking the divine, points readers back to the impoverished environment that the novel's characters inhabit. The final scene of *Underworld,* with its overt religious content (a nun witnessing a miraculous vision) suggests that waste is religious insofar as it is the unseen, nearly mythical by-product of American capitalism's incessant drive toward total efficiency and hygiene. In her work on American modernity and depression, Jani Scandura tracks the changing relationship with rubbish from the late nineteenth century through the 1930s. She discusses the landfill as a site of "complex masking" in which trash could be "contained, ordered, and regulated," exiled to "a space that could be distinguished and set at the margin of American industrial life."[17]

DeLillo displaces his protagonist at the end of the novel and instead narrates the final scene in which this exile of waste is undone through the eyes of a more minor character. We follow Sister Edgar, a nun who appears in the sections of the novel set in the Bronx, as she confronts the "uncanny occurrence" that springs forth at the city's margins (818). Why conclude the novel in this way? Clearly the fact that Edgar is a Catholic nun is important: she is uniquely positioned to comment on matters of faith and transubstantiation. Many scholars have written astutely about the many religious belief systems that involve animate objects. As Caroline Bynum argues in her study of the holy body parts, saintly fragments, "contact relics," and sacred sculptures that suddenly came to life during the early modern period, there is a long history in which matter has been an "insistent and problematic locus of the sacred."[18] But Edgar's gender is also material to this story. Like Oedipa Maas in *The Crying of Lot 49,* Edgar turns out to be something of a "sensitive" who learns to read the signs and symbols of her environment. Like Oedipa, Edgar undergoes a kind of conversion that reorients her toward a community she had previously disdained. Although this turn to women is problematic insofar as it romanticizes their role as empaths and community builders, it also implies a critique of the male characters who are unable to read the world with such acuity. DeLillo certainly signals the importance of gender with the name he has given Sister Edgar. Unlike her friend Sister Grace, who is feminine and tenderhearted from the beginning, Sister Edgar is a cruel disciplinarian (she is a terror to her students) and a strict traditionalist (she still wears a habit in the pre–Second Vatican Council style), and she is afraid that the poor she serves will contaminate her (she wears latex gloves to touch them). But she is deeply affected when a girl whom she has been trying to help is murdered in the housing project where she lives. During her trips to deliver food to people living in "the inner ghetto, a slice of the South Bronx called the Wall," Sister Edgar notices Esmeralda, a girl who "forages in empty lots for discarded clothes, plucks spoiled fruit from garbage bags behind bodegas, who is sometimes seen running through the trees and weeds, a shadow on the rubbled walls of demolished structures" (810). Instead of the usual repulsion that she feels for the Wall's residents, Sister Edgar sees Esmeralda, who lives on and amidst waste, as a "creature of sylvan myth," "a reprieve from the Wall's endless distress," "a source of personal hope" (811).[19] The elderly nun wants to save "the radiant grace in the girl," to "save her from danger, bring her to candles and ashes and palms, to belief in the mystical body" (811). But after her brutal murder, Esmeralda becomes the mystical body herself, and in a reversal of roles, it is the girl who brings Sister Edgar a kind of redemption.

Shortly after Esmeralda's death, people begin to see a mysterious image of the girl on a billboard above the Harlem River. Crowds gather to witness the ghostly apparition, which is visible for fleeting moments when oncoming commuter trains shine their headlights onto the billboard. When Sister Edgar stands with the crowd and witnesses the vision, she strips off her gloves and shakes hands with and embraces the people around her. No longer set apart like a refuse worker shielded by protective garb, she at last enters into the state of communion that, until this moment, has been missing from her aseptic religious life. Sister Edgar's epiphany here at the novel's end represents only one conversion among many. Far from the orderly, glittering grid of moneyed Manhattan, the vision of Esmeralda calls pilgrims to the industrial ruins at the city's margins, to a landscape that seems brutally mined to feed the gluttony of the island's wealthier inhabitants. An abandoned place, a fractured community, and a senseless death are momentarily transformed by this conclusion. Those who come to see the apparition assemble in a forgotten pocket of New York City's northern limits. They cram "onto a traffic island in the bottommost Bronx," amidst "all that old industrial muscle with its fretful desolation—the ramps that shoot tall weeds and the waste burner coughing toxic fumes and the old railroad bridge spanning the Harlem River, an openwork tower at either end" (818). DeLillo's description of the neglected freight yard and eerie structures paints a portrait of a no-man's-land, forgotten except as a place to pass through.

Once stationed here, the people on the traffic island gaze upward, at "a billboard floating in the gloom—an advertising sign scaffolded high above the riverbank meant to attract the doped-over glances of commuters on the trains that run incessantly down from the northern suburbs into the thick of Manhattan money and glut" (818). The apparition draws readers' attention and that of two hundred pilgrims to this overlooked place. Esmeralda appears on the billboard and remakes its surface, inflecting the ephemeral with the eternal and also exposing the dark ironies of consumer culture that DeLillo has chronicled throughout the entire novel. The extensive description of the billboard highlights these ironies:

> The billboard is unevenly lighted, dim in spots, several bulbs blown and unreplaced, but the central elements are clear, a vast cascade of orange juice pouring diagonally from top right into a goblet that is handheld at lower left—the perfectly formed hand of a female Caucasian of the middle suburbs. Distant willows and a vaguish lake view set the social locus. But it is the juice that commands the eye, thick and pulpy with a ruddled flush that matches the madder moon. And the first detailed drops splashing at the bottom of the goblet with a scatter of spindrift, each fleck embellished with the finicky rigor of some precisionist painting. What a lavishment of effort and technique, no refinement spared—the equivalent, Edgar thinks, of medieval church and architecture. And the six-ounce cans of Minute Maid arrayed across the bottom of the board, a hundred identical cans so familiar in design and color and typeface that they have personality, the convivial cuteness of little orange-and-black people. (820)

The "perfectly formed" white hand, the cliché willows and lake of the background, and the nearly pornographic contours of the juice itself make the billboard a cruel reminder of plenty that sails above a community of people living in dire poverty. Sister Edgar's association of the image's lavish details with the art and architecture of the medieval church implies what Nick Shay and the novel as a whole have already told us: unchecked capitalism is the doctrine of twentieth-century America; waste its relic.

From today's vantage point, the billboard seems like a particularly twentieth-century medium: a relic of America's romance with "open roads" and family road trips. As Mike Chasar details in his account of what is perhaps the most famous billboard campaign in advertising history, the sequenced "Burma-Shave" billboards that dotted pre-interstate highways from 1926 to 1963, the driving encounter structured "a dynamic that encouraged driver-readers to cruise the text, to read backward as well as forward, and to cocreate the poem . . . while riding in the white space or extended line breaks between signs."[20] Reading the clever rhymes of the Burma-Shave billboards ("The answer to/A maiden's/Prayer/Is not a chin/Of stubby hair/ Burma-Shave") and even reflecting on DeLillo's billboard for orange juice can feel like a study of a quaint and increasingly obsolete form, but both examples combine motion and message, word and text, attention and distraction in ways that remain relevant.[21] With the way that billboards work on the consumer's senses briefly, and sometimes subliminally, as they pass through space, the signs are the infrastructural precursors to the "semantic priming" of subliminal film and television advertising, something like analogue older siblings to today's online pop-up ads. In their discussion of William Poundstone's work of electronic literature that uses semantic priming, *Project for Tachistocope,* Jessica Pressman, Mark Marino, and Jeremy Douglass argue that the narrative and its formal properties force us to reflect on "how we see, read, and know."[22] The billboard at the end of *Underworld* is similarly self-reflexive, not only alluding to the history of advertising and consumption that has created a toxic culture of waste but also commenting on the novel's multiple threads.

The orange juice in the advertisement in *Underworld* links the billboard to the many histories that the novel unearths and weaves together. In *American Magic and Dread,* Osteen tracks the previous appearances of orange that appear throughout the novel in a "complex skein [that] indicates a unity linking advertising, war, religion, and underground art."[23] Most significant in this skein is a moment in Vietnam when the protagonist's younger brother, Matt Shay, notices "black drums near the perimeter" (462) of his military compound. The drums, he says, "resembled cans of frozen Minute Maid" (463) and prompt him to wonder, "how can you tell the difference between orange juice and agent orange if the same massive system connects them at levels outside your comprehension?" (465). The novel works to bring the "massive system" of global capitalism into some kind of relief for its readers, at least enough so that they understand that consumerism, war, racial violence, and environmental degradation are all interlinked. The racialized cans, sprung forth from a white hand, evoke the novel's specters and stories that jar with the description of cuteness. If the cans are "so familiar" that they become congenial beings, the appearance of Esmeralda defamiliarizes these objects so that they allow onlookers and readers to see anew.

This consumerist spectacle of the billboard and the cans themselves recall Andy Warhol's art of the 1960s. Reading the role of the supermarket in DeLillo's *White Noise* as a "site of interaction between humans and nonhumans," David Alworth draws a connection to Warhol's pop art pieces that mimic the forms of product packaging: Brillo pads, Coke and Heinz bottles, and Campbell's soup cans.[24] Like Warhol, DeLillo faces midcentury mass consumerism; unlike Warhol, DeLillo wants to preserve the affective charge of the consumer objects he depicts. Joshua Shannon points out that Warhol's soup cans and Brillo boxes "provide the barest of reminders of the material specificity of the world onto which the system of signs is projected," but DeLillo's juice cans insist on the specificity of the materials onto and by which they are (literally) projected.[25] The apparition does not externalize or exoticize the cans of juice; it instead recasts them so that the loss and human grief they carry are made visible. Boxall writes that the apparition "transform[s] a marker of banal multinational capital into a sign of divine redemption."[26] This emphasis on redemption has the effect of understating the social import of the scene. The apparition does not simply convert the refuse of capitalism into something holy; it articulates a claim for political agency. DeLillo uncovers the way the billboard speaks the language of loss and grief such that the vision that subsequently appears there makes demands as much as it offers redemption. Those demands include visibility for marginalized subjects and recognition of the interminable and overlooked decay of the infrastructure on which those subjects depend. Bruce Robbins ends his essay "Orange Juice and Agent Orange" with an open question about what the apparition is meant to tell us about the welfare state: "In the midst of his billboard epiphany, is DeLillo really interested in arguing that [American welfare] institutions are not an example of systemic toxicity but a fragile stay against it, and it would be better if they were stronger?"[27] If *Underworld* doesn't quite offer an unequivocally affirmative answer to this question, it certainly insists that we need new ways of seeing, ways of attuning to strange and transient objects that mediate collective calls for agency and action.

This mode of seeing entails a heightened awareness of the world in which Edgar and the crowd are embedded alongside each other. They engage in what Maurice Merleau-Ponty calls "perceptual faith,"[28] a prereflective belief in the perceived world as real and shared. This perceptual faith does not simply confirm the existence of something "beyond," though it may do that; rather it allows communities to form around sensory experiences of mourning and of marginalization. Onlookers stand transfixed, and they direct their eyes into an anxiously focused gaze much different from the "doped-over glances" of the commuters who habitually see the billboard without noticing it. Sister Edgar and the crowd, not knowing "how long they're supposed to wait or exactly what is supposed to happen," stare at the billboard (820). This is an apt description of perceptual faith, which binds the members of the crowd together before the vision even appears. Awaiting the arrival of the unknown, the crowd develops a single consciousness, thrumming with a shared energy like a steadily vibrating tuning fork.[29] The apparition thus promotes a perceptual mode that opposes other forms of attention, like the "freaking network coverage" that sensationalizes and depersonalizes the death of a homeless child. Up until this point, *Underworld* has cataloged and critiqued the "epidemic of seeing" that Pynchon's novels also set forth as a hallmark of postwar American culture. But, because the billboard can be seen only through the kind of attunement that Sister Edgar practices alongside the other people who await the arrival of the unknown, it opposes the fixed stare of the camera, the incessant surveillance of a militaristic gaze. Where Oedipa discovered shadow organizations like the Trystero, never knowing if she was within their reach, Edgar finds her place in the crowd.

The image appears to the waiting crowd when the lights of an oncoming commuter train hit the billboard:

> A face appears above the misty lake and it belongs to the murdered girl. A dozen women clutch their heads, they whoop and sob, a spirit, a godsbreath passing through the crowd. *Esmeralda. Esmeralda.* (821)

Sister Edgar's response to the apparition amounts to a physical transformation. She waits and watches, and waits again, emotion rising within her each time the train lamps illuminate the billboard. Finally, the appearance of the face causes the nun's epiphany and she reaches out for the people around her. The apparition momentarily transforms commuters into community, not only because it is, to some, evidence of the divine, but because it makes legible the grief of those who live in "the Wall," allowing the otherwise unseen pain of poverty and marginalization to be expressed and shared.

Of course, the apparition is a potent instance of the novel's central concern with the recycling and repurposing of waste. The image of Esmeralda, a forgotten girl on a forgotten billboard in a forgotten corner of the city, reflects the endless capacity of the "waste product" to return itself to the heart of the culture that seeks to eliminate it.[30] Sister Edgar knows that the apparition may be nothing more than a fluke wherein an image from a papered-over ad shows through the juice ad, but she nonetheless surrenders to the "sense of someone living in the image, an animating spirit" (822). Though done with less comic effect than the signs in Himes's novels, the billboard's layers likewise insist on the potential for history to unexpectedly animate urban forms. The palimpsest that archived histories of black life in Harlem here metaphorizes the living and the dead that coexist in a single space. In disclosing the past that haunts the present, the apparition gives a structural critique affective force. Infrastructure is once again revealed to hold the charge of history and the potential for its revision. Just as Himes's layered signs testify to social regimes that supersede one another via gentrification, DeLillo's billboard invites readers to apprehend how mass consumerism relies on the invisibility of both waste and marginalized subjects.

Reading this scene today, it's hard not to feel as though DeLillo anticipated the recent scholarly infatuation with agentic objects; after all, he is often hailed as "a prescient and eerily prophetic" novelist whose fictions address ecological end games, terrorism, digital booms, and stock market crashes all before they erupt into public consciousness.[31] Is it possible that what Martin Amis has called DeLillo's "prophetic soul" caught wind of the new materialisms before the new materialists?[32] The apparition does remind us that religious practices have long involved the animation of inert objects. But DeLillo's aim here is not so much to stress the billboard's agency as to suggest that pausing to look at objects differently can create new subject positions and relations. One such relation is the bond between rubbish and relic that is made explicit: even Sister Edgar, whose belief is so great that she experiences a profound transformation, acknowledges the profane means by which the image is actually produced. Her profound transformation lies not so much in the proof that the vision on the billboard might offer of an afterlife for the murdered girl, but in its ability to join the nun to her community through an embodied way of seeing.

But what does it mean that the image is doubly ephemeral? In the train lights, it appears for "less than half a second" before going dark. Then, after a few evenings, it is removed (822). The apparition's fleeting appearance demands the acute attention that causes the community to form; its disappearance paradoxically extends its effects beyond the moment of spectatorship. Or, more precisely, the apparition exposes certain social and material realities because it is ephemeral: its transience is what requires the physical and temporal investment of onlookers. When Esmeralda's likeness disappears, presumably removed by city officials or advertising employees, the elimination seems at first tragic and total: "The next evening the sign is blank. What a hole it makes in space . . . The sign is a white sheet with two lonely words, Space Available, followed by a phone number in tasteful type. When the first train comes, at dusk, the lights show nothing" (824). The hole that the white surface cuts in space, the words that advertise the blank billboard, the train lights that now illuminate nothing indicate that the image had no lasting impact. This is how Osteen reads the scene: "Doubt soon leaches in to taint this moment of rapture. The apparition becomes commercialized and turns into an occasion for phony sentimentality. Finally, the ad is taken down, leaving the lonely words Space Available to represent the void left in the hearts of believers."[33] But the common tag line "Space Available" highlights the very condition that makes the apparition possible. These two words curiously double back upon themselves, declaring the now empty billboard a *tabula rasa,* ready to receive the contours of another projection. The blank space thus preserves the dead girl's afterimage, and most of all it emphasizes the ongoing mutability of urban surfaces that can provide temporary homes for an array of images. This is not a moral narrative of misguided belief or failed community; it is an event that stresses ongoing dynamics of loss in which dying things evoke old spaces while also giving birth to new ones.

The "hole in space" also gives way to a last image—a strange literalization of that amorphous blankness—that moves readers from the city to the screen. After her revelation in the Bronx, Sister Edgar has "nothing left to do but die and this is precisely what she does" (824).

She "awakens" not in Heaven, but in cyberspace, and the very last pages of the novel contain a dreamlike meditation on her afterlife in this virtual state. Her habit now shed, Sister Edgar taps into a "glow, a lustrous rushing force that seems to flow from a billion distant net nodes" (825). As David Cowart describes it, DeLillo's cyberspace is "the contemporary secular world's often paranoid model of universal linkage where again, '[e]verything is connected' amid 'intersecting systems' now virtualized."[34] The power to read and recognize equivalences made manifest on the traffic island in New York City lingers even after the apparition has vanished. Esmeralda on the Lake has caused Sister Edgar to attend to the details of waste and open herself to communion with others; this way of seeing continues in her digitized afterlife. So, although what Sister Edgar sees before her in this cyberheaven are destructive images of atomic bomb explosions, detonating in a symphony of colors, what she feels is "another fusion taking place," a way of joining to other users and other pieces of information that float in the "lunar milk of the data stream" (826). Without her experience at the billboard in the South Bronx, it seems impossible that, in her afterlife, such as it is, Sister Edgar would feel "fusion" in the face of these images. DeLillo himself seems agnostic as to the plausibility of such fusion: projected not only onto Sister Edgar but into the surreal space of the internet, this image of an afterlife is aspirational without being ironic.

As Edgar's desire for communal belonging plays out against the horizon of nuclear fusion, a "single seraphic" word emerges from the sea of pixels. "Peace" appears on the screen and as the final word on the last page of *Underworld*. Among the many scholars who have discussed this ending, Joanne Gass offers a particularly provocative interpretation. She asserts that the word "promises much but is merely another piece of coded information." The word, she argues, can do no more than inspire longing, not unlike the longing Jay Gatsby feels as he gazes at the green light on Daisy's dock. Gass goes on to say that the novel's conclusion thus makes *Underworld* a cautionary tale that ends in cyberspace, "our isolation complete."[35] But the apparition is both material and transient: it invites us to think about this longing as a nondominative orientation toward the world, a way of apprehending the "real" without believing it can be fixed in place. In her work on the Catholic vision of DeLillo's work, Hungerford argues that, in Sister Edgar's internet afterlife, "something close to the traditional

Catholic model of redemption is at work" (74). Hungerford points out that, while DeLillo may retain "only a general mystical sense that nevertheless bears the imprint of the Catholic doctrine," the doctrine of transubstantiation is not entirely irrelevant to an understanding of this final scene.[36] Sister Edgar does appear to learn from the apparition that the divine can hide within the profane: billboards look like medieval churches and homeless girls like angels, strangers whom she has feared become her community, and in the leveling abstractions of the internet, even war can bear a striking resembling to its opposite, peace.

But we might reverse the conventional logic of transubstantiation to make sense of this ending. Instead of insensate matter made animate or divine, here we are once again *returned* to the material world from which DeLillo assembles his visions. If the internet afterlife into which Sister Edgar awakens seems to grant transcendence from the physical limitations of earthly life, this final resonant word assumes undeniably physical dimensions, emerging like another apparition out of the surrounding matter that previously goes unnoticed. As the pixels on the screen assemble to form the word "Peace," what becomes visible for the first time is "the thick lived tenor of things, . . . the plied lives of the simplest surface," and the reader is asked to "imagine the word on the screen becoming a thing in the world" (827). The parting word, shimmering in the ether of the internet, seems to materialize as a thing to be touched. More precisely, the word rematerializes without being reified. The doubling of the word "Peace" itself stresses that attention to nonhuman objects can engender more humane subjects. Its homonym, "piece," reminds readers that for the "asthmatic children and sickle-cell adults, the [people with] AIDS and the cocaine babies" living in the South Bronx, to claim, even for a short time, a small piece of the world is an act of restitution, an act that enables mourning and a working through of shared grief, an act that initiates a momentary armistice in the midst of unending struggles (811). To attain peace in the debris-strewn underworld of DeLillo's making, one must focus on its pieces: the layered billboards, the swinging train lamps, the quivering pixels. That focus moves the reader from a purely literary investment in DeLillo's language to the power that perception and attention have to reorganize what has been forgotten, discarded, or destroyed. The logics of transience remind us that, even as such things become newly visible, they can only ever appear in an ongoing state of loss.

MARY OF THE UNDERPASS

Novels are often said to be in a perpetual state of disappearance. Novels persist, of course, in a variety of forms, despite the repeated frequency with which they are declared dead or dying. And the more monumental a novel, the more it seems to be fighting against its own ephemeralization. The lengthy compendium novel can feel like an author's attempt not just to represent a world, but to embody it. Paul Saint-Amour makes this argument about long modernist works that he claims seek "to capture a whole city or society within their pages."[37] Novels like *Invisible Man, V.,* and *Underworld* attempt this capture, even as they insist that transience is a crucial dynamic in the cities and societies they depict. DeLillo's efforts in *Underworld* are aimed at returning readers to a kind of vernacular community, one that is best accessed in his works through the temporary objects and assemblages that flash up in America's postwar spaces. But do ephemeral objects generate only ephemeral community? In the rest of this chapter, I want to consider whether the kind of attunement that DeLillo describes—and asks his readers to practice in relation to his novel—occurs in other places. Is it possible to locate such forms of perception and to translate the literary lessons of ephemera into the world? Or is the ephemerality I have theorized purely a representational concept? Is the model of transience derived from Freud and explored variously by American fiction writers only an abstraction about the art and practice of losing, the impossibility of absolute loss? To test the hypothesis formed in DeLillo's fiction, I will turn in the rest of this chapter to an example that offers answers that are quite literally concrete.

In April 2005, a little more than seven years after the publication of *Underworld,* an image said to look like the Virgin Mary appeared in Chicago on the walls of the Fullerton underpass of the Kennedy Expressway (Figure 22). Despite the Department of Transportation's official statement explaining that the apparition was, in fact, a stain created by water leaking from the highway overhead, mixing with the road salt that had been scattered during the winter, and penetrating the concrete walls of the underpass, the image quickly began to attract attention. Media outlets credited Obdulia Delgado with discovering the stain during her drive home from work: "I was so stunned I couldn't move. People were honking. It was a dream. I don't even know how I got home."[38] It wasn't long before word spread and hundreds of visitors flocked to the underpass. Calling themselves the "Fullerton Avenue Pilgrims," they came to touch the image, say prayers in its presence, take photographs and to leave flowers, candles, and other tokens of devotion. Local newspapers relayed the words of these pilgrims, who extolled the virtues of "Underpass Mary" despite others' skepticism. *The Chicago Tribune,* for instance, quoted Irene Munoz: "It's very emotional. It's very real. I never believed anyone who saw these things. But I believe now."[39]

The city was forced to acknowledge the practical problems that the image was causing: police were sent to direct the traffic that slowed to a crawl along the expressway as a result of the growing number of pilgrims. Although visitors wondered whether city officials might try to remove the image, the initial response indicated otherwise: "We're treating this just like we treat any type of roadside memorial," claimed the Illinois Department of Transportation spokesman: "We have no plans to clean this site."[40] But, after her three-week stay, Underpass Mary's fate seemed sealed when a man who was later arrested for damage to state property used black shoe polish to paint "BIG LIE" in large letters across the image. Newspaper articles report that bystanders stood by and "wept as a coat of brown paint was rolled over the stain."[41] The resonance of this curious story with the apparition from *Underworld* reminds us that the visions of fiction can clarify the social meaning of moments when traces of magic seem to animate the object world. Like Esmeralda on the Lake, Underpass Mary is an image born out of the city's waste, an ephemeral figure that highlights spaces and conflicts in the urban environment from which it emerges. Like Esmeralda on the billboard, the image on an underpass wall in Chicago calls attention to its own materiality, its transience, and the ways that it interrupts the hurried rhythms of the city and its inhabitants. Reading it alongside *Underworld* emphasizes the way that the apparitions point toward something divine but also ultimately illuminate dimensions of urban life that are frequently ignored and repressed.

Underpass Mary calls attention to aspects of urban life that usually go unnoticed. Like the billboard and the subway train of *Underworld,* the elements that contribute to the creation of Underpass Mary are visible, daily practices in Chicago: the salting of wintry roads, cars driving along the highway, water running off city streets. But their aggregate effects draw attention to an aspect of the city's infrastructure that normally recedes from sight. Highways have long been distinctly

FIGURE 22. Virgin Mary image appears on Chicago expressway underpass, 2005. Photograph by Scott Olson, Getty Images.

American symbols of mobility and freedom, but the subterranean passages and urban grottos they create are physically and figuratively overlooked. In a city where verticality continues to be the dominant architectural paradigm and the public transportation system, "the el," takes its name from its aboveground elevation, underpasses might be said to constitute Chicago's most chthonic world.[42] The stain also highlights the temporal disjunctions of its surroundings: even the names of the streets that branch out from the underpass allude to a past the city effaces by channeling it into a series of place names whose historical content fades through the daily use of these urban markers: Shakespeare, Webster, and Hamilton avenues intersect with Palmer and Dickens avenues in the shadow of the overhead Kennedy Expressway. While novelists like Doctorow and Roth used ephemera to preserve something of the past's untapped futures, the apparition in Chicago highlights how the past itself marches into the future by way of infrastructure, just as in Ellison's and Himes's work.

Just as the apparition sheds light on a largely neglected space, Underpass Mary also brings the devotional practices of a minority group to the forefront. While Catholicism generally posits Mary as a model intercessor, Latinx Catholics have a long history of seizing upon this fact and engaging it in material ways.[43] Even if we doubt the accuracy of the news stories reporting that the majority of devoted pilgrims visiting the underpass were Latinx, the very fact that the site was incorporated into such a narrative highlights the relevance that the apparition may have for one of Chicago's largest minority groups. A quick glance at the history of Underpass Mary's surroundings suggests that the pilgrimage of Latinx people represents an effort to temporarily (re)claim urban space. Bucktown, the neighborhood where the Fullerton Underpass is located, lies about three miles northwest of downtown Chicago. Originally settled by Polish immigrants in the 1830s, Bucktown saw an influx of Germans in the 1840s and 1850s, followed by European Jews at the end of the nineteenth century and Mexican and Puerto Rican immigrants beginning in the twentieth century. From the 1950s to the 1980s, the neighborhood was predominantly Latinx. Beginning in the 1990s, the number of Latinx residents in Bucktown began to decline. Over the past three decades, the cost of living in Bucktown has increased dramatically, pricing out many.[44] As in chapter 3, here again we encounter the forces of gentrification, such as rising home prices, an influx of high-end shops, and frequent "teardowns" of older housing stock, and see how they have displaced many of the neighborhood's Latinx residents. But, for the brief moment that Underpass Mary takes up residence in Bucktown, that displacement is undone. The apparition in the underpass reorganizes movement and seems to enable a new collective to claim both visibility and space.

Shortly after the image made news, a visitor to the site placed a painting directly next to the stain. The painting does not depict a traditional, Roman-Catholic version of Mary (the one most readers will know from Renaissance art: a dark-haired woman wearing blue veil); instead, it shows Our Lady of Guadalupe with her head bowed and veiled in a manner similar to the figure on the underpass wall. To offer a sort of legend to readers and viewers, several news outlets ran a photograph of a statue of a Virgin Mary alongside one of the underpass (Figure 23). However, unintentionally perhaps, the statue shown is most certainly one of Our Lady of Guadalupe, who is said to have appeared as an apparition to a peasant on Tepeyac Hill, near Mexico City. If, as Michael Taussig claims, apparitions can be understood as forces of translation "between home and shrine, between profane and sacred, and not least between official and unofficial voices," the Lady of Guadalupe is especially suited to signify these transformations. *La Virgen Morena*—the dark-skinned virgin—syncretically represents both the Virgin Mary and the indigenous Mexican goddess Tonantzin.[45] Both a figure of colonization (during the conquest, Spaniards used this aspect of the Virgin's multiplicity to gain converts) and of resistance (Mexicans continued to worship their deities in the guise of a Catholic icon), this mestiza Mary sustains the "in-between" state of translation.[46]

The media's visual instruction seems to target viewers disinclined to see anything divine in the stain, but the pairing of images has the distinct effect of creating a lasting link between them. Once the stain is identified as a Marian apparition, it becomes nearly impossible *not* to see the supplicating figure: the down-turned head, the folded arms, the flowing veil. Viewers are drawn into the kind of "perceptual faith" that DeLillo depicts. And, while an average viewer may not be drawn into the community of believers that the image assembles, these mediated scenes disseminate the culturally specific claims to legitimacy that the Latinx pilgrims enact in their visits to the underpass. As religious historian Robert Orsi has explained, "acting upon the urban environment in [religious] ways [allows] immigrants and migrants to deny the arrangements of space, the understanding of poverty, the

FIGURE 23. Virgin of Guadalupe. Artist unknown.

marginalization or ostracism of the foreign, and the alienation of the streets built into the urban landscape by law and architecture."[47] Pilgrimages to Underpass Mary do this as well, but with a crucial difference: because the apparition appears "of its own accord," it is as if the urban environment authorizes the pilgrims' claims independent of their own actions. This is, of course, a defining characteristic of apparitions: their seemingly autonomous materialization gives them a special legitimizing force, from Tepeyac Hill to a traffic island in the Bronx in DeLillo's *Underworld* to the streets of Chicago. Rather than a site that must be built, the underpass emerges unexpectedly as a space where religious beliefs and secular frustrations can be expressed. Underpass Mary binds the energies of pilgrims together such that each is joined to the community occupying the underpass.

By equating the site with a roadside memorial ("We're treating this just like we treat any type of roadside memorial"), city officials reveal the structural and affective parallels between Esmeralda on the Lake and Underpass Mary. Although the billboard in DeLillo's novel is more explicitly a roadside memorial insofar as it commemorates Esmeralda's death, the Chicago underpass also becomes a site where grief may be expressed and shared. The spontaneous shrine in the underpass bears flowers, candles, and written prayers: the same items found at memorials commemorating the dead. And, while the crowd in DeLillo's novel mourns a particular loss, the visitors to the underpass in Chicago make visible the losses that gentrification and displacement cause. Apparitions' transience and the way that, in these cases, they bring waste, inequality, and neglect into view give onlookers a simultaneous impression of the divine and the impoverished. Like the used cars in Mucho's lot in *The Crying of Lot 49* and the Provos' belongings thrust out on the sidewalk in *Invisible Man*, the stain in the underpass presents itself as a spectacle not quite meant to be seen. The apparition is, in a sense, not overheard but overseen, a glimpse of something transient, something that conjoins becoming and loss in a single image. It exposes something we might want to believe in as well as things we might wish did not exist.

But what are we to make of the fact that this image is ephemeral and that the community it engenders might therefore be temporary as well? The surprising conclusion to the story of the stain in the underpass complicates this question. Despite ongoing complaints that the image was causing excessive traffic, it was not until the stain was written over with the words "BIG LIE" that the city took action and painted over the site. The meaning of the "big lie" remains unclear. Is the "lie" the belief in the water stain as a miraculous image? Or the doctrine of the Immaculate Conception? Or the idea that Mary could help anyone in the modern world? Or is the statement a disgruntled complaint about Chicago's infrastructure? Whatever the case, it was this act of vandalism, rather than the stain itself, that could not be overlooked by the city. Although we might conclude that the violation of public ordinances poses a greater threat to the city's logics than the so-called apparitional sensibility of a minority group, it seems equally possible that the official response shows reluctance to intervene with the original image. The city tolerates the stain, the shrine built around it, and the pilgrimages to the underpass. This tolerance seems to endorse the image as a natural event. It is the defacement of the stain that finally prompts the paint-over.

The image also survives in photographs printed in newspapers, posted on the internet, and captured by visitors' cameras and flip-phone cameras of the early 2000s (Figure 24). This phenomenon recalls the opening scene of DeLillo's *White Noise,* when the main character visits a tourist attraction known as "the most photographed barn in America." Standing among the droves of people with cameras, a friend says to the narrator: "We're not here to capture an image, we're here to maintain one. Every photograph reinforces the aura. Can you feel it, Jack? An accumulation of nameless energies."[48] In his essay on the practice of "sacred photography" by pilgrims to a Marian apparition site in Flushing Meadows Corona Park, Daniel Wojcik calls these photographs "miraculous mementos, created on sacred grounds, which then become accessories to personal devotion."[49] Thanks to technologies of pictures and pixels, mobiles and message boards, the energies gathered in the underpass are spread even after the image's disappearance. But the reproductions of Underpass Mary online seem less like "miraculous mementos" than reminders that the apparition is of a material order that cannot be so easily archived. The story of Underpass Mary, like that of Esmeralda, leads onlookers from the city streets into cyberspace. The image from the underpass becomes, like the word "Peace" at the end of *Underworld,* "a sequence of pulses on a dullish screen" (827). And like that word, online images of the stain seem stripped of the magic that might come with physical proximity

FIGURE 24. Documenting Underpass Mary. Photograph by Scott Olson, Getty Images.

to the apparition and other onlookers, such that the remaining function of these pictures on a screen is ambivalent. The cyber-afterlife of Underpass Mary preserves a vision of the image, but it also preserves something of the loss that the image evokes. The painted-over wall also serves as a reminder that the city's surfaces remain ready to receive the outline of another projection. The underpass, like DeLillo's billboard, is another "space available."

The mediated afterlife of the object gives the community that gathered in the underpass a particular kind of afterlife as well. People are bound to, and bound together by, objects that are neither fully lost nor entirely present, objects with the quality of impermanence that this book has been investigating. The community that forms around the apparition has neither an entirely nostalgic formation (around a lost object) nor a fetishistic or consumerist orientation (toward a present object). The community is transient in the sense that it must grapple with the in-between status of the apparition, accepting the ongoing loss it signals and undergoes. This transience inheres as well in the digital afterimages that themselves become a kind of fictional representation. Like novels that narrate the death of things, images of Underpass Mary transmit an awareness of loss: they remind us that the stain no longer exists in its original form and that the photograph is only a residual trace of the object itself. Though novels, even an encyclopedic one like *Underworld,* "know" in some sense that they are representational and always offer a mediated experience of the world, photographs of the Chicago apparition expose the way that real (and surreal) things often become fictional as well. In Marilynne Robinson's *Housekeeping,* the narrator Ruth makes a similar claim when she notes that "everything that falls upon the eye is an apparition."[50] Objects remind us, as they shuttle between the factual and the fictional, that they are rarely present to us as fully or as permanently as we might like them to be.

These kinds of claims about fictionality and mediation can seem to flatten all objects into an indistinct mass of loss. If all representations are imperfect, don't they all address the death of things? Even as all literary objects might testify to their own inadequacy, this kind of Derridean claim we have inherited from poststructuralism doesn't address the particularity of the novels that are the subject of this book. What Underpass Mary helps us understand with greater precision is the way that some American novelists bring readers into proximity with the constant becoming and vanishing of a certain class of objects. This proximity grows even more vexing when that class of objects appears online, in a cyber-afterlife like Sister Edgar's or the photos of Underpass Mary that circulate on the web. These digital traces compound the contradictory logics that I have described as they bring us into a realm that promises both infinite storage and complete immateriality. I will turn to this tension in my coda, but now I want to consider another afterlife of the stain in the underpass.

As if to affirm that the image was possessed of its own will, determined to refuse the city's decision, the stain's contours began to reemerge over time through the layer of brown paint. People carefully scraped the paint from the wall and cleaned off the shoe polish graffiti, and months after her disappearance, Underpass Mary made her miraculous return (Figure 25). Upon its second appearance, the stain no longer looked quite the same, and its slight mutations became a new topic of conversation. In May 2009, Teatro Vista, a Latino production company in Chicago, staged playwright Tanya Saracho's *Our Lady of the Underpass.* The play, a sort of docudrama compiled from a number of interviews that Saracho conducted at the site, unfolds in front of a large set piece: a re-creation of the underpass wall (Figure 26). In the final act of the play, Saracho's characters address the apparition's

FIGURE 25. Underpass Mary returns in underpass, April 4, 2007. Photograph by Daniel X. O'Neill.

FIGURE 26. Staging of Tanya Saracho's *Our Lady of the Underpass* at Teatro Vista, Chicago, Illinois, 2010. Photograph by Carillo Photo.

"second coming." One character, a woman called Terri and described in the script as a "young Latina woman in her late 20s, maybe early 30s," examines the recently uncovered image: "Now it doesn't look like when I first drove by. You know what it looks like now? Like that painting of the guy doing this (puts hands on cheeks and opens mouth and eyes). And he looks like he's melting?"[51] Terri's allusion to Munch's *The Scream* causes the first real rupture in the forms of belief that the stain has otherwise catalyzed. Terri's comparison, played for laughs, finally brings the strange humor that has been latent in the story of Underpass Mary to the surface. Saracho's joke equates the water stain with an iconic image of Western art but also deflates the apparition by highlighting its arbitrary, even absurd nature.

Admittedly, it can be difficult to take apparitions seriously. It's tempting to explain Underpass Mary with something like a pejorative "secularization thesis," one that argues that the devotion to apparitions like this one are the residue of immigrant culture. In this line of thought, the found shrine or pop-up temple reveals the vernacular, transient leftovers of assimilation, the magical thinking that has yet to be displaced by normative, supposedly secular skepticism. But, as the novels I have considered throughout this book remind us, images and objects reflect magical thinking of many kinds, including the fantasy that we might cheat death through them. Here we see how they also consolidate communities that see and make seen the material and social inequalities of life in the United States. Pilgrimages to the underpass also work against an unspoken norm of liberal multiculturalism: that immigrants are welcome but must subscribe to a matrix of dominant beliefs and practices. The underpass, like the novel, can harbor beliefs that have not been assimilated. Instead of reading these beliefs as fantastical or backward, fiction can help us understand them as expressions of political being. Dipesh Chakrabarty has made a similar point in his critique of dominant narratives about modernization. In *Provincializing Europe,* he argues that secularization is never a complete project, that magical thinking is always coeval with modernization. On this point he writes: "Gods and spirits are not dependent on human beliefs for their own existence; what brings them to presence are our practices. They are parts of the different ways of being through which we make the present manifold; it is precisely the disjunctures in the present that allow us to be with them."[52]

DeLillo himself wonders what becomes of an apparition once it is undone by a joke, papered over, or erased by a coat of paint. As the narrator asks at the end of *Underworld*: "What do you remember, finally, when everyone has gone home and the streets are empty of devotion and hope, swept by river wind? Is the memory thin and bitter and does it shame you with its fundamental untruth—all nuance and wishful silhouette? Or does the power of transcendence linger?" (827). The binary DeLillo establishes here suggests that he himself may fail to grasp what it is that makes his story of the apparition so resonant. The fact that we cannot state whether the apparition was "never really there" or whether it is always hiding, ready to materialize in and through any number of urban forms, is precisely what gives apparitions their power.

ELEGY AS FORMAL DESIGN

Although DeLillo has published five novels and one collection of short stories since 2000, his stature as prophet and elegist of the twentieth century has made his twenty-first-century works somewhat challenging to critics. His 2003 novel *Cosmopolis,* about a twenty-eight-year-old multibillionaire asset manager crossing Manhattan in a limousine, received some attention after the 2008 financial crisis and was made into a film by David Cronenberg in 2011. *The Body Artist* (2001), *Falling Man* (2003), *Point Omega* (2010), and *Zero K* (2016) have faced lukewarm reception. Writing about *Point Omega* for *New York Magazine,* Sam Anderson said the novel was the latest in a "recent stretch of post-*Underworld* metaphysical anti-thrillers—*The Body Artist, Cosmopolis, Falling Man*—[that] has reached a whole new level of inertia."[53] Other critics have lamented what Anderson calls DeLillo's "glacial aesthetic." Michiko Kakutani called *Cosmopolis* "a major dud, as lugubrious and heavy-handed as a bad Wim Wenders film, as dated as an old issue of *Interview* magazine."[54] Pundits used to play an annual game of speculation about whether the year's Nobel Prize in literature would go to DeLillo, but they now play it much less, and his star within the academy has begun to recede, as if it has been relegated to the twentieth century that his novels historicize.

Despite this critical ambivalence, DeLillo's fiction has been evolving, reflecting the author's efforts to respond to the first decades of the twenty-first century. Many of these changes have involved a reconception of matter, a turning away from the accumulating debris of his earlier novels toward a world haunted by a pervasive sense of the immaterial. Boxall suggests that, "if *Underworld* is a novel which is attuned to the time of the age, then DeLillo's novels of the twenty-first century—the first novels, perhaps, of DeLillo's own 'late' phase—speak an extraordinary lack of spatial or temporal awareness, a sudden and drastic failure of the bonds that hold us in time and space."[55] What Boxall diagnoses as the condition of time in DeLillo's recent novels—"thin," "fragile," and "insubstantial"—also describes the novels' treatment of objects. Gone is the object density that gives *Underworld* its heft; in its place is a sustained interest in human bodies as they die, disappear, and dematerialize. These bodies, like the ephemera of DeLillo's early novels, trouble easy distinctions between presence and absence, grief and desire, even life and death. But there is a clear shift in attention away from what Jack Gladney in *White Noise* calls "the immensity of things, an overburdening weight" and toward a sense that all objects, including the human body, are moving toward total weightlessness.[56]

In *Zero K*, DeLillo's sixteenth and latest novel, a man named Jeffrey Lockhart travels at the behest of his father to a remote compound called The Convergence. Located in a desert somewhere in Kyrgyzstan, The Convergence is a cryogenic suspension facility where people are frozen (just) before death so that they may be reanimated in a future where reanimation technology exists. We learn that Jeff has come to The Convergence to bid farewell to his stepmother, the archaeologist Artis Martineau, who is dying of several painful and terminal diseases. The Convergence is, as Joshua Ferris describes it, "a cross between a think tank and a state-of-the-art hospice: the Santa Fe Institute meets Sloan Kettering, with a dollop of Heaven's Gate, all of it given over to Christo for interior decorating."[57] The compound's aesthetics are a kind of hygienic minimalism: sterile, spare, evoking the precision and mystery of a high-tech laboratory. This is also an apt description of DeLillo's prose, which is stripped down and uncharacteristically stark in places. Even a quick glance at the pages in the novel confirms this: copious blank space, paragraphs made of single sentences, chapters that end with enigmatic koans like: "Once the dark is total, I will simply stand and wait, trying hard to think of nothing."[58]

DeLillo makes it clear at several moments that *Zero K* is meant to offer a different take on the world of things than his previous novels.

After he has confessed his plan to freeze himself along with his wife, Jeffrey's father tells his son:

> People getting older become more fond of objects. I think this is true. Particular things. A leather-bound book, a piece of furniture, a photograph, a painting, the frame that holds the painting. These things make the past seem permanent. A baseball signed by a famous player, long dead. A simple coffee mug. Things we trust. They tell an important story. (150)

The baseball is, of course, an explicit reference to one of the central objects in *Underworld*: the ball from the game-winning three-run homer hit by Bobby Thomson in the 1951 National League game between the New York Giants and the Brooklyn Dodgers. Although the statement about people growing "more fond of objects" is not overly critical, it is said in an elegiac mode, as though DeLillo wants to remind readers that, like the dead who cannot take their cherished objects with them, writers cannot repeat and revive their earlier works. Those previous works turned to objects to narrate the dusk of the twentieth century while also showing how many of its promises and practices endure. *Zero K*, though, stages the passing of this earlier representational mode altogether. Ferris astutely notes that, even as the novel moves from the subterranean spaces of The Convergence ("Zero K" is a reference to absolute zero, but in the novel it names the elite level of cryogenics, deep underground) to Jeff's daily life in bustling Manhattan, we can never forget that "the dying part came first." "This," Ferris remarks, "is elegy as formal design." What it elegizes is the twentieth century that remains, in DeLillo's earlier works, passing but never past. *Zero K* forgoes the dual logic of transience in favor of a one-way process wherein subjects and objects move toward a vanishing point. Given that, as a character in the novel says, the world "is being lost to the systems, . . . to the transparent networks that slowly occlude the flow of all those aspects of nature and character that distinguish humans from elevator buttons and doorbells," this makes sense. DeLillo's objects crystallize and condense, but ultimately evaporate to reflect the "sense of being virtualized" he names as a hallmark of the twenty-first century (239).

Whether DeLillo understands the new century or 9/11 or the expansion of digital technology to mark the beginning of a new era that requires a new literary orientation toward objects, scholars need not replicate this impulse and should, in fact, question it. Revisiting *Underworld* now, not as a historical relic but as a text that has relevance in the "real world" and in our current debates about posthumans and post-postmodernity, can remedy the tendency of contemporary scholars to ephemeralize the literature that is still very much with us. DeLillo's writing, like that of the other writers in this study, is at its most revelatory when it tackles the magical structural ambiguity between subjects and objects that cannot be represented easily in other media. The mess of transience and its perpetual in-betweenness make these writers compelling; it is what animates their unusual historiography. Novels like *Underworld* relay something profound about what humans borrow from objects. They remind us that, if we look to objects to comfort us in the face of our mortality, there will at some point come a reckoning with the death of things. As they vanish, ephemera thwart our desires for permanence: even the things we thought could not die do. But the fiction I have considered here also maintains the traces of the things we imagine have disappeared. If we want to slough our humanity onto objects, these novels remind us, then we must accept that it includes the ways we linger *and* decay, persist *and* vanish.

At the beginning of this book, I argued that we should not imagine, in a moment of posthumanist longing or object-oriented infatuation, that the human subject disappears. Literary meditations on transience stress that humans are always entangled with objects. Fiction shows us that condensation into thinghood is not a simple act of concretion, but one that produces its dialectic opposite. Portraits of ephemera dispel the fantasy that we might selectively attribute human values to objects and find in them better, more enduring versions of ourselves. The unexpected mortality of objects, their tendency to vanish, is captured by authors interested in the transit between humans and things that is never one-directional. DeLillo's late work, with its tendency to trace a line that moves only from human to object, from all that is solid to air, raises the question of whether the dialectic notion of transience that this book describes has itself been made obsolete by our shift to digital media. What does it mean, after all, to contemplate the ephemeral at a moment when so many actual things are migrating into the digital ether? Or, rather, what becomes of the American postwar novel, with its object catalogs, in the digital age? Media scholars remind us that the digital is material—the glass of touch screens, the factories where they are produced, the server farms that make up the cloud—all have heft.[59] When writing a history of the American novel and its objects, it is possible to imagine that writing it at different times would produce different results. Theodore Dreiser's playbills and F. Scott Fitzgerald's green light; Roth's stamps and Doctorow's ticket stubs; Ellison's blueprints and Himes's signs: each of these objects would mean something distinct if theorized, for instance, during the decade in which they were first described. But to write this literary history of ephemera now requires recognizing that digital technologies and practices inevitably inflect questions of matter. Holding out the promise of infinite storage, the internet seems poised to eradicate the very existence of ephemera while also dematerializing all things, turning them into apparitions that do not appear on billboards or underpass walls, but merely flit across the screen. We wander today through a digital landscape and are left to wonder whether we should, like the young poet from Freud's countryside, imagine that it too shall one day all be lost to us. Perhaps unlike the poet, we also understand that it is our particular fate to watch this loss as it happens, to confront at every turn not so much the death of things, but their perpetual dying.

Coda: The Afterlife of Things

EPHEMERA IN THE DIGITAL AGE

At the beginning of *Mao II* (1991), Don DeLillo describes a character seduced by books:

> He walked among the bookstore shelves, hearing Muzak in the air. There were rows of handsome covers, prosperous and assured. He felt a fine excitement hefting a new book, fitting hand over sleek spine, seeing lines of type jitter past his thumb as he let the pages fall. He was a young man, shrewd in his fervors, who knew there were books he wanted to read and others he absolutely had to own, the ones that gesture in special ways, that have a rareness or daring, a charge of heat that stains the air around them.[1]

The sensuous nature of these books—their bindings, paper, and ink—appeals to Scott Martineau, the personal assistant of the novel's protagonist, before he knows what they contain. By now, this scene of analog print and bookstores and Muzak comes to us like a relic of the past, a familiar but waning ecosystem. Throughout this book, I have considered how novels stage questions of print decay and their own obsolescence. Long-standing debates about the ostensible death of the book hardly require rehearsal, but they have been animated and invigorated anew by the digitization of everyday life. Early efforts to digitize books represented a relatively straightforward effort to preserve, to transcribe the contents of books so they could live longer on hard drives and websites. But more pervasive and creative uses of digital publishing have led scholars to consider not only digitized books, but digital ones. In the introduction to *Book Presence in the Digital Age,* Kiene Brillenburg Wurth deftly surveys the scholarship from the last two decades that has considered the shift from print to digital media.[2] Sven Birkerts, Johanna Drucker, N. Katherine Hayles, Alan Liu, Matthew Kirschenbaum, Jerome McGann, Andrew Piper, and Jessica

Pressman are just a few of the scholars whose work has paved the way toward a robust conceptualization of the book as it exists in new and continually shifting forms.

These scholars have illuminated the many ways that the physical book has always existed in a multitude of forms. Drucker, for instance, points out that current thinking about the difference between the printed and digital book often depends on faulty distinctions:

> The issue that has galvanized the greatest amount of critical attention in contrasting electronic and traditional media . . . is . . . the notion of a distinction between linear conventions of the printed text and possible alternatives. Most of these discussions mistake the fixed form of print support for a rigid programmatic determination of reading. The experience of browsing a book, of flipping from index to notes to marginality and back, let alone of reading a tabloid newspaper, with its deliberately fragmented and polylinear pathways through its pages, quickly belies the myth of this convention.[3]

Seeing such continuity between the printed text and its newer iterations supports the argument that digitization will not "kill" the book, but allow it instead to multiply and proliferate. Leah Price memorably points out that, because "one constant in the history of books is their power to take new forms," we must admit that, "if the book is dying, its funeral appears to be open casket."[4] As Pressman writes: "The book will not become obsolete with new reading platforms, but rather, will change and develop new incarnations and readerships; it will continue to serve certain kinds of literacy needs and literary desires—specifically those related to its book-bound physicality and potentiality."[5] If printed and digital books have more in common than we might assume, then this includes their ephemerality.

Books are always tricky objects to pin down in conversations about durability, precisely because we think of them as simultaneously fragile and immortal. For every claim that the book will last, there is a counterargument attesting to its destruction. So too, for the digital. Every story about the impossibility of deletion has a twin narrative of accidental erasure, bit rot, and technological failure. Amaranth Borsuk names this overlap in her evocative history of the book when she notes: "While we might assume that digital books will have a longer shelf life than print, the proliferation of reading devices coupled with the pace of technological development virtually ensures the obsolescence of e-books tied to particular software or hardware. Ephemerality is thus a concern shared by physical and digital books."[6] And Wendy Chun makes this point forcefully when she notes that we often believe in "our machines as more stable and permanent and, thus, better record holders than human memory." But she claims: "This belief is remarkably at odds with the material transience of discrete information and the internet. Digital media is not always there. We suffer daily frustrations with digital sources that just disappear. Digital media is degenerative, forgetful, eraseable."[7] This all makes good sense, but it is nonetheless difficult for many people *not* to mourn the potential or imminent passing away of the printed book. We know well the lament for the bookstore's disappearance, the vanishing of the gleaming spines and beckoning pages that DeLillo describes. In a 2011 essay about the perpetual death of the book, Ben Ehrenreich sums up that perennial grief: "Books were once such handsome things. Suddenly they seem clunky, heavy, almost fleshy in their gross materiality. Their pages grow brittle. Their ink fades. Their spines collapse. They are so pitiful, they might as well be human."[8]

In previous chapters, I have discussed the way that humans often invest objects with a fantasy of immortality, the hope that they might be agentic but permanent, housing only what we see as our positive values. This is one reason why, no matter how compelling the arguments are that the book will live on even as it is digitized, we still find pathos in its transition to another form. Even as postwar novels reflect on the transience of print, they also suggest the paradoxical endurance of the book through their treatment of ephemera. Ephemera thus help us see that, even while books persist, we can mourn their passing. Books are ephemeral in the same way as many of the objects that appear in them. My aim in these final pages is not to pronounce a verdict on the fate of the book, but rather to suggest how the theory of ephemera I have developed can inflect the ongoing debates about digitization. The central lessons of this book are: an expanded definition of ephemera that reminds us that such objects may be intentionally or accidentally preserved; a sense of the novel as a storage medium that can save ephemera from the ravages of time and capitalism while simultaneously speaking to their disappearance, an awareness that infrastructure is inflected by such dynamics more than we expect; and a clearer view of the consumerist culture of disposability that takes hold in postwar America. And these lessons are more relevant than ever as the twenty-first century marches on. The ambivalence of ephemera offers a useful lens on the contradictions of the digital because it is seemingly immaterial and ever-present, temporary and permanent. Throughout this book, I have defined ephemera as objects destined for disappearance or destruction. But, as I have also demonstrated, these transient objects endure in a variety of forms: novels, museums, libraries, and digital archives. From curated repositories like the New York Public Library's Biblion app to personal photo archives stored on Facebook or Instagram, the internet is rapidly transforming our understanding of ephemera. As John Durham Peters notes, "in recent decades the really big growth in computation has been in storage capacity rather than transmission speed."[9] As storage costs approach zero and storage capacity approaches infinity, the ability to document the world has been expanding to unprecedented levels of detail. Beyond medium-specific questions about the future of the book, the internet seems poised to preserve all ephemera long past their "natural" lives. In this era of expanding hard drives, a tweet archive held by the Library of Congress, and the proliferation of cloud computing, it seems as though loss itself might become obsolete. Is ephemerality an outmoded concept? Can literature help us understand the new forms of transience that are emerging in this digital age?

A central lesson of ephemerality conveyed by the novels I have studied is that fictions of preservation have long underwritten our ideas of loss. In other words, loss as a concept depends on the desire for things to endure. The technologies and tools we create for preserving such things arise out of this sense of loss and then shape our understanding of what loss is. This is a dialectic that remains hidden but feels obvious the minute it is uncovered. The fantasy of "prosthetic memory" and infinite storage stands as an intimate counterpart to the confrontations with ongoing loss that novelists depict. As the internet begins to appear more frequently as the subject of contemporary novels, from David Foster Wallace's *Infinite Jest* and Gary Shteyngart's *Super Sad True Love Story* to Sally Rooney's *Conversations with Friends* and Chimamanda Adichie's *Americanah,* writers are growing attuned to the web's twinned dynamics of loss and preservation. The internet appears in these works not as an unbounded archive, but as a medium for (mis)communication. Like Edgar's time capsule, Philip's stamp collection, and the muted postal horn that Oedipa tracks, representations of the internet can encode desires for proximity and authenticity that can never be entirely fulfilled. Such a trajectory is implicitly mapped in this project, as the green light shining at the end of Daisy's pier in *The Great Gatsby* culminates in the train's headlamps that illuminate the billboard at the end of *Underworld*. Both scenes, as I understand them, are partly about the futility of attempts to get closer to an object of desire that, if it ever existed, is forever receding from our grasp. The object's transience and its unattainability are what incite our desire; we may never reach or possess the object, but we hope that technology might bring it, or at least its generating mechanisms of desire, into clearer focus. The point, then, is not, as DeLillo would have it, that "everything is connected," but that the familiar ache of disconnection and disappearance persists along with the fleeting objects fixed in the internet's massive memory.

To that end, I want to turn now to an example, a strange literary-internet hybrid object that might help us see how digital preservation can illuminate new forms and old attachments. At a moment when literary scholars are eager to import the lessons of media studies, not least because those lessons seem attuned to the shift from print to digital forms, this example is a helpful reminder that the methods and modes of literary analysis also can and should be brought to bear on media objects. Put another way, this example shows that digital forms might not remediate books themselves, but rather their concerns. In January 2011, a website appeared featuring an eight-bit video game adaptation of *The Great Gatsby*. The site claims that the vintage two-dimensional Nintendo game is an unreleased Japanese creation called "Doki Doki Toshokan: Gatsby no Monogatari," and that the website's creators, Charlie Hoey and Peter Malamud Smith, purchased it for fifty cents at a garage sale. The site reproduces images of the original cartridge and the user's manual, which dates the game to around 1989–1990 (Figure 27).

In the game, you play as Nick Carraway and traverse New York from the Valley of Ashes to West Egg. To fight off the baddies (flappers, hobos, gangsters, and waiters) at one of Gatsby's bacchanalian parties, you simply fling Nick's hat at the intended target. The game lifts text directly from the novel (Figure 28); it asks you to best the drunken tantrums of Tom Buchanan and defeat the laser-shooting eyes of Dr. Eckleberg.[10] Is the recovery of this game and its subsequent

FIGURE 27. User's manual for *The Great Gatsby* NES game, created by Charlie Hoey and Peter Malamud Smith. Artwork by Michael DiMotta.

FIGURE 28. In the library at Gatsby's party. Screenshot of *The Great Gatsby* NES game, created by Charlie Hoey and Peter Malamud Smith.

popularity just a recent example of the kind of nostalgia that Simon Reynolds calls "retromania," an obsession with the recent past that has come to dominate pop culture in recent years? Reynolds argues that this trend involves an element of "exact recall: the ready availability of archived documentation (photographic, video, music recordings, the Internet) allows for precision replication of the old style."[11] Since the passing of time has become increasingly indexed to the procession of rapidly obsolescing trends and objects, the popularity of this "old school" video game might well be the marker of an impulse to slow down technological progress or cling to even trivial things that we once found meaningful and important.

But the strange thing about the game, the thing that makes us laugh and press the spacebar to toss Nick's hat, even if we're not gamers and never were, is the dissonance that arises from the translation of a literary classic into this dated format.[12] Is this dissonance so striking because the novel is supposed to feel timeless? Or is it because *The Great Gatsby* is in fact so marked by its time ("the great Jazz Era novel") that seeing it pressed into pixels and set to the beeping, tinny tones of a Nintendo soundtrack is intensely anachronistic? As the website's creators relayed in an interview, the curious effects of translation seem intrinsic to the game itself: "NES games were like these weird, badly translated artifacts from another planet, often really surreal and mysterious with this oddball internal logic of their own."[13] Rather than simply enticing us with access to the past, the game's internal logic seduces us and offers us a chance at immersion. The game does not idealize or sentimentalize the past as much as it charms and amuses us. If we press "start" because we are seeking a portal to the past, it quickly becomes clear that playing the game is an experience that unfolds in the present, as we maneuver through obstacles and anticipate how the next frame will adapt favorite scenes from the novel (Figure 29). Reynolds writes that this kind of playfulness "is related to the fact that the retro is actually more about the present than the past it appears to revere and revive."[14]

Indeed, when we learn that this game is *not* some found object from the past, but an idea conceived and coded by two literature-loving computer programmers in Philadelphia, we leave the realm of recovery and restoration and return to the novel's own questions about shrouded origins and the waning of authenticity. The novel's preoccupation with failed adaptation, with forgery and simulacra, is perfectly

FIGURE 29. Start screen for *The Great Gatsby* NES game, created by Charlie Hoey and Peter Malamud Smith.

captured by the success of the game's discovery myth and the curious effect of the obsolete Nintendo form. Even the game's Japanese title refers to digital mimicry and to one of the novel's principle symbols of fakery: Doki Doki (ドキドキ) refers to the onomatopoetic sound of heartbeats often associated with comics and video games, while Toshokan (図書館) means library. A library of fake heartbeats—what could be more Gatsby-like?

About one week after the game went viral on the strength of its nostalgic garage sale story, the truth emerged about the game's creators. Initially, the game seemed like proof that something lost could be resurrected, that the internet could do away with the ephemeral by ensuring that everything, no matter how trivial, can be stored. But this act of preservation, which turns out to be an act of creation, also incites a double longing for the past: a sense that Gatsby's era and the "naïve" technology of the late 1980s might be lost to us. Even more important is the way that the hoax illuminates the possibility that the internet might eliminate the very need for the original, authentic artifact. The game, I would argue, speaks precisely to this pervasive concern that if everything can exist on the web, in the cloud, or on some server that we access through the wonderfully named "Wayback Machine" (the "Internet Archive"), why would we need "the real thing?" And would we even know it anymore if we saw it? So this is where the game leaves us: online, navigating the "green light jump," returned to the same questions that structure Fitzgerald's novel in the first place (Figure 30).

Lest it seem that I am simply espousing a *plus ça change* conservative outlook, let me reiterate that I find the curious conclusion of this story a meaningful one. When the truth about the Gatsby game's origins is revealed, it gently chastises us for our nostalgia and for our faith in the internet as a redemptive repository or treasure trove of all things vanished. It's worth remembering too, that, in 2013, Baz Luhrmann's highly hyped 3D film *The Great Gatbsy* hit theaters. If the game and the film taken together represent something like a recent "Gatsby resurgence," one in which Fitzgerald's story was translated into contemporary forms

FIGURE 30. The "Green Light Jump." Screenshot of *The Great Gatsby* NES game, created by Charlie Hoey and Peter Malamud Smith.

because it captures an impulse in American culture, it is not difficult to imagine why. Almost a century after its publication, the story of lavish spending and fabricated fortunes leading up to financial collapse felt very relevant in the wake of the "Great Recession" of 2007–8, as it continues to feel now, given the dubious fortunes of America's current president. That the video game evokes the late 1980s and early 1990s, the years of Reaganite deregulation and Wall Street booms, seems like yet another marker of Gatsby's timeliness.[15]

This suggests that, even when objects transition from the material to the digital, they can elicit the same sorts of competing desires that have been the subject of this study. The internet does not necessarily transform those desires so much as it reveals dynamics peculiar to our own cultural moment. Ultimately, this anecdote about a video game resonates with one of the central challenges of reading and writing about ephemera that I have encountered frequently throughout this project. Theories and representations of ephemera ask us to inhabit a present that is informed by our understanding of the past and our projections of the future but not dictated by it either. I have tried to employ a methodology that attends to this present without fixing it in space or time, an interpretive approach to transient objects that does not overwrite their disappearing. If this sounds increasingly vague, as if the way of being in the world in which representations of ephemera help us to imagine is all poetic ambivalence and no substance, then let us reconsider. If we return, after this long detour through white cities, urban undergrounds, overpasses and underpasses, to the countryside where Freud and his morose companions contemplated the transience of nature, we can understand the full force of the demand made by writers and filmmakers to orient ourselves toward a vanishing present. Freud writes that, when we apprehend the transience of our environment, we cling "with all the greater intensity to what is left to us," and that we should not be surprised "that our love of country, our affection for those nearest us and our pride in what is common to us have suddenly grown stronger." By now we are familiar with the dangers inherent in such intense attachments: the misplaced fetishism, the suffocating love, the blinding nostalgia, the virulent nationalism. What novelists reveal is that recognizing the ephemeral and its powerful place in our world and in our psyches might actually prevent us from this compensatory clinging. Ironically, through attention to the past—in this case, to a history of fiction that takes seriously vanishing objects and the affects they shape—we are better positioned to see which of our attachments can and should be let go. Novels push and pull us in two directions to show us that, while permanence is a fiction, the past cannot simply be discarded. They invite us to loosen our grip on fantasies about the past and projections of the future so that we may begin to love without fixing our loved objects in a place where we always knew they could never last.

Acknowledgments

Writing this book was incredibly hard. I am so fortunate to be where I am now, but I began this book during a period of professional precarity and finished it during a pandemic. Many kinds of privilege and luck allowed me to complete this project, but most of all it was friends' and colleagues' kindness and support that saw me through. Truly, this book would not exist if it weren't for the people who sustained me throughout its writing. In the very long time I have spent on a book about, of all things, disappearance, I have happily accrued lasting debts of gratitude to many people.

This project began as a dissertation and my advisors, Anne Cheng, Zahid Chaudhary, and Valerie Smith, remain my intellectual north stars. Anne's humble brilliance, Zahid's intellectual acuity, and Val's courage are never far from my mind as I write, teach, and advise. I still can't believe my luck that I was taught by such incredible thinkers who have turned out to be such incredible friends.

Sabine Sielke, Christian Klöckner, Elisabeth Schäfer-Wünsche, and Justin Sully sustained me during a postdoctoral fellowship in Bonn. Hanjo Berressem was a fast friend who gave me opportunities to strengthen my thinking when I really needed them (and to throw Twinkies at his students). In Berlin I had the good fortune of working with and learning from Martin Lüthe, Frank Kelleter, Florian Sedlmeier, and Alexander Starre at the John F. Kennedy Institute. I miss you guys!

At the University of Delaware, Zara Anishanslin, Jill Flynn, Sandy Isenstadt, Ed Larkin, Laura Helton, Stephanie Kerschbaum, McKay Jenkins, Kristen Poole, Keerthi Potluri, Lance Winn, and Julian Yates have been wonderful colleagues and friends. Kaylee Olney and Jessica Venturi have helped with all the things. My students inspire me and give me hope. The graduate students in my "Material Losses" seminar in fall 2016 invigorated my thinking about this project. Joseph Nash served as my research assistant and did heroic work tracking down scattered references and formatting an early version of the manuscript. Michael

Doss and Jack Truschel did last-minute editing as well. Tori Aquilone did stellar work helping me with image permissions. Mostly, though, I am grateful to all four of them for their curiosity and kindness.

John Ernest has been my department's chair since I began at UD and his unflagging support has made all the difference. He made a manuscript review possible, and the generous feedback I received there from Martin Brückner, Kate Marshall, and Paul Saint-Amour transformed this project. They helped me see what could be cut, what could be added, and how to take ownership of the ideas I care most about. To Martin I add my thanks for his mentorship at UD—he's taught me how to be a better historicist, a better steward of literary objects, and, most of all, a rigorous but kind colleague.

Jackie Goldsby taught me so much when I knew so little, John Durham Peters reminded me of the untrammeled joy of ideas, and Jim English vouched for me at crucial moments. Bill Brown's exacting but patient and profoundly generous feedback have been invaluable, at both early stages and late ones. This book exists on ground that his work cleared.

A version of chapter 3 was published in *PMLA*. I am thankful for the extensive suggestions from the manuscript's two readers, Daylanne English and Justin Gifford, as well as from the journal's editor, Wai Chee Dimock. Eve Dunbar commented on the piece with her characteristic incisiveness and encouragement. Members of the 2018–19 Mellon Research Seminar at University of Pennsylvania's Wolf Humanities Center asked great questions about this chapter and shared work all year long that helped me refine my methodological thinking. An early version of chapter 6 was published in *The Journal of American Studies.* Thanks are due to the anonymous readers there who worked on it with me. *Merci bien* to Greg Pierrot, who offered comments on a draft of chapter 2 and good humor the whole way through. Charlie Hoey and Peter Malamud Smith, the Gatsby guys, are as generous as they are genius. Micah Kraus's photographs gave me some much needed visual inspiration.

At the University of Minnesota Press, my manuscript landed in exactly the right hands at exactly the right time. How does anyone actually publish a book without Doug Armato? His faith in the project helped me finish it; his feedback made it better. The thorough, attentive reports I received from readers for the Press were the stuff of writers' dreams. So many people at the Press had a hand in bringing this book into being. I am deeply grateful for Merle Brett Kendall's meticulous editing. Ana Bichanich, Gabriel Levin, Zenyse Miller, and Mike Stoffel made sure everything came together. Derek Gottlieb worked indexing magic. Thanks to John Gerrard for letting me use his astonishing artwork for the book's cover.

My friends—my chosen family—have carried me along in ways big and small so that I could complete this book. In Germany, Rieke Jordan and Cornelius Reiber keep me modern and make me laugh. Nina Wegscheider has been there since the first word of this thing; I am so happy that she's there for the last (and doesn't have to edit it!). Amy Liu, Pat Moran, and Mary Robertson keep my thinking about things creative. Amy Jersild taught me so much about finding my voice. Dylan Ceglowski taught me to stay in the fight. Jess Horton's solidarity keeps me going at UD. It's a gift to be in this profession with Kinohi Nishikawa, who asks the right questions and gives the best talks. Jed Esty was this book's most devoted and enthusiastic reader, finding a way to make all of my ideas stronger while always making sure they were my own. I never imagined I could learn so much from someone. Whitney Trettien's dazzling mind and uncompromising attitude make me feel all things are possible. Truth! It's not an exaggeration to say I wouldn't have survived the past couple years in Philadelphia without her. David Kim's friendship is everything. Emily Hyde has written and thought alongside me at every turn since 2006. Her feedback, especially on my Introduction, made this book better, but more important, her friendship has made me a better person. I am grateful to her amazing daughters, Lydia and Jo Shelov, who remind me that sometimes a game of spoons and a trip to Igloo are more necessary than another hour of work. The best copy editor on the planet, Gaga (Martha Hyde), was kind enough to look over my proofs.

Max can't read, but he's been the most loyal (and furry) writing companion. I am sad that Lillian and Jim Broderick, whose curiosity and passion for literature shaped my own, are not here to see this book. But I am so happy that their daughter, Sophie, my older-sister-by-choice, is. My brother Henry has always pushed me to be smarter and stronger. Finally, not a word of this book would exist without the unconditional love and endless support of my parents, Margery and Forrest Wasserman. Thank you, Mom and Dad. This is for you.

Notes

INTRODUCTION

1. Edward W. Soja, *Postmodern Geographies* (New York: Verso, 1989), 11.

2. "Ephemera," *Oxford English Dictionary Online.*

3. Bodleian Libraries, University of Oxford, "About the Collection," John Johnson Collection of Printed Ephemera, accessed July 11, 2019, https://www.bodleian.ox.ac.uk/johnson/about.

4. Bodleian Libraries, "About the Collection."

5. Lisa Gitelman, *Paper Knowledge: Toward a Media History of Documents* (Durham, N.C.: Duke University Press, 2014), 3.

6. Jacques Derrida, *Paper Machine,* trans. Rachel Bowlby (Stanford, Calif.: Stanford University Press, 2005), 42.

7. Margreta de Grazia and Peter Stallybrass, "The Materiality of the Shakespearian Text," *Shakespeare Quarterly,* 44, no. 3 (1993): 255–83; de Grazia, "The Essential Author and the Material Book, *Textual Practice* 2 (1988): 69–86.

8. Jonathan Senchyne, *The Intimacy of Paper in Early and Nineteenth-Century American Literature* (Amherst: University of Massachusetts Press, 2019).

9. Theodore Dreiser, *Sister Carrie* (New York: Barnes & Noble Classics, 2005), 20. Further page references will be parenthetical.

10. Caitlin DeSilvey, *Curated Decay: Heritage Beyond Saving* (Minneapolis: University of Minnesota Press, 2017), 19.

11. For more on the distinct character of obsolescence, see *Cultures of Obsolescence: History, Materiality, and the Digital Age,* ed. Babette Tischleder and Sarah Wasserman (New York: Palgrave Macmillan, 2015).

12. Raymond Malewitz, *The Practice of Misuse: Rugged Consumerism in Contemporary American Culture* (Stanford, Calif.: Stanford University Press, 2014).

13. Though "thingness" is a persistent concern across Heidegger's work, it is explored as distinct from objecthood in *What Is a Thing?,* trans. W. B. Barton Jr. and Vera Deutsch (Chicago: Henry Regnery, 1967). The German edition is *Die Frage nach dem Ding* (Tübingen: Max Niemeyer, 1962).

14. Bill Brown, *Other Things* (Chicago: University of Chicago Press, 2016), 5.

15. Don DeLillo, *Zero K* (New York: Scribner, 2016), 214.

16. See *October* no. 155 (Winter 2016): 3–110. This is a symposium entitled "A Questionnaire on Materialisms" that was edited by David Joselit, Carrie Lambert-Beatty, and Hal Foster. The entries by Emily Apter, Jeff Dolven, and Helmut Draxler are especially provocative in their claims about the relevance—ascending or waning—of Heidegger to the new materialisms.

17. Lisa Gitelman's *Always Already New: Media, History, and the Data of Culture* (Cambridge, Mass.: MIT Press, 2006), Yuk Hui's *On the Existence of Digital Objects* (Minneapolis: University of Minnesota Press, 2016), and Matthew Kirschenbaum's *Mechanisms: New Media and the Forensic Imagination* (Cambridge, Mass.: MIT Press, 2008) all insist, in different registers, on the materiality of digital practices and devices. John Durham Peters's *The Marvelous Clouds: Toward a Philosophy of Elemental Media* (Chicago: University of Chicago Press, 2015) also reminds readers that digital forms are physical forms, albeit by pointing out how environments and atmosphere are themselves forms of media. Already in 1963, the media critic Vilém Flusser noted that things were receding into the background of our areas of concern. "Non-things," as he called them, "flood our environment from all directions, displacing things." For Flusser, *information*, which is electronic and digital in his thinking, is immaterial because it is "impossible to get hold of" (*The Shape of Things: A Philosophy of Design,* trans. Anthony Mathews [London: Reaktion, 1999], 86).

18. Brown gives such an explanation in *Other Things* when he argues that the digitization of the world has resulted in efforts to forestall feelings of disappearance: "If one can posit a material unconscious that has provoked this thing about things, I suspect that it is troubled by a 'dematerialization of the world'" (13).

19. Matthew Kirschenbaum's work on everything from word-processor documents to floppy disks offers examples of how media archaeology brings the materiality of contemporary technologies into historical focus; see *Mechanisms* and *Track Changes* (Cambridge, Mass.: Harvard University Press, 2016). For an overview of media archaeology methods, see *Media Archaeology: Approaches, Applications, and Implications.* ed. Erkki Huhtamo and Jussi Parikka (Los Angeles: University of California Press, 2011).

20. Peter Schwenger, *The Tears of Things: Melancholy and Physical Objects* (Minneapolis: University of Minnesota Press, 2006), 3.

21. Schwenger, 2.

22. Anne Anlin Cheng, *Ornamentalism* (New York: Oxford University Press, 2019), 17.

23. In his unfinished work *The Dialectics of Nature,* Friedrich Engels attempts to apply Marxist ideas to science. Engels discusses matter as becoming rather than being: "All nature, from the smallest thing to the biggest, from

a grain of sand to the sun, from the Protista to man, is in a constant state of coming into being and going into being, in a constant flux, in a ceaseless state of movement and change" ("Introduction"; full text available at marxists.org/archive/marx/works/1883/don/ch01.htm). Throughout the work, Engels somewhat enigmatically suggests that any understanding of material requires an understanding of dematerialization.

24. See, for instance, Jean Baudrillard, *The System of Objects* (1968; repr. New York: Verso, 1996; originally 1968), and Pierre Bourdieu, *Outline of a Theory of Practice* (New York: Cambridge University Press, 1977).

25. For examples of work with a focus on consumption and exchange, see: Arjun Appadurai, *The Social Life of Things: Commodities in Cultural Perspective* (New York: Cambridge University Press, 1986), which includes Igor Kopytoff's essay "The Cultural Biography of Things: Commodification as Process"; Daniel Miller, *Material Culture and Mass Consumption* (New York: Blackwell, 1987); and *Acknowledging Consumption: A Review of New Studies*, ed. Daniel Miller (New York: Routledge, 1995).

26. Appadurai, *The Social Life of Things*, 17.

27. Appadurai, 13.

28. See Susan Strasser, *Waste and Want: A Social History of Trash* (New York: Metropolitan, 1999), William Rathje and Cullen Murphy, *Rubbish! The Archaeology of Garbage* (Tucson: University of Arizona Press, 2001), and Giles Slade, *Made to Break: Technology and Obsolescence in America* (Cambridge, Mass.: Harvard University Press, 2006). For books on literary treatments of waste, see Susan Morrison, *The Literature of Waste: Material Ecopoetics and Ethical Matter* (New York: Palgrave Macmillan, 2015), and *Filth: Dirt, Disgust, and Modern Life*, ed. William A. Cohen and Ryan Johnson (Minneapolis: University of Minnesota Press, 2005).

29. Jules David Prown, "Mind in Matter: An Introduction to Material Culture Theory and Method," *Winterthur Portfolio* 17, no. 1 (Spring 1982): 1–19.

30. Jennifer Roberts, "Lucubrations on a Lava Lamp," in *American Artifacts: Essays in Material Culture*, ed. Jules David Prown and Kenneth Haltman (East Lansing: Michigan State University Press, 2000), 167–89.

31. Susan Stewart, *On Longing: Narrative of the Miniature, the Gigantic, the Souvenir, the Collection* (Baltimore, Md.: Johns Hopkins University Press, 1984).

32. Diana Fuss, *The Sense of an Interior: Four Writers and the Rooms that Shaped Them* (New York: Routledge, 2004), 15.

33. Bill Brown, *The Material Unconscious: American Amusement, Stephen Crane, and the Economies of Play* (Cambridge, Mass.: Harvard University Press, 1996) and *A Sense of Things: The Object Matter of American Literature* (Chicago: University of Chicago Press, 2003).

34. Elaine Freedgood, *The Ideas in Things: Fugitive Meaning in the Victorian*

Novel (Chicago: University of Chicago Press, 2006); John Plotz, *Portable Property: Victorian Culture on the Move* (Princeton, N.J.: Princeton University Press, 2008); Mary Jacobus, *Romantic Things: A Tree, A Rock, A Cloud* (Chicago: University of Chicago Press, 2012); Matthew Mullins, *Postmodernism in Pieces: Materializing the Social in U.S. Fiction* (New York: Oxford University Press, 2016).

35. Jane Bennett, *Vibrant Matter* (Durham, N.C.: Duke University Press, 2010); *New Materialisms: Ontology, Agency, Politics,* ed. Diana Coole and Samantha Frost (Durham, N.C.: Duke University Press, 2010); *Political Matter: Technoscience, Democracy, and Public Life,* ed. Bruce Braun and Sarah J. Whatmore (Minneapolis: University of Minnesota Press, 2010).

36. Bennett, *Vibrant Matter,* 4.

37. Graham Harman, *Tool-Being: Heidegger and the Metaphysics of Objects* (Peru, IL: Open Court, 2002); *The Speculative Turn: Continenal Materialism and Realism,* ed. Levi Bryant, Nick Srnicek, and Graham Harman (Melbourne: re.press, 2011); Timothy Morton, *Hyperobjects: Philosophy and Ecology After the End of the World* (Minneapolis: University of Minnesota Press, 2013); Ian Bogost, *Alien Phenomenology, or What It's Like to Be a Thing* (Minneapolis: University of Minnesota Press, 2012).

38. Maurizia Boscagli, *Stuff Theory: Everyday Objects, Radical Materialism* (New York: Bloomsbury Academic, 2014), 24.

39. Charles Acland makes this statement about Benjamin in the introduction to his edited volume *Residual Media* (Minneapolis: University of Minnesota Press, 2007), xvii. Many of the essays in the volume draw on Benjamin's work to rethink the persistence of once new media artifacts.

40. *Vergänglichkeit* translates well as "transience" but also contains within it the sense of perishability and even volatility; see Sigmund Freud, "On Transience," trans. James Strachey, in *The Standard Edition of the Complete Psychological Works of Sigmund Freud,* vol. 14, *On the History of the Psycho-Analytic Movement, Papers on Metapsychology and Other Works* (London: Hogarth, 1957), 304–7.

41. Matthew von Unwerth traces this meeting and its implications in his compelling history of the composition of "On Transience" in *Freud's Requiem: Mourning, Memory, and the Invisible History of a Summer Walk* (New York: River Head, 2005).

42. In his first seminar at the École Normale Supérieure in March 1964, Lacan told an anecdote with which many readers will be familiar. He described a boat outing with fishermen. One of them pointed to an empty sardine can floating in the water, glittering in the sin. The man then said to Lacan, "You see that can [*boîte de conserve*]? Do you see it? Well it doesn't see you!" and burst out laughing (*The Four Fundamental Concepts of Psychoanalysis,* trans. Alan Sheridan [New York: Norton, 1981], 95). Lacan, quite aware that

the fisherman's comment implied that he, the bourgeois tourist, was the odd man out among a group of workers, added that, to be more precise, even if the can did not see him (*voir*), it was in fact gazing at him (*régarder*) all the time. The sardine can allegorizes the idea of an Other's gaze that frames the subject and the objects in his field of perception from the outside. But Lacan does not comment on why it is a can that condenses light and plays a central role in the story of the gaze. It is not insignificant that the can preserves the fruit of the fisherman's labor. More important though, is the fact that Lacan's attraction to the fishermen might be due to what he sees as their precarious existence under industrialization.

43. Sigmund Freud, "The Sexual Aberrations," in *The Freud Reader,* ed. Peter Gay (New York: Norton, 1989), 240.

44. Jean Laplanche and Jean-Bertrand Pontalis, *The Language of Psycho-Analysis,* trans. Donald Nicholson-Smith (New York: Norton, 1973), 273.

45. Sigmund Freud, "Mourning and Melancholia," trans. James Strachey, in *The Standard Edition,* vol. 15, *Introductory Letters on Psycho-analysis (Parts I and II* (London: Hogarth, 1957), 247.

46. Erich Heller, *The Artist's Journey into the Interior, and Other Essays* (New York: Harcourt, 1985), 103.

47. Freud, "Mourning and Melancholia," 249.

48. Freud, "On Transience," 307.

49. Freud's own collection of "the riches of civilizations" in the form of Egyptian scarabs, Roman death masks, Etruscan funeral vases, and various sculptures from antiquity has been well documented. Fuss considers the effect of these objects in Freud's Vienna office, "the exteriorized theater of Freud's own emotional history" (*Sense of an Interior,* 79).

50. This difference, it must be said, also depends upon a fictional construction. In *Freud's Requiem,* von Unwerth makes a convincing case that, if a conversation about mourning ever transpired between Freud, Rilke, and Salomé, it is unlikely that it unfolded during a walk. The countryside is likely an instance of poetic license, the proper backdrop to cast Rilke as an archromantic.

51. Leo Bersani's *The Freudian Body: Psyschoanalysis and Art* (New York: Columbia University Press, 1986) cleared the way for generations of scholars to read psychoanalytically without "doing psychoanalysis" to characters or forms.

52. Paul K. Saint-Amour, *Tense Future: Modernism, Total War, Encyclopedic Form* (New York: Oxford University Press, 2015), 7–8.

53. Henry James, *New York Revisited* (New York: Franklin Square, 1994), 34 (originally published in 1906 in *Harper's Monthly*). James laments that New York City is "crowned not only with no history, but with no credible possibility of time for history" (62).

54. Le Corbusier, *When the Cathedrals Were White,* trans. Francis Edwin Hyslop (New York: Reynal and Hitchcock, 1947), 45.

55. Michel de Certeau, *The Practice of Everyday Life,* trans. Steven Rendall (Berkeley: University of California Press, 1984), 91.

56. Alexis de Tocqueville, *Democracy in America,* vol. 2, trans. Phillips Bradley (1840; repr. New York: Vintage), 105–6.

57. See T. J. Jackson Lears, *Rebirth of a Nation: The Making of Modern America, 1877–1920* (New York: Harper Collins, 2009).

58. Theodore Dreiser, *Sister Carrie,* 146.

59. F. Scott Fitzgerald, *The Great Gatsby* (New York: Scribner, 2004), 98. Further page references will be parenthetical.

60. Walter Benjamin, *The Arcades Project,* trans. Howard Eiland and Kevin McLaughlin (Cambridge, Mass.: Harvard University Press, 1999), 462.

61. In his essay, "Marx; or, The Universal Exposition," Giorgio Agamben extrapolates this point from a reading of the guide to the Paris Exposition of 1867. The guide uses the language of enchantment and Agamben thus concludes: "At the Universal Exposition was celebrated, for the first time, the mystery that has now become familiar to anyone who has entered a supermarket or been exposed to the manipulation of an advertisement: the epiphany of the unattainable" (in Agamben, *Stanzas: Word and Phantasm in Western Culture,* trans. Ronald L. Martinez, Theory and History of Literature 69 [Minneapolis: University of Minnesota Press, 1993], 36–40, at 38).

62. Jean Baudrillard, *System of Objects,* 1.

63. Karl Marx and Friedrich Engels, "Manifesto of the Communist Party," *The Marx-Engels Reader,* ed. Robert C. Tucker (New York: Norton, 1978), 476.

64. Baudrillard, *System of Objects,* 158.

65. Baudrillard, 157.

66. Susan Strasser, *Waste and Want*; Lizabeth Cohen, *A Consumer's Republic: The Politics of Mass Consumption in Postwar America* (New York: Knopf, 2003); Ellen Ruppell Shell, *Cheap: The High Cost of Discount Culture* (New York: Penguin, 2009).

67. Fredric Jameson, *Post-modernism, or the Cultural Logic of Late Capitalism* (Durham, N.C.: Duke University Press, 1991).

68. Jameson, 309.

69. See: James F. English, *The Economy of Prestige: Prizes, Awards, and the Circulation of Cultural Value* (Cambridge, Mass.: Harvard University Press, 2008); Mark McGurl, "Everything and Less: Fiction in the Age of Amazon," *Modern Language Quarterly* 77, no. 3 (2016): 447–71; Laura B. McGrath, "Comping White," *The Los Angeles Review of Books,* January 21, 2019, lareviewofbooks.org/article/comping-white; Dan Sinykin, "How Capitalism

Changed American Literature," *Public Books,* July 17, 2019, publicbooks.org/how-capitalism-changed-american-literature/.

70. Kinohi Nishikawa, *Street Players: Black Pulp Fiction and the Making of a Literary Underground* (Chicago: University of Chicago Press, 2018).

71. Boscagli, *Stuff Theory,* 14.

72. Brown's *Other Things* begins with a meditation on Achilles's Shield, which Brown calls "Western literature's most magnificent object" (1).

73. William Butler Yeats, "Ephemera," in *The Collected Poems of W.B. Yeats,* ed. Richard J. Finneran (New York: Scribner Paperback Poetry: 1996), 15.

74. J. Paul Hunter, *Before Novels: The Cultural Contexts of Eighteenth-Century English Fiction* (New York: Norton, 1990), 58.

75. Kathleen Fitzpatrick, "The Future History of the Book: Time, Attention, Convention," in Tischleder and Wasserman, *Cultures of Obsolescence,* 111.

76. Jessica Pressman, "Jonathan Safran Foer's *Tree of Codes* : Memorial, Fetish, Bookishness," *ASAP/Journal* 3, no. 1 (January 2018): 97.

77. David Foster Wallace, "E Unibus Pluram: Telvision and U.S. Fiction," *Review of Contemporary Fiction* 13, no. 2 (Summer 1993): 166.

78. Peter Schwenger, *Tears of Things,* 1.

79. Using the term "critical futurities" to name scholarship that considers various instantiations of "the future," Saint-Amour traces a genealogy from poststructuralist literary theorists and nuclear critics to scholars studying queer temporalities (*Tense Future,* 23–30). He points to the special "Queer Temporalities" issue of *GLQ: A Journal of Lesbian and Gay Studies* 12, nos. 2–3 (2007), ed. Elisabeth Freeman, and to Lee Edelman's *No Future: Queer Theory and the Death Drive* (Durham, N.C.: Duke University Press, 2004) as key texts in imagining distinctly queer relationships to constructions of the future.

80. Walter Benn Michaels takes up the differential materialities of reading and readers in *The Shape of the Signifier: 1967 to the End of History* (Princeton, N.J.: Princeton University Press, 2007). More broadly, this divergence between "real" and "represented" objects has been the subject of many of the major theoretical movements in literary studies, including structuralism, poststructuralism and deconstruction, and phenomenology.

81. Andrew Piper, *Book Was There: Reading in Electronic Times* (Chicago: University of Chicago Press, 2012), 20.

82. Rebecca Solnit, "Whose Story (and Country) is This? On the Myth of a 'Real' America," *Literary Hub,* April 18, 2018, lithub.com/rebecca-solnit-the-myth-of-real-america-just-wont-go-away/.

83. Yetta Howard's work attests to the importance of minor sentiments and marginalized aesthetics to a feminist, queer politics; see *Ugly Differences: Queer Female Sexuality in the Underground* (Urbana: University of Illinois Press, 2018).

84. In *The Melancholy of Race* (New York: Oxford University Press, 2000), Anne Anlin Cheng astutely argues that Freud's notion of melancholia helps explain the dialectic of racial assimilation and disavowal in America: "In a sense, the racial other is in fact quite 'assimilated' into—or, more accurately, most uneasily digested by American nationality." She explains here that American melancholia is "particularly acute" because, "even as the economic, material, and philosophical advances of the nation are built on a series of legalized exclusions (of African Americans, Jewish Americans, Chinese Americans, Japanese Americans, and so on) and the labor provided by those excluded, it is also a history busily disavowing those repudiations" (10).

85. Sandy Alexandre, "'[The] Things What Happened with Our Family': Property and Inheritance in August Wilson's *The Piano Lesson*," *Modern Drama* 52, no. 1 (Spring 2009): 73–98 (Alexandre's forthcoming book, *Up From Chattels: Thinghood in an Ethics of Black Curation,* promises to offer a robust portrait of black material culture); Robin Bernstein, "Dances with Things: Material Culture and the Performance of Race," *Social Text* 27, no. 4 (2009): 67–94; Tavia Nyong'o, "Racial Kitsch and Black Performance," *The Yale Journal of Criticism* 15, no. 2 (Fall 2002): 371–91.

86. Uri McMillan, "Objecthood, Avatars, and the Limits of the Human," *GLQ: A Journal of Lesbian and Gay Studies* 21, no. 2–3 (June 2015): 224. McMillan's book *Embodied Avatars* (New York: New York University Press, 2015) develops this critique of the new materialisms and offers readings of black feminist art and performance.

87. Alexander Galloway, "History Is What Hurts: On Old Materialism," *Social Text* 34, no. 2 (2016): 129. Galloway is glossing the phrase in Fredric Jameson, *Political Unconscious: Narrative as Socially Symbolic Act* (Ithaca, N.Y.: Cornell University Press, 1982), 102.

1. YESTERDAY'S TOMORROWLAND

1. Georg Simmel, "Berliner Gewerbeaustellung," *Die Zeit,* Vienna 7, no. 91 (1896): 204, trans. in full by Sam Whimster in *Theory, Culture & Society* 8, no. 3 (1991): 119.

2. For more on the history of the Berlin exhibition and the role that it played in shaping Simmel's theories of urban life, see Dorothy Rowe, "Georg Simmel and the Berlin Trade Exhibition of 1896," *Urban History* 22, no. 2 (1995): 216–28.

3. Benjamin, *Arcades Project,* 184, 189.

4. See James Gilbert, *Perfect Cities: Chicago's Utopias of 1893* (Chicago: University of Chicago Press, 1991).

5. Bill Cotter, *The 1984 New Orleans World's Fair* (Charleston, S.C.: Arcadia, 2008).

6. John Pickles, *A History of Spaces: Cartographic Reason, Mapping, and the Geo-coded World* (New York: Routledge, 2004), 138.

7. Bill Brown, *Sense of Things*, 35.

8. Burton Benedict, quoted in *Fair America: World's Fairs in the United States*, ed. Robert W. Rydell, John E. Findling, and Kimberly D. Pelle (Washington, D.C.: Smithsonian Insitution, 2000), 6.

9. The number of publications on world's fairs is staggering. The range of topics is equally vast: readers can find biographies of the fairs' creators, studies of particular objects and technologies displayed at the fairs, and monographs about the fairs' imperial dimensions. Some of the most important cultural histories include Neil Harris, *Cultural Excursions: Marketing Appetites and Cultural Tastes in Modern America* (Chicago: University of Chicago Press, 1990), and Robert Rydell, *All the World's a Fair: Visions of Empire at American International Expositions* (Chicago, University of Chicago Press, 1984), as well as the volume *Fair Representations: World's Fairs and the Modern World*, ed. Robert Rydell and Nancy Gwinn (Amsterdam: VU University Press, 1994). A key text in postcolonial studies, Timothy Mitchell's *Colonising Egypt* (Berkeley: University of California Press, 1991) offers an incisive reading of the way fairs were used to negotiate Europe's colonial encounter with nineteenth-century Egypt.

10. Quoted in Charles Moore, *The Life and Times of Charles Follen McKim* (Cambridge, Mass.: Da Capo, 1970), 126.

11. Hjalmar Hjorth Boyensen, "A New World Fable," *The Cosmopolitan*, 16, no. 2 (December 1893).

12. Gilbert, *Perfect Cities*, 85. Gilbert discusses the importance of the White City's whiteness, the pristine façade that alluded not only to a scrupulously clean city but also to one "scrubbed" of its ethnic and racial character.

13. Ida B. Wells, *The Reason Why the Colored American Is Not in the World's Columbian Exposition: The Afro-American's Contribution to Columbian Literature*, ed. Frederick Douglass (1893), ed. Robert W. Rydell (Urbana: University of Illinois Press, 1999), i.

14. Robert Herrick, *The Web of Life* (New York: Grosset & Dunlap, 1900), 135.

15. In 1925, Fitzgerald writes in *The Great Gatsby*: "About halfway between West Egg and New York the motor road hastily joins the railroad and runs beside it for a quarter of a mile, so as to shrink away from a certain desolate area of land. This is a valley of ashes   a fantastic farm where ashes grow like wheat into ridges and hills and grotesque gardens; where ashes take the forms of houses and chimneys and rising smoke and, finally, with a transcendent effort, of ash-grey men who move dimly and already crumbling through the powdery air" (24). It seems that the fair's planners understood their chosen site as, once again in Fitzgerald's words, "a solemn dumping ground," and

therefore envisioned their transformation as all the more potent. For more on this point, see chapter 1 of Bill Cotter's *The 1939–1940 New York World's Fair* (Chicago: Arcadia, 2009).

16. H. G. Wells, "World of Tomorrow," *The New York Times,* March 5, 1939, 4 (emphases mine).

17. Marshall Bruce Gentry, "The First Three Full-Length Studies of E. L. Doctorow," *Modern Language Studies* 22, no. 3 (1992): 112. Gentry reviews Carol Harter's and James Thompson's *E. L. Doctorow* (1990), John Parks's *E. L. Doctorow* (1991), and Christopher Morris's *Models of Misrepresentations: On the Fiction of E. L. Doctorow* (1991). All published during the first years of the 1990s, when Doctorow had reached the height of critical attention, the three books indeed classify Doctorow as a postmodern writer, invested in historiographic critique and formal experimentation.

18. Michael Robertson, "Cultural Hegemony Goes to the Fair: The Case of E. L. Doctorow's *World's Fair,*" *American Studies* 33, no. 1 (1992): 32.

19. Bruce Weber, "The Myth Maker: The Creative Mind of Novelist E. L. Doctorow," *The New York Times Magazine,* October 20, 1985, 76; Alvin P. Sanoff, "A Conversation with E. L. Doctorow: 'Writing Is Often a Desperate Act,'" *U.S. News and World Report,* December 16, 1985, 73.

20. Anne Tyler, from the back cover of E. L. Doctorow's *World's Fair* (New York: Random House, 1985). Further citations of Doctorow's novel refer to this edition and are included parenthetically within the text.

21. Harris, *Cultural Excursions,* 116.

22. For more on the midways and the way they were explicitly racialized, see Gilbert's *Perfect Cities* and Harris's *Cultural Excursions.*

23. Quoted in Cotter, *1939–1940 New York World's Fair,* 101.

24. Richard Powers, *Prisoner's Dilemma* (New York: Harper Collins, 1988), 43.

25. Robertson discusses the contrast between Edgar's fictional essay and Roberts's real one in "Cultural Hegemony Goes to the Fair."

26. Westinghouse Electric Corporation, *Book of Record of the Time Capsule of Cupaloy: Deemed Capable of Resisting the Effects of Time for Five Thousand Years, Preserving an Account of Universal Achievements, Embedded in the Grounds of the New York World's Fair, 1939* (Utica, N.Y.: G. Leonard Gold, 1938), 18.

27. Saint-Amour, *Tense Future,* 181.

28. Westinghouse Electric Corporation, *Book of Record,* 49.

29. Westinghouse Electric Corporation, 17.

30. Westinghouse Electric Corporation, 17.

31. James Mauro, *Twilight at the World of Tomorrow: Genius, Madness, Murder, and the 1939 World's Fair on the Brink of War* (New York: Ballantine, 2010), 346.

32. Michael Chabon, *The Amazing Adventures of Kavalier and Clay* (New York: Picador, 2000), 15. Further references are to this edition and will be included parenthetically.

33. Hillary Chute, "*Ragtime, Kavalier and Clay,* And the Framing of Comics," *Modern Fiction Studies* 2, no. 54 (2008): 280.

34. Andrew Hoberek, *Considering Watchmen: Poetics, Property, Politics* (New Brunswick, N.J.: Rutgers University Press, 2014), 163.

35. Chute, "*Ragtime, Kavalier and Clay,* And the Framing of Comics," 282.

36. The New York Public Library, "Biblion: The Boundless Library," video, 2:57, May 16, 2011, youtube.com/watch?v=vNlxyLLNi1g.

37. Saint-Amour, *Tense Future,* 31.

38. Fredric Jameson, "Progress versus Utopia, or Can We Imagine the Future?" in *Archaeologies of the Future* (New York: Verso, 2005), 286.

39. Michael Sahlins, "Infrastructuralism," *Critical Inquiry* 36, no. 3 (2010): 374.

2. COUNTERHISTORY, COUNTERFACT, COUNTEROBJECT

1. Catherine Gallagher, *Telling It Like It Wasn't: The Counterfactual Imagination in History and Fiction* (Chicago: University of Chicago Press, 2018). Distinguishing the genre from "the historical counterfactual" and "alternate history," Gallagher defines the alternate-history novel as a fiction that "invents not only alternative-historical trajectories but also fictional characters" (3).

2. Brown, *Sense of Things;* Freedgood, *Ideas in Things;* Plotz, *Portable Property;* Mullins, *Postmodernism in Pieces.*

3. Gallagher, *Telling It Like It Wasn't,* 52.

4. Baudrillard, *System of Objects,* 93.

5. Catherine Gallagher, "War, Counterfactual History, and Alternate-History Novels," *Field Day Review* 3 (2007): 58.

6. Judith Thurman, "Philip Roth E-Mails On Trump," *The New Yorker,* January 30, 2017, newyorker.com/magazine/2017/01/30/philip-roth-e-mails-on-trump.

7. Philip Roth, "The Story Behind *The Plot Against America,*" *The New York Times,* September 19, 2004, nytimes.com/2004/09/19/books/review/19ROTHL.html.

8. See Elyse Wanshel. "Trump Supporters Thought a Fake Station Called 'Resistance Radio' Was Real," *The Huffington Post,* March 13, 2017, huffingtonpost.com/entry/trump-supporters-fake-station-resistance-radio-real-amazon-man-in-the-high-castle_us_58c6ebcce4b0428c7f122cf8.

9. Catherine Gallagher, Mark Maslan, Paul K. Saint-Amour, "Forum: Counterfactual Realities," *Representations* 98, no. 1 (2007): 51.

10. Quentin Meillassoux, *After Finitude: An Essay on the Necessity of Contingency* (New York: Continuum, 2008).

11. Meillassoux, 90.

12. Ursula K. Le Guin, "Introduction," in *The Left Hand of Darkness* (New York: Penguin Random House, 1976), ii.

13. Jameson, *Archaeologies*, 381.

14. To name just a few of the many book-length studies of Dick that are not cited elsewhere in this chapter, see: Kyle Arnold, *The Divine Madness of Philip K. Dick* (New York: Oxford University Press, 2016); Andrew M. Butler, *Philip K. Dick* (Chicago: Pocket Essentials, 2000); Douglas Mackey, *Philip K. Dick* (Boston: Twayne, 1988); Christopher Palmer, *Philip K. Dick: Exhilaration and Terror of the Postmodern* (Liverpool: Liverpool University Press, 2003); Kim Stanley Robinson, *The Novels of Philip K. Dick* (Ann Arbor: University of Michigan Research Press, 1989).

15. See Eric Carl Link, *Understanding Philip K. Dick* (Columbia: University of South Carolina Press, 2010).

16. Jameson, *Archaeologies*, 345.

17. Brown, *Other Things*, 148.

18. Skinner Auctioneers and Appraisers, skinnerinc.com/specialty-areas/antique-books/ephemera-auction.

19. Philip K. Dick, *The Man in the High Castle* (1962; repr. New York: Penguin Classics, 2001), 10. Further references are to this edition and will be cited parenthetically in text.

20. Racialized anxiety about Japanese powers of imitation continue today. See Tom Downey, "How Japan Copied American Culture and Made it Better," *Smithsonian Magazine*, April 2014, smithsonianmag.com/travel/how-japan-copied-american-culture-and-made-it-better-180950189/.

21. Cassie Carter, "The Metacolonization of Dick's *The Man in the High Castle:* Mimicry, Parasitism, and Americanism in the PSA," *Science Fiction Studies* 22 (1995): 333.

22. See Dave Jamieson, *Mint Condition: How Baseball Cards Became an American Obsession* (New York: Atlantic Monthly Press, 2010). Gum Inc., later known as the Bowman Gum Company and eventually purchased by Topps Chewing Gum, was once the leading producer of baseball cards. In 1929, Gum Inc.'s "Blony Bubble Gum" was the top-selling penny bubblegum in the United States.

23. Umberto Eco, *Travels in Hyperreality* (New York: Harcourt, 1986), 8.

24. Jameson, *Archaeologies*, 378; Brown, *Other Things*, 146.

25. Although the novel does not mention it, the title of Abendsen's novel references Ecclesiastes, the biblical book that characterizes all human actions as fleeting. In Ecclesiastes, readers are urged to remember God and repent

throughout their lives, not only in their later years. Those later years, when death looms imminent, are described metaphorically: "Also when they shall be afraid of that which is high, and fears shall be in the way, and the almond trees shall flourish, and the grasshopper shall be a burden, and desire shall fail: because man goeth to his long home, and the mourners go about the streets" (Eccles. 12:5, AV). When even the grasshopper is a burden—when it lies heavy—only then do humans perceive the transience of the world they have built.

26. Paul K. Saint-Amour, "Counterfactual States of America: On Parallel Worlds and Longing for the Law," *Post45*, September 20, 2011, post45.research.yale.edu/2011/09/counterfactual-states-of-america-on-parallel-worlds-and-longing-for-the-law/.

27. See, for example, Patricia S. Warrick, *Mind in Motion: The Fiction of Philip K. Dick* (Carbondale: Southern Illinois University Press, 1987), and Paul William's essay in the November 6, 1975, issue of *Rolling Stone*, "The Most Brilliant Sci-Fi Mind of Any Planet: Philip K. Dick." Also, in his introduction to the 1979 edition of *Man in the High Castle*, (Boston: Gregg, 1979), Joseph Milicia cites personal correspondence from Dick where he states that he "used the *I Ching* only when one of the characters made use of it, which in effect meant I used it for plot developments" (vii).

28. N. B. (Katherine) Hayles, "Metaphysics and Metafiction in *The Man in the High Castle*," in *Writers of the 21st Century: Philip K. Dick*, ed. Martin Harry Greenberg and Joseph D. Oleander (New York: Taplinger, 1983), 67.

29. The *I Ching* or "Yì Jīng," also known as the *Classic of Changes, Book of Changes* and *Zhouyi*, is one of the oldest of the Chinese classic texts. The book contains a divination system comparable to Western geomancy; in Western cultures and modern East Asia, it is still widely used for this purpose. The text of the I Ching is a set of oracular statements represented by sixty-four sets of six lines each called hexagrams. For an engaging, contemporary interpretation of the *I Ching*, see Jack M. Balkin's *The Laws of Change: I Ching and the Philosophy of Life* (New York: Schocken Books, 2002). When asked in an interview if he used the *I Ching* as a plotting device, Dick replied: "I used it in *The Man in the High Castle* because a number of characters used it. In each case when they asked a question, I threw the coins and wrote the hexagram lines they got. That governed the direction of the book. Like in the end when Juliana Frink is deciding whether or not to tell Hawthorne Abendsen that he is the target of assassins, the answer indicated that she should. Now if it had said not to tell him, I would have had her not go there. But I would not do that in any other book" (Arthur Byron Cover, "Vertex Interview with Philip K. Dick," *Vertex* 1, no. 6 [February 1974], accessed February 28, 2020, philipkdickfans.com/literary-criticism/frank-views-archive/vertex-interview-with-philip-k-dick/). This

comment makes it seem that where Philip Roth makes one change (Lindbergh's election) that alters history, Dick abdicates narrative agency and allows the plot to unfold counterfactually at every turn.

30. For more on this, see "The Fictions of Nazi Britain" in Gallagher, *Telling It Like It Wasn't.*

31. Robinson, *Novels of Philip K. Dick,* 170.

32. Nathan Englander, "What We Talk about When We Talk about Anne Frank," *The New Yorker,* December 12, 2011, newyorker.com/magazine/2011/12/12/what-we-talk-about-when-we-talk-about-anne-frank.

33. There are too many texts on this topic to name. A few foundational works include Alan Cooper, *Philip Roth and the Jews* (Albany: State University of New York Press, 1996), Ross Posnock, *Philip Roth's Rude Truth: The Art of Immaturity* (Princeton, N.J.: Princeton University Press, 2006), and three chapters in *The Cambridge Companion to Philip Roth,* ed. Timothy Parrish (New York: Cambridge University Press, 2007): Victoria Aarons, "American-Jewish Identity in Roth's Short Fiction"; Michael Rothberg, "Roth and the Holocaust"; Timothy Parrish, "Roth and Ethnic Identity."

34. Hana Wirth-Nesher, "Roth's Autobiographical Writings," in Parrish, *Cambridge Companion to Philip Roth,* 167.

35. Timothy Parrish, "Review of *The Plot Against America,*" *Philip Roth Studies* 1, no. 1 (2005): 95.

36. Roth, "The Story Behind *The Plot Against America.*"

37. Philip Roth, *The Plot Against America* (New York: Random House, 2004), 1. Further references are to this edition and will be cited parenthetically in the text.

38. Stewart, *On Longing,* 154.

39. Debra Shostak, *Philip Roth: Countertexts, Counterlives* (Columbia: University of South Carolina Press, 2004), 170.

40. Although Einstein is the first Jewish person to be pictured alone on a U.S. postage stamp, the "Four Chaplains" stamp issued in 1948 featured four U.S. Army chaplains who died saving other civilian and military personnel as the troop ship SS *Dorchester* sank on February 3, 1943, during World War II. Among them is Rabbi and Lieutenant Alexander D. Goode (see fourchaplains.org).

41. Walter Benn Michaels, "Plots Against America: Neoliberalism and Antiracism," *American Literary History* 18, no. 2 (2006): 288.

42. Michaels, 289. In his essay "Ralph Ellison: The Invisible Man in Philip Roth's *The Human Stain,*" Timothy Parrish considers how, in the 2000 novel, Roth reflects on his (literary) relationship to Ralph Ellison and offers a critique of American multiculturalism (*Contemporary Literature* 45, no. 3 [2004]: 421–59).

43. The "Inverted Jenny" remains a coveted stamp for collectors. A single

Inverted Jenny was sold at a Robert A. Siegel auction in November 2007 for $977,500 ("Sale 946a: The 1918 24¢ Inverted 'Jenny,'" Robert A. Siegel Auction Galleries, siegelauctions.com/2007/946a/s946a.htm). For the full story of the stamp, see George Amick, *The Inverted Jenny: Mystery, Money, Mania* (Sidney, Ohio: Amos Press, 1987).

44. Gilles Auliard, "Maiden of the Skies," *Air Classics* 45, no. 4 (2009): 44.

45. Curiously enough, in 2001, for the centenary of the inverts issue, the U.S. Postal Service produced a souvenir sheet that contained reproductions of the three original inverts, along with four eighty-cent stamps based on a souvenir stamp circulated at the original Pan-American Exposition (see mysticstamp.com/Products/United-States/C3/USA/).

46. Non-denominated postage was first issued in the United States in 1975, when there was uncertainty as to the timing and extent of a rate increase for first-class postage as the end of the year approached. In 2007, the U.S. Postal Service introduced the "forever stamp," which depicts the Liberty Bell and is marked "USA First-Class Forever." In an instance of (unintentional) irony, in 2012, the U.S. Postal Service released a forever stamp featuring an image of Alaska's Bear Glacier, one of the fastest shrinking glaciers in the world (Joe Romm, "Irony Alert: Postal Service's New 'Forever' Stamp Is Shrinking Alaskan Glacier!," *ThinkProgress,* October 1, 2012, thinkprogress.org/irony-alert-postal-services-new-forever-stamp-is-shrinking-alaskan-glacier-3a14d4793165/).

47. Jason Siegel, "*The Plot Against America:* Philip Roth's Counter-Plot to American History," *MELUS* 37, no. 1 (2012): 147.

48. Saint-Amour, "Counterfactual States of America."

49. Jean Baudrillard, "The System of Collecting," trans. Roger Cardinal, in *The Cultures of Collecting,* ed. John Elsner and Roger Cardinal (Cambridge, Mass.: Harvard University Press, 1994), 17.

50. See Susan Stewart's discussion of the collection as a means of private containment in *On Longing.*

3. ZONED OUT

1. James Baldwin, "The Harlem Ghetto," in *Notes of a Native Son,* repr. in *James Baldwin: Collected Essays,* ed. Toni Morrison (New York: The Library of America, 1998), 42.

2. Baldwin, 42.

3. James Baldwin, "Fifth Avenue, Uptown" in *Nobody Knows My Name,* repr. in *Collected Essays,* 170.

4. Baldwin, 170.

5. Ann Petry's *The Street* (1946) considers the changing landscape of Harlem during the Second World War. Petry's depiction of the tenement on

116th Street in Harlem where Lutie, the novel's protagonist, lives attests to the sexism and racism built into the urban environment. Rather than an emblem of both persistence and change, however, the building comes to represent a trap that Lutie must ultimately flee. Unlike Ellison's and Himes's male protagonists, who have some mobility within Harlem, Petry stresses that Lutie must endure the burden of poverty and the threat of sexual violence as long as she remains there.

6. Recent novels of gentrification set in New York include Paul Auster's *The Brooklyn Follies* (2005), Kitty Florey's *Solos* (2015), Jonathan Lethem's *Motherless Brooklyn* (2000), Joanna Rakoff's *A Fortunate Age* (2010), and Amy Sohn's *Prospect Park West* (2009).

7. At the risk of reducing complex scholarship on urban life to two oversimplified poles, I would suggest that scholars such as David Harvey and Lewis Mumford focus on structural change while Michel de Certeau and Kevin Lynch consider urban structure from the city-dweller perspective.

8. If structural thinking entails an awareness of historical conditions (the legacy of slavery that shapes race relations today or the system of capitalism that determines the means of production and the constitution of labor forces), while "structure" usually names the physical environment, as in "Manhattan," then infrastructure is a scaled-down instantiation of those structural relations.

9. For an account of urban renewal programs in the twentieth century, see Christopher Klemek's 2011 *The Transatlantic Collapse of Urban Renewal.* As Justin Gifford notes in his work on Himes in *Pimping Fictions: African American Crime Literature and the Untold Story of Black Pulp Publishing* (Philadelphia: Temple University Press, 2013), one of the most famous agents of urban renewal, Robert Moses, spearheaded racially divisive redevelopment in New York between 1930 and 1970 (36).

10. Myka Tucker-Abramson, *Novel Shocks: Urban Renewal and the Origins of Neoliberalism* (New York: Fordham University Press, 2018), 6

11. James Baldwin, *Conversations with James Baldwin,* ed. Fred L. Standley and Louis H. Pratt (Jackson, Miss.: University Press of Mississippi, 1989), 42.

12. See Glass's introduction in *London: Aspects of Change,* ed. Ruth Glass (London: MacGibbon and Kee, 1964). Glass studied London's working-class neighborhoods. She meant "gentrification" to evoke the British social class of the "landed gentry."

13. Jane Jacobs, *Dark Age Ahead* (New York: Vintage, 2004), 214.

14. In urban studies, infrastructure has been considered from a number of perspectives by scholars including Neil Brenner, David Harvey, and Michael Porter.

15. Caroline Levine, "'The Strange Familiar': Structure, Infrastructure, and Adichie's *Americanah,*" *MFS Modern Fiction Studies* 61, no. 4 (2015): 588.

16. Kate Marshall, *Corridor: Media Architectures in American Fiction* (Minneapolis: University of Minnesota Press, 2013), 28–29.

17. Samuel Delany, *Times Square Red, Times Square Blue* (New York: New York University Press, 1999), 144.

18. Delany, 162.

19. In March 1925, the magazine *Survey Graphic* published an issue entitled *Harlem: Mecca of the New Negro,* guest-edited by Alain Locke. Much of the material from the issue appears in Locke's 1925 anthology *The New Negro.* See Seth Scheiner's 1965 *Negro Mecca: A History of the Negro in New York City, 1865–1920* and Sharifa Rhodes-Pitt's 2011 *Harlem Is Nowhere: A Journey to the Mecca of Black America.*

20. James Weldon Johnson, *Black Manhattan* (New York: Atheneum, 1968), 3. Neither Johnson nor Blair discusses Spanish Harlem, the area north of the Upper East Side that has its own complex history of racial and ethnic settlement and displacement.

21. Sara Blair, *Harlem Crossroads: Black Writers and the Photograph in the Twentieth Century* (Princeton, N.J.: Princeton University Press, 2007), 8.

22. Johnson, *Black Manhattan,* 4.

23. Myka Tucker-Abramson, "Blueprints: *Invisible Man* and the Housing Act of 1949," *American Studies* 54, no. 3 (2015): 16.

24. Christopher Breu, "Freudian Knot or Gordian Knot?: The Contradictions of Racialized Masculinity in Chester Himes' *If He Hollers Let Him Go,*" *Callaloo* 26, no. 3 (2003): 767.

25. Clare Rolens, "Write Like a Man: Chester Himes and the Criminal Text Beyond Bars," *Callaloo* 37, no. 2 (2014): 432.

26. Lawrence P. Jackson, *Chester B. Himes: A Biography* (New York: Norton, 2017), 377.

27. Ralph Ellison, "Harlem Is Nowhere," in *The Collected Essays of Ralph Ellison,* ed. John F. Callahan (New York: Random House, 2003), 322.

28. Chester Himes, *My Life of Absurdity: The Autobiography of Chester Himes, Volume II* (New York: Doubleday, 1976), 109.

29. Eve Dunbar, *Black Regions of the Imagination: African American Writers Between the Nation and the World* (Philadelphia: Temple University Press, 2013), 135, 129.

30. Michael Denning, "Topographies of Violence: Chester Himes's Harlem Detective Novels," in *The Critical Response to Chester Himes,* ed. Charles L. P. Silet (Westport, Conn.: Greenwood, 1999), 157.

31. As Dunbar discusses in *Black Regions of the Imagination* (153–71), a ninth, unpublished novel entitled *Plan B* was to have been the final novel of the Harlem Cycle. In 1967, Himes wrote to a friend that, in the novel, he planned to kill off Coffin Ed Johnson and Grave Digger Jones. The novel remained unfinished when Himes died in 1984 but was finally published in

1993. Dunbar reads the novel in the context of black nationalism and argues that the detectives' incompatibility with the politics of the 1960s and 1970s necessitated their erasure.

32. Raymond Nelson, "Domestic Harlem: The Detective Fiction on Chester Himes," in Silet, *Critical Response to Chester Himes*, 54.

33. Chester Himes, *The Real Cool Killers* (New York: Random House, 1988), 5.

34. Thomas Heise, "Harlem Is Burning: Urban Rioting and the 'Black Underclass' in Chester Himes's *Blind Man with a Pistol*," *African American Review* 41, no. 3 (2007): 493.

35. Chester Himes, *Blind Man with a Pistol* (New York: Random House, 1989), 19–20.

36. Himes, 21.

37. Himes, 57.

38. Himes, 7.

39. Although it is beyond the scope of this chapter, Himes's 1960 *Run Man Run* features a murder weapon that is similar to the Colt .44 that Tagomi uses in *Man in the High Castle*. A corrupt white police officer, Walker, can't use his service weapon to commit crime, so he instead uses a pistol with a silencer poached from "the homicide museum." Walker says the gun is "the rod Baby Face killed Jew Mike with." (*Run Man Run* [1960; repr. New York: Carroll & Graf, 1995], 188). The backstory calls up America's history of organized crime and ethnic hatred. Most striking, though, is the plausible detail that the gun was on display in a museum: like the Colt .44, the pistol is an artifact of violent history and of America's fascination with it. Walker's gun, like Tagomi's, is awakened from a historical slumber and put to use in murders that scrambles the myths attached to the weapon.

40. Chester Himes, *A Rage in Harlem* (1957; repr. New York: Random House, 1991), 90–1.

41. Jonathan P. Eburne, *Surrealism and the Art of Crime* (Ithaca, N.Y.: Cornell University Press, 2008), 264.

42. Himes, *A Rage in Harlem*, 109.

43. Ralph Ellison, *Invisible Man* (1952; repr. New York: Penguin Classics, 2001), 158–59. Further references are to this edition and will be cited parenthetically in text.

44. One exception is Tucker-Abramson, who argues that the blueprints are a key to reading *Invisible Man* as a novel whose context and form is shaped by postwar urban planning ("Blueprints: *Invisible Man* and the Housing Act of 1949"). In *Wrestling with the Left* (Durham, N.C.: Duke University Press, 2010), Barbara Foley also considers the blueprints and suggests that they allegorize the utter disregard or disposal of American democracy.

45. Brown, *Other Things*, 266.

46. Julia Sun-Joo Lee, "Knuckelbones and Knocking-Bones: The Accidental Trickster in Ellison's *Invisible Man*," *African American Review* 40, no. 3 (2006): 470.

47. According to Lukács, novelists *narrate* when they present a world in flux, riven by forces of change, change in which the novelist and the narrator have a vested interest. Narration is therefore committed to action, interior or external. By contrast, novelists *describe* when they enumerate the details of a world in which those details ultimately are mere backdrop or setting, absent the kind of meaning that they would have in narration. György Lukács, "Narrate or Describe?" in *Writer and Critic and Other Essays*, ed. and trans. Arthur Kahn (London: Merlin Press, 1970), 131. Ellison frustrates this distinction because Harlem is both setting and source of action; gentrification entails the stasis of social conditions and the change of the built environment.

48. Blair, *Harlem Crossroads*, 140.

49. Thomas Heise, *Urban Underworlds: A Geography of Twentieth-Century American Literature and Culture* (New Brunswick, N.J.: Rutgers University Press, 2010), 157.

50. Himes, *Blind Man with a Pistol*, 187.

51. Himes, 187.

52. Himes, 187.

53. For more on the novel's riot scenes in relation to Ellison's reporting of the riots, see Foley's *Wrestling with the Left*, in which she discusses the specific ways in which Ellison's rewriting of historical events in *Invisible Man* critiques the left for its inadequate understanding of Marxism.

54. Robert B. Stepto, "Literacy and Hibernation: Ralph Ellison's *Invisible Man*," in *Speaking For You: The Vision of Ralph Ellison*, ed. Kimberly W. Benston (Washington, D.C.: Howard University Press, 1987), 387.

55. See, for instance, Heise: "The invisible man's plunge into the underground removes him from history and from the surface, where history is being made on the streets" (*Urban Underworlds*, 161). Foley, on the other hand, notes that "the narrator's marijuana-scented den is haunted by history—not only the suppressed history of slavery and abolition, . . . but also the currents roiling the aboveground world where a 'socially responsible role' (581) awaits him when he chooses to return" (*Wrestling with the Left*, 326).

56. For one example, see John S. Wright's essay "Ellison's Experimental Attitude and the Technologies of Illumination," in which he writes that *Invisible Man* is uniquely concerned with "the immediate effects of the technological environment on the human imagination and spirit, and on the blurring line between reality and illusion, the natural and the artificial" (*The*

Cambridge Companion to Ralph Ellison, ed. Ross Posnock [New York: Cambridge University Press, 2005], 163).

57. Kate Marshall, *Corridor: Media Architectures in American Fiction* (Minneapolis: University of Minnesota Press, 2013), 80–81.

58. Canadian artist Jeff Wall's well-known staged photograph "After *Invisible Man* by Ralph Ellison, the Prologue" also enforces this point that the narrator's hidden space is deeply imbricated in the city's infrastructure. In the image, Wall has materialized the narrator's description of 1,369 light bulbs. The photograph reminds viewers, to put it very simply, that this is an astonishing number of bulbs, and thus a massive amount of electricity.

59. Himes, *Blind Man with a Pistol,* 97.

60. Science fiction has become a major area of study, in particular for scholars interested in "Afrofuturism," a term first used in print by Mark Dery in 1994. In *Speculative Blackness: The Future of Race in Science Fiction* (Minneapolis: University of Minnesota Press, 2016), andré m. carrington argues that both histories of genre and medium and histories of enslavement often animate the future visions of science fiction. Arguments for the renewed significance of genre to the study of twentieth-century and contemporary fiction are set forth by Jeremy Rosen in *Minor Characters Have Their Day* (2016) and Theodore Martin in *Contemporary Drift* (2017).

4. TIME, STAMPED

1. In his biography of Himes, Lawrence Jackson details Chester and Jean Himes's move in 1941 to Los Angeles, "a West Coast metropolis that was a migrant's beacon but becoming increasingly like the American South" (*Chester B. Himes,* 147). Jackson chronicles Himes's efforts at publication in L.A. and his interactions with Hollywood screenwriters and the black literati, including Zora Neale Hurston.

2. Chester Himes, *The Quality of Hurt: The Autobiography of Chester Himes* (Garden City, N.Y.: Doubleday, 1972), 73–74.

3. Thomas Pynchon, "A Journey Into the Mind of Watts," *New York Times,* June 12, 1966, nytimes.com/books/97/05/18/reviews/pynchon-watts.html.

4. Pynchon.

5. Pynchon.

6. Pynchon.

7. Pynchon.

8. See Norman M. Klein, *The History of Forgetting: Los Angeles and the Erasure of Memory* (New York: Verso, 1997; repr. 2008). In his extensive survey of literary treatments of Los Angeles, *Imagining Los Angeles: A City in Fiction* (Reno: University of Nevada Press, 2000), David Fine remarks that

fiction about the city often plays "at times obsessively on themes of unreality, masquerade, and deception" (16). Fine charts a long lineage of L.A. writers, from Upton Sinclair and Nathanael West to Norman Mailer, Joan Didion, and Walter Mosley, detailing the city's role in dystopic fictions, noir novels, and stories of racial conflict.

9. California serves as the backdrop for the three Pynchon novels that make up what Brian McHale ("Pynchon's Postmodernism," in *The Cambridge Companion to Thomas Pynchon,* ed. Inger H. Dalsgaard, Luc Herman, and Brian McHale [New York: Cambridge University Press, 2012]) calls Pynchon's accidental trilogy: *The Crying of Lot 49* (1966), *Vineland* (1990), and *Inherent Vice* (2009; adapted for the screen in 2014).

10. McHale, 97.

11. Hanjo Berressem, "Coda: How to read Pynchon," in Dalsgaard, Herman, and McHale, *Cambridge Companion to Thomas Pynchon,* 170.

12. See Inger H. Dalsgaard, "Science and Technology," in Dalsgaard, Herman, and McHale, *Cambridge Companion to Thomas Pynchon,* 156–67.

13. Amy J. Elias, "History," in Dalsgaard, Herman, and McHale, *Cambridge Companion to Thomas Pynchon,* 123–35.

14. David J. Alworth, *Site Reading* (Princeton, N.J.: Princeton University Press, 2015), 113.

15. Mark Greif, *The Age of the Crisis of Man: Thought and Fiction in America, 1933–1973* (Princeton, N.J.: Princeton University Press, 2015), 229–30.

16. In their efforts to define and delineate contemporary literature, several scholars have insisted that recent novels take a stance toward history that is decidedly unlike that of postmodern writers. Alexander Manshel argues that, while the recent historical novel takes catastrophe seriously and sincerely, disaster is cause for "Pynchon's jest" ("The Rise of the Recent Historical Novel," Post45, September 29, 2017 post45.research.yale.edu/2017/09/the-rise-of-the-recent-historical-novel/). Similarly, Amy Elias has claimed that the longing for the past—the knowledge and truth that we might gain from history—cannot be taken seriously by postmodern writers (*Sublime Desire* [Baltimore, Md.: Johns Hopkins University Press, 2001], 22–23).

17. Fredric Jameson, *A Singular Modernity* (New York: Verso, 2012), 123.

18. Thomas Pynchon, *V.* (New York: Harper, 1961), 1. Further citations are to this edition and will be included parenthetically in the text.

19. The Yiddish term comes from the 1814 German text *Peter Schlemihl's Remarkable Story* by Adelbert Von Chamisso. The *Faust*-like fairytale follows the titular character who sells his shadow to the devil without realizing that this loss will cause him unexpected difficulties. He refuses to restore the shadow in exchange for his soul and instead wanders the world searching for the peace of mind he never reclaims. The novel is often interpreted as an allegory of

Chamisso's own fate as a French-born exile in Germany. Certainly the term allegorizes Benny's wanderings as well, but it also resonates with Pynchon's sustained interest in Jewishness as a marker of high European culture *and* of profound victimhood in the wake of the Holocaust. The Levi's are of a piece with this interest, invoking the Jewish German American businessman Levi Strauss who founded the jeans company in California. Though scholarly examinations of Pynchon's interest in Judaism (or, more precisely, in Jewishness) mostly focus on *Bleeding Edge,* some earlier criticism addresses his representation of the Holocaust. See, for instance, Amy J. Elias, "Paranoia, Theology, and Inductive Style," *Soundings* 86, no. 3/4 (2003): 281–313, for a consideration of how Pynchon's theological interests relate to his paranoid postmodernism, see Katalin Orban, *Ethical Diversions: The Post-Holocaust Narratives of Pynchon, Abish, DeLillo, and Spiegelman* (New York: Routledge, 2013).

20. Lacan, *Four Fundamental Concepts,* 222.

21. Anne Anlin Cheng, "Shine: On Race, Glamour, and the Modern," *PMLA* 126, no. 4 (2011): 1022–41.

22. Katherine Behar, "An Introduction to OOF," in *Object-Oriented Feminism,* ed. Katherine Behar (Minneapolis: University of Minnesota Press, 2016), 3.

23. Sigmund Freud, "Fetishism," in *Sexuality and the Psychology of Love,* ed. Philip Rieff (New York: Simon & Schuster, 1997), 206. This notion that the fetish congeals and conceals human values is also true of the Marxist fetish. Rachel's relationship with her car is symptomatic of a culture enamored with the products of its alienated labor (the car is available as a sexual fetish because it already is a fetish in the Marxist sense).

24. Jacques Lacan, *Le Séminaire,* vol. 4, *La relation d'objet, 1956–57,* ed. Jacques-Alain Miller (Paris: Seuil, 1991), 154 (translation mine).

25. Linda Hutcheon, "Historiographic Metafiction: Parody and the Intertextuality of History," in *Intertextuality and Contemporary American Fiction,* ed. P. O'Donnell and Robert Con Davis (Baltimore, Md.: Johns Hopkins University Press), 5.

26. Luc Herman, "Early Pynchon," in Dalsgaard, Herman, and McHale, *Cambridge Companion to Thomas Pynchon,* 24.

27. Thomas Pynchon, *The Crying of Lot 49* (London: Vintage, 2000), 10. Further references are to this edition and will be included parenthetically in the text.

28. See Stefan Mattessich, *Lines of Flight: Discursive Time and Countercultural Desire in the Work of Thomas Pynchon* (Durham. N.C.: Duke University Press, 2002). For a discussion of Pynchon's own encounters with Varo's paintings, see David Cowart, "Pynchon's *The Crying of Lot 49* and the Paintings of Remdios Varo," *Critique* 18, no. 3 (1977): 19–26.

29. Roger Bellin, "Pynchon's Dustbin of History: Collecting, Collectivity,

and Care for the Past," *Amerikastudien / American Studies* 57, no. 2 (2012): 292.

30. Greif, *Age of the Crisis of Man,* 230.

31. See, for instance, Edward Mendelson, "The Sacred, the Profane, and *The Crying of Lot 49,*" in *Individual and Community: Variations on a Theme in American Fiction,* ed. Kenneth H. Baldwin and David K. Kirby (Durham, N.C.: Duke University Press, 1975), 182–222, and Thomas Hill Schaub, "*The Crying of Lot 49* and other California Novels," in Dalsgaard, Herman, and McHale, *Cambridge Companion to Thomas Pynchon,* 30–43.

32. Bernhard Siegert, *Relays: Literature as an Epoch of the Postal System,* trans. Kevin Repp (Stanford, Calif.: Stanford University Press, 1999), 2.

33. Marshall, *Corridor,* 177.

34. Peters, *Marvelous Clouds,* 265.

35. David M. Henkin, *The Postal Age: The Emergence of Modern Communications in Nineteenth-Century America* (Chicago: University of Chicago Press, 2006), ix.

36. Henkin, 40.

37. Gitelman, *Paper Knowledge,* 3. In developing this point about paper's duality, Gitelman cites Derrida, whose *Paper Machine* makes a similar claim.

38. Saint-Amour, *Tense Future,* 308.

39. See Francisco Collado-Rodríguez, "Intratextuality, Trauma, and the Posthuman in Thomas Pynchon's *Bleeding Edge,*" *Critique: Studies in Contemporary Fiction* 57 (2016): 229–41, and Jason Siegel, "Meatspace is Cyberspace: The Pynchonian Posthuman in *Bleeding Edge,*" *Orbit: A Journal of American Literature* 4, no. 2 (2016), doi.org/10.16995/orbit.187.

40. Brown, *Other Things,* 135. Brown is referring here to Latour's work in *The Politics of Nature: How to Bring the Sciences into Democracy,* trans. Catherine Porter (Cambridge, Mass.: Harvard University Press, 2004). In *We Have Never Been Modern* (Cambridge, Mass.: Harvard University Press, 1993), Latour uses the term "hybrids" (the mixtures of nature and culture that the modern constitution both denies and allows to proliferate) and "quasi-objects" (the entities between the poles of the dialectic that places objects below or above human subjects and society).

41. One recent example is Anna Lowenhaupt Tsing's *The Mushroom at the End of the World: On the Possibility of Life in Capitalist Ruins* (Princeton, N.J.: Princeton University Press, 2015), an anthropological study of Matsutake, a rare mushroom that Tsing tracks as it persists through capitalist destruction. Peter Godfrey-Smith's *Other Minds: The Octopus, the Sea, and the Deep Origins of Consciousness* (New York: Farrar, Straus, and Giroux, 2016), about the intelligence of the Octopus, might also be said to be a kind of posthuman foray into the deep, one that presents biological history and evolution in great detail. It is telling that, in both of these examples, history is not a nonhuman

construct, but a crucial factor in narrating the development and lifecycles of nonhuman organisms.

42. Graham Harman uses this example in "Elements of an Object-Oriented Philosophy," chapter 3 in his book *Tool-Being: Heidegger and the Metaphysics of Objects* (Chicago: Open Court, 2002), 217–88.

5. THE DISORDER OF THINGS

1. Marilynne Robinson, *Housekeeping* (New York: Picador, 1980), 51. Further references are to this edition and will be included parenthetically in the text.

2. Elizabeth Klaver, "Hobo Time and Marilynne Robinson's *Housekeeping*," *The Journal of the Midwest Modern Language Association* 43, no. 1 (2010): 28.

3. Paula E. Geyh, "Burning down the House? Domestic Space and Feminine Subjectivity in Marilynne Robinson's *Housekeeping*," *Contemporary Literature* 34, no. 1 (1993), 103–22.

4. Elizabeth A. Meese, *Crossing the Double-Cross: The Practice of Feminist Criticism* (Chapel Hill: University of North Carolina Press, 1986).

5. Geyh, "Burning down the House?" 104.

6. Christine Caver, "Nothing Left to Lose: *Housekeeping*'s Strange Freedoms," *American Literature* 68, no. 1 (1996): 112.

7. In order of citation: Sinead McDermott, "Future-Perfect: Gender, Nostalgia, and the Not Yet Presented in Marilynne Robinson's *Housekeeping*," *Journal of Gender Studies* 13, no. 3. (2004): 262.; Geyh, "Burning down the House?" 107; Sarah D. Hartshorne, "Lake Fingerbone and Walden Pond: A Commentary on Marilynne Robinson's *Housekeeping*," *Mondern Language Studies* 20, no. 3 (1990): 52; Kristin King, "Resurfacings of 'The Deeps': Semiotic Balance in Marilynne Robinson's *Housekeeping*," *Studies in the Novel* 28, no. 4 (1996): 571; Klaver, "Hobo Time," 35.

8. Rebecca Falkoff, "Hoarding," *Discard Studies Compendium*, January 22, 2016, discardstudies.com/discard-studies-compendium/#Hoarding; *Histories of the Dustheap Waste, Material Cultures, Social Justice*, ed. Stephanie Foote and Elizabeth Mazzolini (Cambridge, Mass.: MIT Press, 2012); Priyanka Jacob, "The Relic and the Ruin: Equivocal Objects and the Presence of the Past in *Daniel Deronda*," *Victorian Literature and Culture*, 44, no. 4 (2016): 855–74; Patrick Moran, "The Collyer Brothers and the Fictional Lives of Hoarders," *MFS Modern Fiction Studies*. 62 (2016): 272–91.

9. Marshall, *Corridor*, 5.

10. See "Good Housekeeping," in *Women's Periodicals in the United States: Consumer Magazines*, ed. Kathleen T. Endress and Therese L. Lueck (Westport, Conn.: Greenwood, 1995), 123–30, and Frank Luther Mott, "Good

Housekeeping," *A History of American Magazines*, vol. 5 (Cambridge, Mass.: Harvard University Press, 1968), 125–43.

11. Emily Dickinson, "I heard a Fly buzz—when I died-" (no. 465), in *The Complete Poems of Emily Dickinson*, ed. Thomas H. Johnson (New York: Little, Brown and Company, 1960), 223.

12. Susan Howe, *The Birth-Mark: Unsettling the Wilderness in American Literary History* (Middletown, Conn.: Wesleyan University Press, 1993), 1.

13. Bill Brown, "[Concept/Object] [Text/Event]," *English Literary History* 81, no. 2 (2014): 536.

14. Emily Dickinson, "Perception of an object costs" (no. 1071), in Johnson, *Complete Poems of Emily Dickinson*, 486.

15. Peter Schwenger's reading of this poem in *The Tears of Things* draws on Maurice Merleau-Ponty's notions of sense perception to come to similar conclusions (2).

16. Marilynne Robinson, "Writers and the Nostalgic Fallacy," *New York Times Book Review*, October 13, 1985, nytimes.com/1985/10/13/books/writers-and-the-nostalgic-fallacy.html.

17. Laura E. Tanner, *Lost Bodies: Inhabiting the Borders of Life and Death* (Ithaca, N.Y.: Cornell University Press, 2006).

18. Thomas Foster, "History, Critical Theory, and Women's Social Practices: 'Women's Time' and *Housekeeping*," *Signs: Journal of Women in Culture and Society* 14, no. 1 (1988): 74.

19. Julia Kristeva, "Women's Time," trans. Alice Jardine and Harry Blake, in *Feminist Theory: A Critique of Ideology*, ed. Nannerl O. Keohane, Michelle Z. Rosaldo, and Barbara C. Gelpi (Chicago: University of Chicago Press, 1982), 32.

20. It is tempting, perhaps, to turn to Melanie Klein's theories to help make sense of *Housekeeping*. Could the various objects Robinson describes be transitional objects? Could the house itself be one? Klein frequently diagnoses object-relations as structures that compensate for the loss of the mother—her withdrawal or her actual death—as in her 1938 essay "Mourning and Manic-Depressive States." In it, she illustrates the role of anxiety in mourning by discussing the case of D., "a man in his early 40s" whose fears and phantasies, Klein says, "were stirred . . . by the death of his mother" (*The Selected Melanie Klein*, ed. Juliet Mitchell [New York: Free Press, 1986], 167). But even as Klein revises Freud's map of the gendered formation of the psyche and Freud's reductive concept of female sexuality, her account of objects still amounts to a pathologizing discourse of bad and good, symptom and cure. Robinson, I am arguing, instead refuses to absolutize the gendered logic of what is preserved (as symptom) or discarded (in the cure).

21. Heather Love, *Feeling Backward: Loss and the Politics of Queer History* (Cambridge, Mass.: Harvard University Press, 2007), 27.

22. Lauren Berlant, *Cruel Optimism* (Durham, N.C.: Duke University Press, 2011), 2.

23. Klaver, "Hobo Time," summarizes the very different positions that scholars have taken on the ending of the novel. Though some scholars, such as Martha Ravits and Gary Williams, find the conclusion entirely positive, most suggest that it is to some degree distressing. Caver, for instance, writes that, to escape Fingerbone, Sylvie and Ruth pay the price of "a silenced voice and a disappearing body" ("Nothing Left to Lose," 112").

24. Jonathan Kramnick, *Paper Minds: Literature and the Ecology of Consciousness* (Chicago: University of Chicago Press, 2018), 152.

25. Amy Hungerford, *Postmodern Belief: American Literature and Religion since 1960* (Princeton, N.J.: Princeton University Press, 2010), 120.

6. EPHEMERAL GODS, BILLBOARD SAINTS

1. Peter Boxall, *Twenty-First-Century Fiction: A Critical Introduction* (New York: Cambridge University Press, 2013), 27.

2. John N. Duvall, "Introduction: The Power of History and the Persistence of Mystery," in *The Cambridge Companion to Don DeLillo,* ed. John Duvall (New York: Cambridge University Press, 2008), 3.

3. Phillip Löffler, *Pluralist Desires: Contemporary Historical Fiction and the End of the Cold War* (Rochester, N.Y.: Camden House, 2015), 34.

4. Stefano Ercolino, "The Maximalist Novel," *Comparative Literature* 64, no. 3 (2012): 245.

5. Boxall, *Twenty-First-Century Fiction,* 26.

6. Mark McGurl, *The Program Era* (Cambridge, Mass.: Harvard University Press, 2009), 63.

7. James Wood, "Human, All Too Inhuman," *The New Republic,* July 24, 2000, newrepublic.com/article/61361/human-inhuman.

8. Amy Hungerford, "Don DeLillo's Latin Mass," *Contemporary Literature* 47, no. 3 (2006): 376.

9. John A. McClure, *Partial Faiths: Postsecular Fiction in the Age of Pynchon and Morrison* (Athens: University of Georgia Press, 2007), 66; Jeffrey T. Nealon, *Post-Postmodernism: Or, the Cultural Logic of Just-In-Time Capitalism* (Stanford, Calif.: Stanford University Press, 2012), 156.

10. Hungerford, *Postmodern Belief.*

11. McClure, *Partial Faiths,* 65.

12. Anne Anlin Cheng, *The Melancholy of Race: Psychoanalysis, Assimilation, and Hidden Grief* (New York: Oxford University Press, 2000), 174.

13. Benjamin, *Arcades Project,* 462.

14. Jason S. Polley, *Jane Smiley, Jonathan Franzen, Don DeLillo: Narratives of Everyday Justice* (New York: Peter Lang, 2012), 184.

15. Don DeLillo, *Underworld* (New York: Scribner, 1997), 791. All further references are to this edition and will be cited parenthetically.

16. Among postmodern artists, Jasper Johns and Robert Rauschenberg frequently repurposed trash to comment on the changing American landscape. For a comprehensive account of how New York artists engaged the economic and architectural transformation of the city during the 1960s by creating art with obsolete and discarded objects, see Joshua Shannon's *The Disappearance of Objects: New York Art and the Rise of the Postmodern City* (New Haven, Conn.: Yale University Press, 2009).

17. Jani Scandura, *Down in the Dumps* (Durham, N.C.: Duke University Press, 1997), 19.

18. Caroline Walker Bynum, *Christian Materiality: An Essay on Religion in Late Medieval Europe* (New York: Zone, 2011), 19.

19. Certainly DeLillo's decision to name the girl Esmeralda calls to mind the young, barefoot "gypsy dancer" of Victor Hugo's *The Hunchback of Notre-Dame* (1831). Hugo's Esmeralda, hanged by the king in a desperate attempt to quell the chaos growing in Paris, is often read as an unjustly vilified, innocent girl whose death illuminates the inhumane conditions of the city at the time of Hugo's writing.

20. Mike Chasar, *Everyday Reading: Poetry and Popular Culture in Modern America* (New York: Columbia University Press, 2012), 136.

21. From the pamphlet *Burma-Shave Jingle Book* (1936), quoted in Chasar, 149.

22. Jessica Pressman, Mark C. Marino, Jeremy Douglass, *Reading Project: A Collaborative Analysis of William Poundstone's Project for Tachistoscope {Bottomless Pit}* (Iowa City: University of Iowa Press, 2015), 3. To view Poundstone's Project, visit collection.eliterature.org/1/works/poundstone__project_for_tachistoscope_bottomless_pit.html.

23. Mark Osteen, *American Magic and Dread: Don DeLillo's Dialogue with Culture* (Philadelphia: University of Pennsylvania Press, 2000), 215.

24. Alworth, *Site Reading*, 41.

25. Shannon, *Disappearance of Objects*, 90.

26. Peter Boxall, *Don DeLillo: The Possibility of Fiction* (New York: Routledge, 2006), 180. Boxall links the apparition to the Pieter Bruegel painting, *The Triumph of Death*, that appears throughout the novel: "As the face of the dead Esmeralda miraculously reveals itself at the close of the novel, . . . so the Bruegel pushes up to the surface throughout the novel, revealing the apocalyptic dimensions that lie latent in the quotidian" (180).

27. Bruce Robbins, "Orange Juice and Agent Orange," *Occasion: Interdisciplinary Studies in the Humanities* 2 (December 20, 2010): 14, arcade.stanford.edu/sites/default/files/article_pdfs/Occasion_v02_Robbins_122010_0_0.pdf.

28. Maurice Merleau-Ponty, *The Visible and the Invisible,* ed. Claude Lefort, trans. Alphonso Lingis (Evanston, Ill.: Northwestern University Press, 1968), 3.

29. This mode of perception recalls the type of engagement that Walter Benjamin described in his explorations of mimesis and innervation: the onlookers demonstrate the embodied presence of mind that Benjamin attributed to the gambler and also the "innervation of the collective" that he saw as characteristic of urban modernity; see "Short Shadows (I)" and "Surrealism: The Last Snapshot of the European Intelligentsia," in *Selected Writings,* vol. 2, *1927–1934,* ed. Michael W. Jennings, Howard Eiland, and Gary Smith, trans. Rodney Livingstone and Others (Cambridge, Mass.: Harvard University Press, 1999).

30. Many critics have written on the theme of recycling in *Underworld.* David Cowart, for instance, traces the repetition of themes and objects themselves throughout the novel in *Don DeLillo: The Physics of Language* (Athens: University of Georgia Press, 2002). See also David H. Evans's "Taking out the Trash: Don DeLillo's *Underworld,* Liquid Modernity, and the End of Garbage," *Cambridge Quarterly* 35, no. 2 (2006): 103–32.

31. Michiko Kakutani, "A Man, a Woman, and a Day of Terror," review of *Falling Man* by Don DeLillo, *New York Times,* May 9, 2007, Books, nytimes.com/2007/05/09/books/09kaku.html.

32. Martin Amis, "Laureate of Terror," *The New Yorker,* November 21, 2011, newyorker.com/magazine/2011/11/21/laureate-of-terror.

33. Osteen, *American Magic and Dread,* 258.

34. David Cowart, *Don DeLillo,* 55.

35. Joanne Gass, "In the Nick of Time: DeLillo's Nick Shay, Fitzgerald's Nick Caraway and the Myth of the American Adam," in *UnderWords: Perspectives on Don DeLillo's Underworld,* ed. Joseph Dewey, Stephen G. Kellman, and Irving Malin (Newark: University of Delaware Press, 2002), 128.

36. Hungerford, "Don DeLillo's Latin Mass," 374.

37. Saint-Amour, *Tense Future,* 9.

38. Jennifer Lebovich, "Faithful See Mary on Underpass Wall," *Chicago Tribune,* April 19, 2005, chicagotribune.com/chi-0504190294apr19-story.html.

39. Lebovich.

40. Dan Collins, "Faithful See Image of Virgin Mary," CBS News, April 20, 2005, cbsnews.com/news/faithful-see-image-of-virgin-mary/.

41. Reuters, "'Virgin Mary' Stain Defaced, Covered in Chicago," ABC News, May 6, 2005, abc.net.au/news/2005-05-07/virgin-mary-stain-defaced-covered/1565452.

42. The Council on Tall Buildings and Urban Habitat (CTBUH) reports that Chicago is the eighth most vertical city in the world, based on the num-

ber of completed buildings that are greater than 150 meters in height (skyscrapercenter.com/cities).

43. For more on the material practices of Latinx Catholics in the United States, see: Thomas Tweed, *Our Lady of the Exile: Diasporic Religion at a Cuban Catholic Shrine in Miami* (New York: Oxford University Press, 1997); Eva Sperling Cockcroft and Holly Barnet-Sánchez, *Signs from the Heart: California Chicano Murals* (Albuquerque: University of New Mexico Press, 1990).

44. See Martha Bayne, "A Tale of Two Villages," *Chicago Reader*, May 8, 2008, chicagoreader.com/chicago/ukrainian-village-and-east-village-chicago-history/Content?oid=1486780. For more on Chicago's changing demographics, see John P. Koval's *The New Chicago: A Social and Cultural Analysis* (Philadelphia: Temple University Press, 2006).

45. Michael Taussig, *The Magic of the State* (New York: Routledge, 1997), 197.

46. For a thorough history of Our Lady of Guadalupe and her iconography, see D. A. Brading, *Mexican Phoenix: Image and Tradition across Five Centuries* (New York: Cambridge University Press, 2001).

47. Robert Orsi, *Gods of the City: Religion and the American Urban Landscape* (Bloomington: Indiana University Press, 1999), 41.

48. Don DeLillo, *White Noise* (New York: Penguin, 1985), 12.

49. Daniel Wojcik, "'Polaroids from Heaven': Photography, Folk Religion, and the Miraculous Image Tradition at a Marian Apparition Site," *Journal of American Folklore* 109, no. 432 (1996): 142.

50. Robinson, *Housekeeping*, 116.

51. Tanya Saracho, *Our Lady of the Underpass*, 2006, MS provided by Teatro Vista, Chicago, p. 34.

52. Dipesh Chakrabarty, *Provincializing Europe* (Princeton, N.J.: Princeton University Press, 2000), 112.

53. Sam Anderson, review of *Point Omega* by Don DeLillo, *New York Magazine*, January 24, 2010, The Book Review, nymag.com/arts/books/reviews/63210/.

54. Michiko Kakutani, "Headed Toward a Crash, Of Sorts, in a Stretch Limo," review of *Cosmopolis* by Don DeLillo, *New York Times*, March 24, 2003, Books, nytimes.com/2003/03/24/books/books-of-the-times-headed-toward-a-crash-of-sorts-in-a-stretch-limo.html.

55. Boxall, *Twenty-First-Century Fiction*, 27.

56. Don DeLillo, *White Noise*, 250.

57. Joshua Ferris, review of *Zero K* by Don DeLillo, *The New York Times*, May 2, 2016, Books, nytimes.com/2016/05/08/books/review/don-delillos-zero-k.html.

58. Don DeLillo, *Zero K* (New York: Scribner, 2016), 264. Future references are to this edition and will be cited parenthetically in the text.

59. Kirschenbaum's book *Mechanisms* has been foundational in establishing the materiality of digital storage technologies.

CODA

1. Don DeLillo, *Mao II* (New York: Penguin Books, 1991), 19.

2. Kiene Brillenburg Wurth, "Book Presence: An Introductory Exploration," in *Book Presence in a Digital Age,* ed. Kiene Brillenburg Wurth, Kári Driscoll, Jessica Pressman (New York: Bloomsbury, 2018).

3. Johanna Drucker, "The Self-Conscious Codex: Artists' Books and Electronic Media," *Substance* 26, no. 1 (1997): 104.

4. Leah Price, *What We Talk about When We Talk about Books: The History and Future of Reading* (New York: Basic, 2019), 14, 20.

5. Jessica Pressman, "The Aesthetic of Bookishness in Twenty-first Century Literature," *Michigan Quarterly Review* 48, no. 4 (2009): 465–82.

6. Amaranth Borsuck, *The Book* (Cambridge, Mass.: MIT Press, 2018), 182.

7. Wendy Hui Kyong Chun, "The Enduring Ephemeral, or the Future is a Memory," *Critical Inquiry* 35, no. 1 (2008): 160.

8. Ben Ehrenreich, "The Death of the Book," Los Angeles Review of Books, April 18, 2011, lareviewofbooks.org/article/the-death-of-the-book/#!.

9. John Durham Peters, "Proliferation and Obsolescence," in Tischleder and Wasserman, *Cultures of Obsolescence,* 83.

10. Figure 28 shows a screen shot of the moment in the game when Nick talks to "Owl Eyes" in Gatsby's library. It is telling that the game includes this exchange about the uncut books, a symbol of Jay Gatz's near-but-not-entirely perfect transformation into Gatsby. As I discuss, the game raises the same questions of adaptation and authenticity as the novel. The game can be accessed at greatgatsbygame.com/ and a "playthrough" video with the Owl Eyes scene (11:26) can be found at youtube.com/watch?v=woJqbb7UIiA.

11. Simon Reynolds, *Retromania: Pop Culture's Addiction to Its Own Past* (London: Faber and Faber, 2011), xxx.

12. The Nintendo game is an excellent example of what Sianne Ngai calls "the zany" in her new work. She explains that zaniness is "the only aesthetic category in our repertoire about a strenuous relation to playing that seems to be on a deeper level about work," adding that the zany, a "seemingly lighthearted but strikingly vehement aesthetic, in which the potential for injury always seems right around the corner" is a hallmark of video games" (*Our Aesthetic Categories* [Cambridge, Mass.: Harvard University Press, 2012], 7).

13. Peter Smith, interviewed by Salvatore Pane, "The Rumpus Interview with Peter Smith and Charlie Hoey," *The Rumpus*, therumpus.net/2011/03/the-rumpus-interview-with-peter-smith-and-charlie-hoey-the-brains-behind-the-great-gatsby-game/.

14. Reynolds, *Retromania*, xxx.

15. In a 2003 episode of *The Wire*, the character D'Angelo Barksdale offers a poignant interpretation of *The Great Gatsby* in his prison reading group. In response to the group leader's question about Fitzgerald's view of second chances, D'Angelo replies: "He's saying that the past is always with us. And where we come from, what we go through, how we go through it, all this shit matters. I mean, that's what I thought he meant. Like at the end of the book, you know—boats and tides and all. It's like you can change up, you can say you somebody new, you can give yourself a whole new story. But what came first is who you really are and what happened before is what really happened. And it don't matter that some fool say he different because the only thing that make you different is what you really do or what you really go through. You know, like all them books in his library. Now, he frontin' with all them books but if we pull one down off the shelf, none of the pages ever been opened. He got all them books, and he ain't read one of 'em. And Gatsby, he was who he was and he did what he did and cause he wasn't ready to get real with the story, that shit caught up to him" (*The Wire*, episode "All Prologue," written by David Simon, aired July 6, 2003, on HBO). D'Angelo's reading insists on the endurance of the past and the consequences of imitation, tropes that are both relevant in this coda's discussion of nostalgia and authenticity.

Index

Sarah Wasserman is assistant professor of English and material culture studies at the University of Delaware. She is coeditor of *Cultures of Obsolescence: History, Materiality, and the Digital Age.*